Skeletal Radiography

Skeletal Radiography

A concise introduction to projection radiography

Sheila Bull BA MSc HDCR TDCR

SECOND EDITION

Toolkit
Publications

STANLEY, UNITED KINGDOM 2005

Published by TOOLKIT PUBLICATIONS

© Toolkit Publications 2005

First edition published in 1985 by Butterworths
© Butterworths & Co. (Publishers) Ltd, 1985
Second edition 2005

ISBN 0–9551311–0–3

British Library Cataloguing in Publication Data
A catalogue record for this book is available from the British Library

10   9   8   7   6   5   4   3   2

Typeset by Tech-Set Ltd. (www.tech-set.co.uk)
Printed by Athenaeum Press Ltd. (www.athenaeumpress.co.uk)

Cover and illustrations for the second edition by Nigel Dobbyn
(www.nigeldobbyn.co.uk)

Preface and acknowledgements to the second edition

In this edition I have made changes that include more frequent references to modalities such as magnetic resonance imaging (MRI) and computerized (computed) tomography (CT), the former being in its relative infancy in 1985.

A significant development in recent years has been the migration from film/screen imaging technology to computed radiography. Changes in Chapter 4 (The radiographic examination) have been made to reflect this development. Throughout the book, the phrase 'image receptor' or the term 'cassette' has replaced the word 'film'.

The introduction of degree education for radiographers in the United Kingdom and changes in the National Health Service have meant that there is now a requirement for reference to and knowledge of the evidence base for practice. This has led me to include many references in the text. I trust these will be of help to *all* students of radiography.

In response to comments about the first edition, a number of new illustrations have been included. Some radiographic techniques have been added (or updated) and a few have been removed.

Whilst CT and MRI are now used as gold standard investigations in certain situations, I have thought it fitting to leave some of the potentially outdated radiographic techniques within their relevant chapters. Occasionally radiographers are required to undertake these projections, possibly because conventional projection radiographic imaging supplements the newer modalities. Nevertheless statements about the less-commonly used (or historic) projections will act as a useful resource for researchers and those acting in situations where the 'new' modalities are unavailable.

SB 2005

Acknowledgements

Credit for the knowledge skills of radiography do not belong to any one person. The art and science of this discipline exist in their current state of development because of the labours of many people. Availability of written resources produced by researchers from a range of professional backgrounds provided much of the underpinning knowledge needed to complete this book. In addition, some of these authors will certainly owe a debt to those investigating and writing about radiography in preceding years leading back to the discovery of X-rays in1895. Of equal importance is the fact that I could not have developed my skills base without completing several years of trial, observation and practice in the clinical field, working alongside many highly competent radiographers who passed their knowledge and ideas on to me.

The following individuals kindly agreed to review chapters and offer useful comments and suggestions on content; Ms Lynne Breen, Superintendent Radiographer at Newcastle-upon-Tyne Freeman Hospital; Mr Phil Ferrar, Sales and Marketing Manager, Oncology Imaging Systems Ltd; Mr David Horsfield, Senior Superintendent Radiographer at the Royal National Orthopaedic Hospital, Stanmore; Mr Ken Moore, Senior Radiographer at the Regional Neurological Centre, Newcastle-upon-Tyne; Mr Jason Oakley, Senior Lecturer at the University of Portsmouth; Mr David Stelmach, MA HDCR PGCE Grad IPD, Trauma and Orthopaedic Radiology, St. James's University Hospital, Leeds; Ms Katie Whittam, Professional Lead Radiographer at James Cook University Hospital, South Tees NHS Trust and Mr Miles Woodford, Superintendent Radiographer, Duke of Cornwall Spinal Unit Salisbury District Hospital.

I am grateful to Ms Nicola Glover and Ms Joanne Heslop, Assistant Practitioners at Queen Elizabeth Hospital Gateshead for acting as models for the second edition illustrations. Ms Dorothy Keane, Consultant Radiographer and colleagues at South Tyneside NHS Foundation Trust kindly provided some of the radiographs for this second edition.

Finally, in 1985, when the first edition was written, word processing, e-mail and the Internet were not available to me. These devices have been an invaluable and wonderful help for writing and research. I give a heartfelt thanks to their inventors and developers.

About the author

At publication date, Sheila Bull is Senior Lecturer in medical imaging at Teesside University, Middlesbrough, United Kingdom. She has lectured in radiography and other subjects at Newcastle Schools of Radiography and Northumbria University, Newcastle upon Tyne and is a practising radiographer.

How to use this book

Part I includes general information on the subject of bone and associated tissues, skeletal trauma, pathology and the radiographic examination.

Part II is arranged on a regional basis and radiographic techniques for these regions are listed in a table at the beginning of each chapter. Statements about effective radiation doses are derived from RCR Working Party (2003) *Making the Best Use of a Department of Clinical Radiology: Guidelines for Doctors (5th Edition)* London: Royal College of Radiologists

Information on essential anatomical terminology is included; however readers should have at least a basic working knowledge of anatomy and medical terminology and are expected to consult other works on these subjects.

Descriptions of skeletal trauma and pathology specific to each region are included as potential indications for the X-ray examination and cross-reference should be made to general comments made about these 'conditions' in Chapters 2 and 3.

Radiographic techniques are numbered to allow cross-referencing, and where appropriate techniques related to specific indications are included.

References to literature and further reading are listed at the end of each chapter and numbered within the text, along with the page number if available. For example [ref 7: 29] is page number 29 of citation 7.

This book is intended as a concise guide rather than a free-standing instruction manual and must be used in conjunction with other texts. Students of radiography are required to undertake appropriate training under supervision and must have suitable professional guidance when applying the techniques listed in this book.

Scientific knowledge and technology related to radiography and radiology are subject to rapid change. As new information becomes available, changes in procedures and equipment become necessary. Every effort has been made by the author to make the contents as accurate as possible, both typographical and in content. Readers are advised to confirm that the information, especially with regard to radiation protection and safety of patients complies with the latest legislation and standards of practice. In addition, readers must bear in mind that professional opinions do vary on approaches to radiography. Many current opinions are supported by scientific research, however others may not be substantiated in this way and remain potential subjects for further investigation.

Contents

Part I
Introduction

The tissues of the skeleton

CHAPTER CONTENTS

Introduction

In 1895 Roentgen was the first person to see the shadow of living bones cast by what were to become known as 'X-rays'; thus skeletal radiography is as old as the discovery of the new radiation. Later in the twentieth century, the science of medical imaging expanded to embrace a range of modalities with radiography being complemented or eclipsed by these new developments.

In the contemporary field of musculo-skeletal medical imaging, radiography retains its importance in the examination of bone and joints, however it has clear limitations when it comes to imaging associated soft tissues and cartilaginous structures. Nevertheless the new modalities, notably magnetic resonance imaging, have successfully made up for this deficit.

Skeletal radiography is 'X-raying' bone to demonstrate the unique form of anatomy and morphology provided by radiographs. Bone makes a very good subject for radiography provided that the X-ray beam used for the imaging process is of

the appropriate energy and the image receptor and associated processing is geared to render high quality radiographs. In order to appreciate the rationales for radiography of the skeleton and its joints, some understanding of the nature of the subject is required.

THE SKELETON

Each bone of the skeleton is a complex, living organ made of specialised *connective tissue*. Collectively they are rigid members of lever systems concerned with body movements and hence they form part of the *locomotor system*. In addition, some bony structures such as the skull and ribs protect vulnerable organs from damage.

There are said to be two hundred and six named bones in the body but *accessory ossicles* are common (*see* – below). Bones also act as a reservoir for certain minerals and play a vital role in the homeostasis of calcium and other ions in the body fluids.

Bone tissue

A characteristic of connective tissues is that they are made up of *cells* embedded in a *matrix* of fibres and amorphous (formless) *ground substance*. In bone the mature cells each lie in a space or lacuna in a collagen matrix heavily impregnated with inorganic minerals collectively known as *apatite*. This includes calcium and magnesium in combination with phosphate and carbonate. These minerals are responsible for the compressive strength of bone. The relatively high atomic number of calcium and the physical density of bone account for its radiopacity as compared with the soft tissues which are not normally radiopaque. Average compact bone contains by weight about 30% matrix and 70% minerals [**ref 3**: 989].

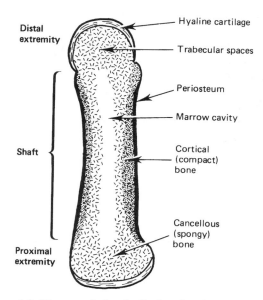

Figure 1.1 Diagram of a longitudinal section through a long bone showing its constituent parts. The shaft is formed mainly by a thickened tube of compact bone while the ends are made of spongy bone with only a thin covering of compact bone.

Lamellar bone

Normal, mature bone is *lamellar bone* which means it is layered. This type of bone contains Haversian systems where concentrically arranged layers of matrix surround a central Haversian canal (*see* below). Fine fibre bundles are arranged in these layers in an orderly direction. Lamellar bone usually replaces cartilage or woven bone in the growing skeleton. Lamellar bone may be classified according to the spaces within it i.e. compact and spongy bone.

Compact (cortical) bone (Figures 1.1 and 1.2)

The external covering of a bone (the *cortex*) is formed by compact bone. Cortex appears in a radiograph as a white line with a sharp and clear outer edge and a less clearly defined inner edge where it merges with the trabecular bone of the medulla. Cortical bone is particularly evident where there are torsional (twisting) stresses in action. In a long bone this layer tends to be thickest in the mid-shaft area and relatively thin over the expanded ends. Compact bone makes up about 80% of the skeleton.

Spongy bone (Figures 1.1 and 1.2)

This is also known as *trabecular* and *cancellous* bone. The word spongy best describes its appearance – a meshwork of *trabeculae* (*trabeculum* means a small beam or bar) surrounded by intercommunicating

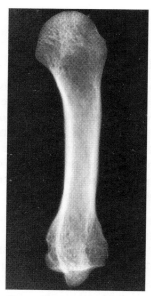

Figure 1.2 Radiograph of a metacarpal. The spongy bone at each end shows the honeycomb pattern of trabeculae.

spaces (*cancelli*). Spongy bone is found in areas of the skeleton where compressional forces are experienced, e.g. chiefly in the ends of long bones; the bodies of vertebrae; and the calcaneus of the heel.

Woven bone

The fibres form an irregular interlacing pattern in a matrix rich in ground substance. The cells are larger than those found in lamellar bone. Woven bone is found wherever bone is rapidly being laid down – for example – in the embryonic skeleton; sub-periosteally in growing bone; in fracture callus and in reactive bone formation in relation to a pathological process. Woven bone is an impermanent structure and is usually replaced by lamellar bone which is mechanically stronger.

Bone cells

Five main types of cell are associated with bone:

(1) *Osteoblasts* that are capable of forming and maintaining bone. They lie on all bone surfaces except those undergoing resorption (*see Figure 1.3*). Osteoblasts are able to respond to stimuli such as changes in the level of parathyroid hormone in the circulation.

(2) *Osteoclasts* are responsible for resorption of bone. They have specific receptors [ref 5: 3] for a blood-borne substance called calcitonin to allow them to directly regulate bone resorption. Calcitonin inhibits the action of osteoclasts.

(3) *Osteocytes* are derived from osteoblasts during bone formation. Each osteocyte occupies a lacuna (space) in the bone and gives out cytoplasmic processes that reach out to adjacent areas of bone and also communicate with similar processes derived from osteoblasts (*Figure 1.4*). Osteocytes have an important role in controlling the extracellular concentration of calcium and phosphorus [ref 5: 2].

(4) *Osteoprogenitor cells* line Haversian canals, endosteum and periosteum awaiting stimulus to differentiate into osteoblasts.

(5) *Lining cells* are narrow flattened cells that form an 'envelope' around bone.

Bone marrow

The thick cylinder of compact bone forming the shaft of a long bone encloses the central marrow cavity which communicates with the cancelli of the spongy bone (*Figure 1.1*). All the spaces are lined

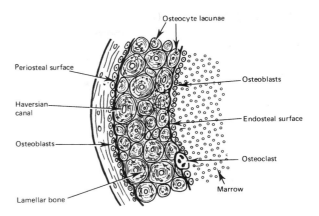

Figure 1.3 Schematic diagram of a section through lamellar bone forming the cortex of a tubular (long) bone. The concentric layers of bone surrounding each Haversian canal are shown (not to scale).

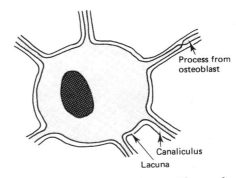

Figure 1.4 Osteocyte occupying a lacuna. The cytoplasmic processes communicate via channels known as canaliculi.

with a tissue – the *endosteum* – and are filled with bone marrow which is either fatty or blood forming (*haemopoietic*). The character of the bone marrow varies with the age of the individual and its location in the skeleton.

Periosteum

This is a tough fibrous membrane that covers the outer surface of the bone except for the articular surface and serves as an attachment for tendons and ligaments (*Figure 1.1*). The inner layer of periosteum contains cells that are capable of becoming osteoblasts (which will form new bone).

Providing that the periosteum remains intact bone formation cannot spread outside it. (Normally the periosteum is not visible on the radiograph). In certain abnormal conditions the periosteum may become elevated due to haemorrhage. This may happen in an injury, or in bone tumours where the tumour itself produces new bone (*see Figure 3.14* Chapter 3).

The formation and growth of bone

Most bones, notably long bones, are preformed in *hyaline cartilage* which is replaced by bone in a process known as *ossification (enchondral ossification)*. In the foetus the cartilage model is roughly the shape of the future bone (*Figure 1.5(a)*). A *primary ossification zone* establishes itself across the width of the shaft and starts extending in both directions towards either end. By birth most of what is later to become the shaft of the bone is ossified but the ends are still cartilaginous (*Figure 1.5(b)*).

During the first few years of life *secondary ossification centres* appear in the cartilaginous ends of the bone (*Figure 1.5(c)*). Eventually the whole of these extremities are replaced by bone except for the articular surfaces which remain covered by cartilage. A thin zone of cartilage also persists between the ends of the bone and its shaft (*Figure 1.5(d)*). It is at these *growth or epiphyseal plates* and adjacent part of the shaft that a long bone will continue to increase in length.

The terms used for the parts of the growing bone are (*Figure 1.5(d)*):

1. Diaphysis.
2. Epiphyseal plate (physis).
3. Epiphysis.

Note: an *apophysis* is a scale of growing bone not contributing to length growth and which in some locations may look like a fracture even if there is no abnormality – for example – the tibial tubercle.

Growth in length (Figure 1.6)

A long bone grows in length by the interstitial growth of the epiphyseal plate cartilage in which the cells (chondrocytes) are arranged in columns lying parallel to the longitudinal axis of the bone. These columns or palisades are produced by repeated cell division. Each row of cells is surrounded by cartilage matrix with thin partitions lying between the cells. As the cells approach the diaphyseal side of the plate they enlarge and the matrix in which they are enclosed becomes calcified. Cells next to the marrow cavity die and

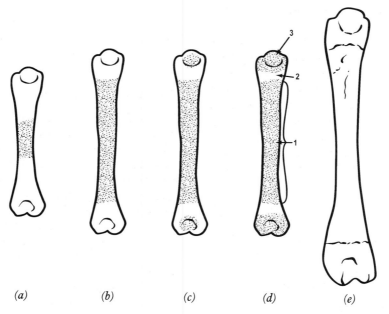

(a)   (b)   (c)   (d)   (e)

Figure 1.5 Stages of ossification in a long bone (see text for key).

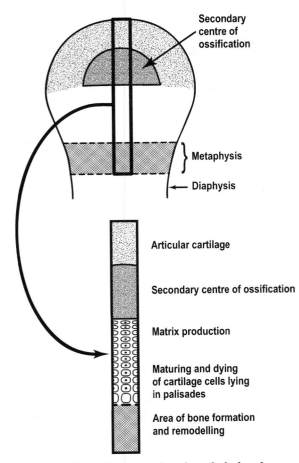

Secondary centre of ossification

Metaphysis

Diaphysis

Articular cartilage

Secondary centre of ossification

Matrix production

Maturing and dying of cartilage cells lying in palisades

Area of bone formation and remodelling

Figure 1.6 Areas of bone growth at the end of a long bone.

the thin transverse partitions of matrix disappear leaving tunnels which are invaded by capillaries and osteoblasts. The osteoblasts put down several layers of bone (lamellae) on the inner walls of the tunnels and this process is repeated until only a narrow channel (Haversian canal) containing a neurovascular bundle remains. Bone-forming cells are now entrapped in their lacunae in the newly formed layers of bone. The cells are now termed osteocytes.

Each concentric arrangement of layers of bone matrix and cells is called an Haversian system. The narrow canaliculi containing the cell cytoplasmic processes pass radially and circumferentially in the Haversian systems conveying nutrients to the enclosed osteocytes (*see Figures 1.3 and 1.4*).

During the growing period the interstitial growth of the epiphyseal cartilage keeps pace with its

replacement by bone so the epiphyseal plate is always present as a thin, radiolucent zone. The actively growing part of the diaphysis adjacent to the epiphyseal cartilage is known as the metaphysis. Fusion of the plate with its neighbouring bony elements halts any further increase in bone length. When this occurs the bone is said to have reached maturity (*Figure 1.5(e)*).

A long bone will grow from both ends but one end will generally grow faster. The lower femoral and upper tibial epiphyses contribute about 60% and the upper humeral about 80% of the limb length [**ref 2**: 33]. A fracture through a growth plate may halt growth on one side resulting in a deformity if untreated. Illness during bone growth may leave *growth arrest lines* (Harris lines) visible on a radiograph.

Growth in width

Growth in width in a long bone and growth in all other bones is achieved by deposition of new bone on the periosteal and endosteal surfaces of the existing bone. This is known as *appositional growth*.

Intramembranous ossification

A few bony elements notably the clavicle and the bones of the skull vault are formed by ossification of connective tissue membranes (mesenchyme). This is known as *intramembranous ossification*.

Measuring the stage of bone maturity

The radiographic appearance (or non-appearance) of the ossification centres in a limb can be used as an indicator of the stage of skeletal maturity. In 1937 an Atlas of Skeletal Maturation of the Hand was published. This was later to be revised by Greulich and Pyle [**ref 4**]. This work recognized the importance of serial changes of maturing ossification centres that were considered to be maturity determinators. In 1967 Tanner, Whitehouse and Healy produced a new method for assessing skeletal maturity that was believed to be more flexible and derived from a more solid mathematical base. In this system each bone of the hand and wrist was classified separately into one of eight or nine stages, to which scores were assigned. These scores were summed to give skeletal maturity. This system has subsequently been revised and the new approach provides separate maturities for the carpal bones and the long bones [**ref 6**]. The determination of skeletal maturity may be used in the diagnosis and treatment of endocrine disorders in children, in the prediction of adult height and in general surveys for public health purposes.

Bone remodelling and turnover

Bone tissue is not static; it is constantly being produced and destroyed by the activity of osteoblasts and osteoclasts. In the process of remodelling, bone tissue is deposited on some surfaces whilst it is removed from others. This turnover rate is much faster in growing bone whose interior structure is changing continually to adjust to increasing size and shape. The effects of remodelling are more startling – for example – in a child with a fracture that has healed with deformity. The deformity is seen to diminish gradually and the bone returns to its 'normal' shape (*see* Chapter 2). Even in the adult, bone is continually being remodelled with accretion and resorption occurring simultaneously. Studies with radioactive isotopes have shown that there is a pool of readily exchangeable calcium within the bone [**ref 1**]. The anatomical site of this pool is not clear but it has been estimated that bone crystal surfaces exposed to extracellular fluid on the walls of the lacunae, canaliculi and Haversian canals amount to 1500–5000 m^2 on average. Exchangeable calcium provides a rapid buffering mechanism to keep the calcium ion concentration in the extracellular fluids from rising or falling to extreme levels under changing conditions of excess or sparcity [**ref 3: 990**]. The continual exchange of the mineral between bone and the extracellular fluid is illustrated by the use of radioisotope scintigraphy (*Figure 1.7*). This technique may be used to indicate areas of the skeleton with increased turnover such as the sites of bony secondaries in malignant disease.

Increased turnover is also seen where there is healing of fractures or at the growing ends of normal bone in children.

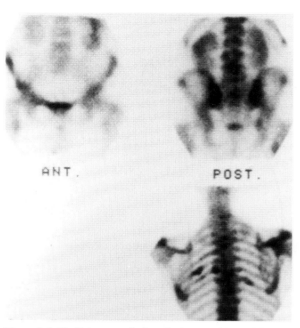

Figure 1.7 Radioisotope scintigraphy image of bone. There are areas of increased activity in the ribs.

Bone morphology (shapes)

Table 1.1   Classification of bone shapes

Shape of bone	Examples
Long bone	Humerus, metacarpal
Cuboidal bone	Carpals
Irregular bone	Vertebrae
Flat bone	Sternum
Sesamoid bone	Patella

Accessory and supernumery ossicles

These are tiny bones resulting in part from altered patterns of ossification. They occur most frequently in the hands, wrists and feet and represent normal variations. Sometimes they need to be distinguished from *avulsion* or *chip* fractures. The notable accessory ossicles are named.

Terminology of general bone features

Table 1.2   Terminology of bone features

Bone feature	Description
Articular surface	Surface for forming joints with neighbouring bone
Articular facet	Small articular surface
Condyle	Knuckle-shaped articular surface
Crest	Elongated elevation
Epicondyle	Projection of bone *next* to a condyle
Fissure	Cleft in or between bones
Foramen	Hole
Fossa	Depression
Head	Expanded proximal end of long bone
Lamina	Thin plate of bone
Process	Projection of bone
Sulcus	Groove
Trochlea	Joint surface grooved like a pulley
Tubercle	Small facet for tendon insertion
Tuberosity	Large facet for tendon insertion

Joints of the skeleton

Synovial joints *(Figure 1.8)*

Joints are functional connections between different bones of the skeleton, and they can be classified according to their structure and degree of movement. The major moving joints of the body are those that have a joint 'cavity'. These may be termed *diarthroses* and are all *synovial* joints. The term 'synovial' refers to the *synovial membrane* that forms part of the joint structure. The ends of the bones forming these articulations are almost invariably covered by *articular (hyaline) cartilage* which is some 2–4 mm thick (in the young). The cartilage's normal radiolucency provides the effective joint 'space' seen on the radiograph as an apparent 'gap' between the bone ends. In reality there is normally little 'space' in a synovial joint.

When damaged, articular cartilage has little power of regeneration. The joint surfaces and the cartilage are lubricated and nourished by *synovial fluid* secreted by synovial membrane.

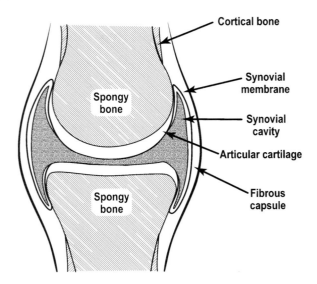

Figure 1.8 Diagram of the constituent features of a synovial joint.

Normal human synovial joints contain less than 1 ml of this fluid. A large intra-articular accumulation of this substance (for example) following a traumatic incident is termed an *effusion*.

The strong surrounding fibrous *capsule* provides structural support for the bone ends. This structure is reinforced by localized thickenings of ligaments and adjacent structures such as tendons or muscles.

Table 1.3   Classification of synovial joints according to articular shape and movement

Type	Example
Ball and socket joint	Hip, shoulder
Hinge joint	Elbow
Plane or gliding joint	Posterior vertebral (facet) joints
Sellar (saddle) joint	First carpometacarpal joint
Pivot joint	Proximal radioulnar joint

Fibrous joints

Joints where the bone margins are united by a layer of fibrous tissue are called fibrous joints. Because they are 'immovable' they may also be termed *synarthroses*. Examples of fibrous joints include the sutures of the skull. The inferior tibiofibular joint is a fibrous joint and provides vital stability for the ankle.

Cartilaginous joints

A third type of joint is known as an *amphiarthrosis* or 'slightly' moving joint and in this case the bone ends are united by cartilage. Examples of these cartilaginous joints include those that lie between the pubic bones and between the vertebral bodies. In both of these locations the bone joint surfaces are covered in hyaline cartilage and are separated by a disc of fibrocartilage which functions as a shock absorber. This type of joint is also known as a *symphysis*.

Ligaments and tendons

Ligaments are designed to prevent the occurrence of excessive or abnormal movements at joints and tendons and are integral parts of the extremities of skeletal muscles. Both are made of dense, fibrous connective tissue and are attached to bone at their origins and insertions by an interweaving of the collagen fibres with those of the periosteum. *Sharpey's fibres* extend from the ligaments and tendons through the periosteum into the substance of the underlying cortical bone. In certain injuries of a tendon or ligament a portion of cortical bone may be pulled away or *avulsed* from the main body of bone due to the firm anchorage provided by Sharpey's fibres (*see* page 10, *avulsion fracture*). Tendons do not tolerate friction well and are protected by *bursae*, *synovial membrane sheaths* or *sesamoid bones*.

Muscles

The active portion of skeletal (striped) muscle consists of specialised long cells that are able to actively shorten, thus exerting a moving force on joints. As well as producing prime movements, muscles work in harmony with each other in balanced groups called *agonists* and *antagonists*. This balance may be lost in certain fractures that separate mechanical linkage between muscle groups (*see Figure 8.2, Chapter 8*, page 121). These fractures are difficult to hold without some form of internal fixation.

Soft tissue visibility on radiographs

Absorption of X-rays is sufficiently different in fat compared with muscle or tendon to allow fat planes to be seen on a radiograph. There are some specific soft tissue signs that may point to injury such as the *fat pad sign* in the elbow (*see* page 66). Soft tissues may also be rendered visible by the presence of foreign bodies, gas, calcification, tattoos and soft tissue tumours.

References

1. Bell GH Emslie-Smith D and Paterson CR (1980) *Textbook of Physiology* Edinburgh: Churchill Livingstone

2. Dandy DJ and Edwards DJ (2003) *Essential Orthopaedics and Trauma (4th Edition)* London: Churchill Livingstone

3. Ganong WF (2003) Review of Medical Physiology New York: McGraw-Hill

4. Gruelich WW and Pyle SI (1959) *Radiographic Atlas of Skeletal Development of the Hand and Wrist* California: Stanford University Press

5. Miller MD (ed) (2000) *Review of Orthopaedics (3rd Edition)* London: WB Saunders

6. Tanner JM Whitehouse RH Marshall WA Healey MJB and Goldstein H (1975) *Assessment of Skeletal Maturity and Prediction of Adult Height* London: Academic Press

Further Reading

1. Bizarro AH (1921) On the sesamoid and supernumery bone of the limbs *Journal of Anatomy (Cambridge)* 55: 256–268

2. Gunn C (2002) *Bones and Joints: A Guide for Students* Edinburgh: Churchill Livingstone

3. Keats TE Anderson MW (2001) Atlas of Normal Roentgen Variants that may Simulate Disease (7th Ed) St Louis: Mosby

4. Miller MD (ed) (2004) *Review of Orthopaedics (4th Edition)* London: Saunders

5. Standing S Ellis H (eds) (2004) *Gray's Anatomy: The Anatomical Basis of Clinical Practice (39th Edition)* Edinburgh: Churchill Livingstone

Fractures and dislocations

CHAPTER CONTENTS

Introduction

Requests for radiography of the skeleton are most often made because of the need to exclude or confirm the presence of bone or joint injury. Skeletal trauma is the commonest problem presented to a musculoskeletal radiologist [ref 8: 1371].

When a normal living bone is subject to trauma sufficient to make it break it is inevitable that the nearby soft tissue will also be damaged. Periosteum is stripped or torn from the bone and there may be considerable bleeding with the result that a *haematoma* (blood swelling) forms around the site. Some damage will also occur to the muscles and tendons near to the bone. Treatment of injuries therefore requires dealing with more than just fractures because complications and soft tissue injuries are able to spoil the results of the finest fracture management [ref 4: 92].

Bony injury is likely to be visible on radiographs and although these images occasionally show related soft tissue signs they will not show complications such as injured muscles, nerves, blood vessels or wound contamination. The majority of injuries can be visualised by ordinary projection radiography however use of other imaging modalities may be required. *Magnetic resonance imaging (MRI)* can – for example – identify occult (hidden) injury to bone and post-traumatic *avascular necrosis* (*see* – below). *Computerized tomography (CT)* with its multi-planar imaging and three-dimensional image reconstruction facilities is of value for subjects of complex structure. *Radionuclide imaging* may be used forty-eight hours after an injury to demonstrate bone activity at a fracture site [ref 6: 29]. For further information on these modalities – *see* Chapter 4.

Fractures of bone

A fracture is a break in the continuity of bone and the bone pieces are referred to as fragments. Any break, even of one bone cortex constitutes a fracture. There is a wide and confusing number of ways to classify fractures and as time progresses and knowledge expands the number of classifications continues to grow [**ref 6**: 21]. Many fractures have been named after the individual who may have first described them (eponymous fractures). Usage of eponymous terminology may be discouraged in image reporting where the focus is aimed at describing the fracture by its site and pattern. There is also a trend towards classifying injuries by the forces causing them.

Closed (simple) fractures

Fractures are classified either as *closed* or *open*. This terminology has generally replaced the older *simple* and *compound*. In a closed fracture there is no direct communication between the fracture and the external environment. The label *simple* can also be applied to fractures where there are only two bone fragments. Use of this latter term may be confusing if the treatment for the injury is not trouble-free.

Open (compound) fractures *(Figure 2.1)*

In an open fracture there is a direct communication between the fracture and the skin surface – for example – a fracture of the tibia with a laceration of the overlying skin. Fractures may become compound *from within* if the sharp bone ends broaches the skin. Open fractures are likely to become infected while simple fractures are not.

Other classifications of fractures

Several other terms are used to describe fractures:

(1) *Incomplete* – an incomplete break occurs mainly in children. On the radiograph the bone may be seen to be buckled (*Figure 2.2*). *Torus* and *greenstick fractures* are types of incomplete fractures.

(2) *Hairline* – these may be difficult to detect on a radiograph. A repeat examination at a later date may show the abnormality where the bone has started the healing process.

(3) *Avulsion* – usually caused by traction of the tendon tearing off a bone fragment at the point of its insertion (at the apohpysis). Examples are; base of fifth metatarsal (by peroneus brevis tendon), tibial tuberosity (by quadriceps tendon).

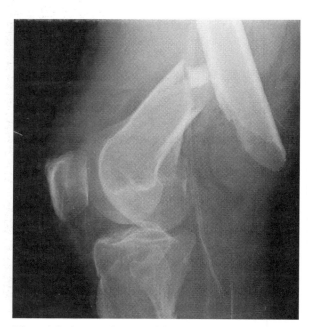

Figure 2.1 An open fracture of the femur.

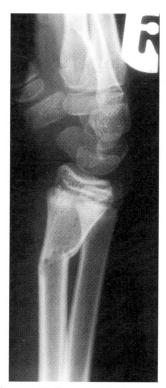

Figure 2.2 A greenstick fracture of the lower end of the radius. The ulnar styloid process is also fractured.

(3) *Stress* – similar to fatigue fractures in metal; this type of fracture results from repeated application of a minor force (*Figure 2.3*) related to abnormal muscular tension on a normal bone [**ref 3**]. Stress fractures occur in 10% of athletes [**ref 5**].

Table 2.1   Locations of some common stress fractures and activities that might cause them

Bone Area	Activities
Femur	Long-distance running
Foot	Marching and running
Hand	Gymnastics
Patella	Hurdling
Pelvis	Bowling
Ribs	Golf
Spine	Weight lifting
Tibia	Running, ballet
Ulna	Wheelchair

(List adapted from [ref 2: 358])

(4) *Pathological* – a fracture occurring through abnormal bone – for example – at the site of a secondary deposit from a carcinoma (*Figure 2.4*) or where there is *osteoporosis*.

(5) *Compression* (*crush*) – where cancellous bone has collapsed due to compressive forces – for example – in a wedge fracture of a vertebral body or the calcaneus.

Nature of the fracture line

The orientation and state of the fracture line are described by further terms such as *transverse, oblique* or *spiral* (*Figure 2.5*). Where the fragments are driven into each other the fracture is termed *impacted*. *Comminuted* means that there is more than two fragments. An alternative name is *multifragmentary* fracture.

The type and direction of the applied force may have some influence on the way in which the bone breaks. If the injuring force is applied directly to the bone then the fracture is more likely to be of the

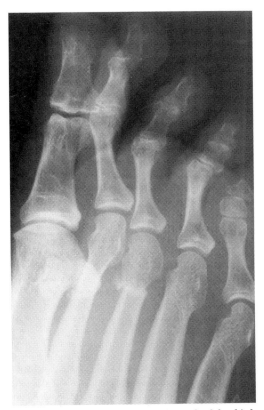

Figure 2.3 A stress fracture through the neck of the third metatarsal.

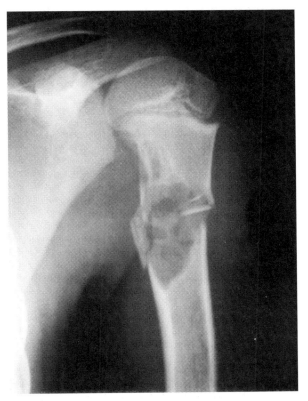

Figure 2.4 A pathological fracture through a bone-destroying lesion in the upper humerus.

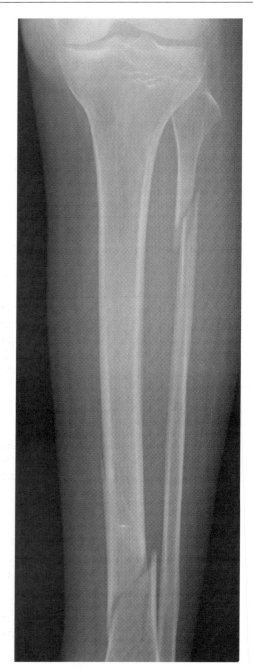

Figure 2.5 A spiral fracture line in lower tibia and upper fibula.

comminuted type and possibly compound. The transmission of violence – for example – by a twisting of the limb, may cause a spiral or oblique fracture. Indirect violence is also the most common cause of dislocation [ref 3: 5].

Continuity and proximity of fracture fragments

Apposition is a term that refers to the position of major fragments with respect to each other. Fractures are defined as *displaced* if the bone ends have shifted in relation to one another. Displacement is described in terms of how the distal fragment has moved in relation to the proximal fragment. *Alignment* refers to the relationship of fragments along the axis of major fragments. The distal fragment is described in terms of how it may be *angled* in relation to the proximal (*angulation*). *Varus and valgus angulation* refers to the alignment of the distal fragment with respect to the midline of the body. *Varus* is angled towards the midline and *valgus* is angled away from the midline.

Epiphyseal injuries

At the growing ends of bone the epiphysis can be separated from the diaphysis forcefully. This is known as fracture separation or displacement of the epiphysis. Salter and Harris [**ref 7**] classified these injuries into four types. Blood supply to the epiphysis may be impaired by the injury leading to *avascular necrosis*. Another adverse effect is that the growth plate may be disturbed and growth affected.

Soft tissue clues of injury on a radiograph

Fractures at a joint may provide evidence in the form of an effusion. A good example is the *fat pad sign* at the elbow (*see* page 66). A *lipohaemarthrosis* (fat-blood fluid level) (*see* page 114) may also be visualised at the knee when the radiograph is made using a horizontal X-ray beam. This is firm presumptive evidence of an intra-articular fracture [**ref 8**: 1373].

Clinical features of a fracture

The radiographer should be aware of the signs and symptoms of a fracture. These may affect the degree of co-operation the patient can achieve and hence alter the approach to the radiographic technique. The patient will be in pain and may lose function of the limb. The fracture site itself may be tender, swollen and bruised. The limb may look *deformed*, owing to displacement, angulation or overlapping of the fragments. There could also be abnormal mobility at the fracture or even *crepitus* (grating sound) at the fragment ends.

Complications

Complications of fractures and the associated soft tissue injuries may be classified according to the timescale of their occurrence and whether they are localised or generalised. *Immediate complications* include bleeding and damage to blood vessels, nerves and viscera.

Table 2.2 Possible blood loss from fractures (litres)

Fracture site	Blood loss
Tibia	1–3
Femur	2–4
Hip	3–5

(Adapted from [ref 4: 101])

Early complications (i.e. within the first few hours) include infection, *fat embolism syndrome* and *compartment syndrome*. *Fat embolism* occurs most frequently after femoral shaft and pelvic fractures as microscopic globules of fat escape into the circulation from the fracture site. They lodge in the lungs and may cause pulmonary insufficiency which can be lethal.

Compartment syndrome – muscles are contained within fascial compartments which prevent injured tissues from swelling. Following injury, pressure rises within the compartment and cell death occurs with fibrosis and contraction of the muscle tissue on healing.

Late complications include osteoarthritis where joint surfaces have been disrupted, or where injuries have altered the mechanical load on the joint. Deformity due to *malunion* (*see* – below) is another late complication along with *avascular necrosis* (*asceptic necrosis*). In the latter the bone dies and collapses due to disruption of blood supply. Avascular necrosis often takes two years to develop and sometimes as long as eight [**ref 4**: 104].

Myositis ossificans (*heterotopic ossification*) is a complication of trauma and the commonest site is the elbow [**ref 6**: 96]. A calcified mass is visible on the radiograph and the condition restricts movement.

Treatment of fractures

The orthopaedic surgeon will make clinical judgements in the management of a fracture. The overall aims are to achieve bony union with no or little limb deformity and restore function. The purpose of radiography is to aid assessment before, during and after treatment. Radiographs can easily show bony alignment and may reveal information concerning the degree and success of the fracture healing with or without the presence of fixation devices.

Reduction

First of all the bone fragments are replaced in their proper alignment. The term 'reduction' refers to the normalizing of any angulation or displacement present. Not all fractures need 'reducing'; some degree of displacement may be acceptable in some anatomical sites (but not in others). Reduction usually takes place under some form of anaesthetic. If the surgeon has to operate and expose the bone fragments before they are re-aligned then this is known as *open reduction*.

Immobilization or fixation

The bone ends must now be held firmly in *apposition* until the fragments unite together. Some fractures need no special support – for example – *avulsion* fractures and *hairline* fractures.

External supports

These include

(1) Non-rigid types of support such as slings, strapping and bandages.

(2) Splints which are usually made of metal or plastic (polymer) and are held on by bandages.

(3) Plaster of Paris (hemi-hydrated calcium sulphate) bandages or casts made of synthetic resin.

(4) Traction. This works by applying a pulling force along the line of the limb to hold the two fragments in position. Where the force is slowly applied over a period of time, traction can be used to reduce a fracture or dislocation.

Internal skeletal fixation

This is the use of special metal 'implants' to hold the bone fragments together. Compression of the fracture site by implants stimulates union. The advantage of fixation is that it allows earlier mobilization of the patient. Many types of internal fixation devices are available, all of which are scientifically designed and utilize advanced engineering principles. Materials in use are high-grade stainless steel and various alloys of chrome, cobalt, molybdenum, tungsten and nickel, carbon fibre and biodegradeables. There are several types of implant (*Figure 2.6 and 2.7*). Some examples are:

(1) Intramedullary nails used for long bones. These may be fixed with interlocking screws to prevent rotation of fragments and assist in maintaining reduction.

(2) Plates held on with screws. Plates have the additional function of compressing the bone ends together.

(3) Cortical and cancellous bone screws to hold fragments together.

External skeletal fixation

Pins are inserted through the skin to hold bone fragments in alignment. This method is used for long bones, maxillofacial fractures and spinal surgery [**ref 4**: 130].

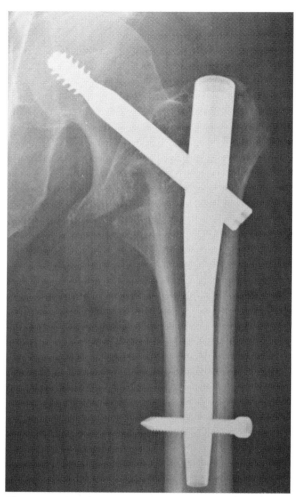

Figure 2.7 Nail for treating trochanteric fractures. The fragments are compressed with a compression screw.

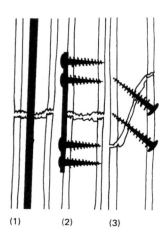

Figure 2.6 Diagram of types of metal implant used in internal fixation of fractures.

Fracture healing processes
(Figure 2.8)

(1) Immediately after the injury the fracture bleeds and a clot is formed. This *haematoma* acts as a bridge along which cells grow.

(2) *Osteoblasts* from the *periosteum* and *endosteum* form a collar of cellular tissue which soon grows to link the ends of both fragments. The haematoma gradually disappears.

(3) The active osteoblasts lay down intercellular matrix (*osteoid*) which becomes impregnated with calcium salts to form primitive *woven bone*. Calcified woven bone (*callus*) is visible on the radiograph.

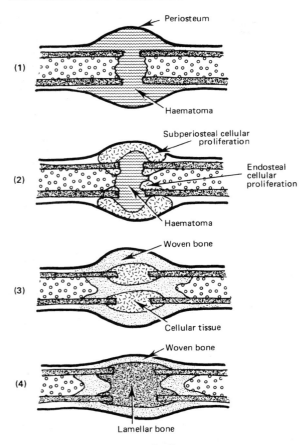

Figure 2.8 Stages in fracture healing.

(4) The woven bone is eventually replaced by mature *lamellar* or *haversian* bone. During this last stage of consolidation, remodelling of the bone takes place (*Figure 2.9*). This means that the callus collar is removed and the bone is effectively reshaped by the action of osteoblasts and osteoclasts. In children remodelling after a fracture is often so perfect that the site becomes indistinguishable on the radiographs.

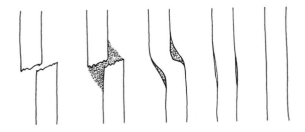

Figure 2.9 Remodelling of a bone after a fracture.

Avascular necrosis (aseptic necrosis)

Bone will die if its blood supply is disrupted by a fracture. If the avascular portion of bone involves a joint surface then the necrosis will lead to *secondary arthritis*. An example of this is in the hip joint following fracture through the neck of femur.

Union of the fragments

A fracture may be described as united when the bone moves as a single unit and is not tender when gently stressed. This is a clinical sign and is not always linked with the appearances on the radiograph. *Radiological union* is when the cortices of the (two) fragments appear to be joined on the radiograph. The time scale for healing varies. Fractures involving (chiefly) cancellous bone unite more quickly than those involving (chiefly) cortical bone. Union in cancellous bone is usually in an advanced stage at six weeks. An adult tibial fracture can take about sixteen weeks to unite, some femoral shaft fractures may take six months to unite. In young children the healing process can take about four to six weeks to reach consolidation.

Union may be delayed for a variety of reasons such as restricted blood supply to the fracture site, local infection or inadequate fixation or immobilization. Healing can be stimulated by bone grafting if the bone fails to unite.

Classes of fracture union problem are:

- *Slow* – union occurs at a slower than normal rate.
- *Delayed* – union is slow with radiological signs of abnormality.
- *Non-union* – complete failure of union. Long bones are susceptible particularly if there is poor blood supply to the bone ends.

On the other hand the fragments may unite in the 'wrong' position, resulting in a deformity that interferes with function or spoils appearances. This is called *mal-union*.

Rehabilitation

Once the fracture has united treatment may continue so that the patient regains full use of the limb. The fracture may have to be protected for a while especially if it is a weight-bearing limb.

Appliances to perform this job include crutches, splints and calipers. Graduated exercises (physiotherapy) are then undertaken to build up muscles that have become wasted owing to disuse.

Joint injuries

Sprains

This is a tearing of the joint capsule or its supporting ligaments. The only radiological evidence of this may be soft tissue swelling over the affected area.

Subluxations

A *subluxation* is a partial displacement of the articular surface of a joint, with the bones still remaining in contact with each other. These occur most commonly in the 'plane' variety of synovial joints such as the acromioclavicular or the facet joints of the spine.

Dislocations (luxations)

This is a complete separation of the articular surfaces of a joint as the result of trauma. The joint capsule is often extensively torn. Pathological dislocation may occur where there is some abnormal muscle pull or where the joint has been destroyed by some pathological process.

Fracture-dislocations

A fracture-dislocation is a combination injury where the bone is fractured at the same time as it is dislocated. These are most frequently seen in severe injuries of the ankle and the elbow joints

References

1. Berquist TH (1991) *Imaging of Orthopaedic Trauma* New York: Raven Press

2. Berquist TH (1992) *Imaging of Sports Injuries* Aspen: Gaithersburg

3. Daffner RH (1978) Stress fractures *Skeletal Radiology* 2: 221–229

4. Dandy DJ and Edwards DJ (2003) *Essential Orthopaedics and Trauma (4th Edition)* Edinburgh: Churchill Livingstone

5. Matheson GO Clement DB McKenzie DC Taunton JE Lloyd-Smith DR MacIntyre JE (1987) Stress fractures in athletes. A study of 320 cases *American Journal of Sports Medicine* 15: 46–58

6. McRae R Esser M (2002) *Practical Fracture Treatment (4th Edition)* Edinburgh: Churchill Livingstone

7. Salter RB Harris WR (1963) Injuries involving the epiphyseal plate *Journal of Bone and Joint Surgery* 45A: 587–622

8. Young JWR in Sutton D (ed) (2003) *Textbook of Radiology and Imaging (Volume 2) (7th Edition)* Edinburgh: Churchill Livingstone

Further Reading

1. Grainger RG Allison DJ Adam A Dixon AK (eds) (2001) *Grainger and Allison's Diagnostic Radiology (Volume 1) (4th Edition)* Edinburgh: Churchill Livingstone

2. Manaster BJ (1997) *Handbook of Skeletal Radiology (2nd Edition)* St Louis: Mosby

3. Miller MD (ed) (2004) *Review of Orthopaedics (4th Edition)* London: Saunders

4. Rogers LF (2002) *Radiology of Skeletal Trauma (3rd Edition)* Edinburgh: Churchill Livingstone

5. Taylor JAM Resnick DMD (2000) *Skeletal Imaging. Atlas of the Spine and Extremities* Philadelphia: Saunders

Pathological conditions of bones and joints

CHAPTER CONTENTS

Introduction

Disease may be defined as an abnormal variation in the structure and function of any part of the body, and pathology may be described as the scientific study of disease. Many factors are known to influence and modify bone production and development. For example, deprivation or excess of raw materials, vitamins and hormonal imbalances can each result in abnormalities. However, there are many diseases of bones (and joints) for which the causes are not clearly understood.

Some pathological processes may significantly alter the rate of bone formation or destruction and this abnormality may become detectable on a radiograph. For example, there may be visible changes in the thickness or physical density of the bone's cortex or alterations in the trabecular pattern (*Figures 3.1 and 3.2*). Joint architecture and bone alignment may also change as a result of disease. It should not be forgotten however, that some soft-tissue abnormalities might also show on radiographs that have been taken principally to exclude skeletal pathology (or injury). For example, increases in fluid content of joints (effusions) may be detected as they displace adjacent structures.

Radiographic examinations of the skeleton are used to exclude or assess the extent of an abnormality.

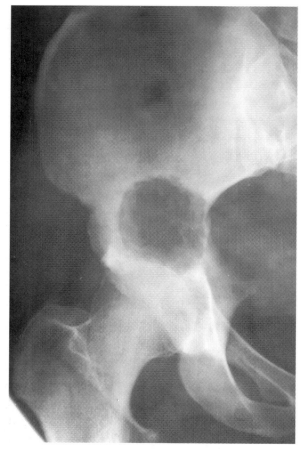

Figure 3.1 A well-demarcated osteolytic (bone-destroying) lesion.

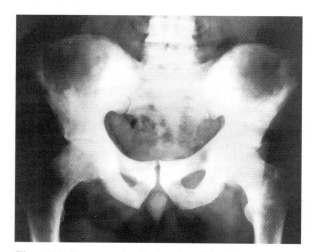

Figure 3.2 Osteopetrosis affecting the pelvis. The radiographic appearance implies that the physical density of the bone is much greater than normal.

These examinations may be part of a range of investigations used in the clinical management of the case. Radiography may be the first-choice imaging modality, however in certain circumstances it may often take second place to or even be disqualified by modalities such as *MRI* or *radioisotope scintigraphy* where sensitivity and specificity are far higher than X-ray imaging (*see* Chapter 4). This is particularly true for MRI used for detecting and characterising soft tissue lesions. However MRI may be combined with plain radiography for assessment of features such as abnormal calcification, ossification, cortical destruction and periosteal reaction (*see* – below).

The remainder of this chapter contains brief descriptions of some the better-known pathological conditions of bone and joints. Some of them are rare. These conditions are mostly of a generalized nature, i.e. they can affect several bones or joints or even the whole of the skeleton at anyone time. Some of the diseases are not necessarily of a generalized nature but could still occur at any location of the skeleton – for example – neoplastic conditions, osteoarthritis. Further comments on these conditions when they affect certain specific areas of the skeleton may be found in Part II of this book.

Diseases of bone due to vitamin deficiency

Vitamin C deficiency

Vitamin C is important in the synthesis of collagen, which is formed in the metaphyses of bone and in the walls of blood vessels. Deficiency of vitamin C causes *scurvy*. In very young children large haematomas may form under the periosteum in response to relatively minor trauma. The osteoblasts on the under-surface proceed to form new bone and considerable time is required for remodelling to occur. Similar haematomas with ossification may be seen on radiographs of the bones of 'battered babies'. In adults, scurvy is dominated by changes of capillary fragility in the skin and mucous membrane; there are rarely any skeletal radiological signs.

Vitamin D deficiency

Bone is built in two stages:

(1) Osteoblasts lay down intercellular substance or matrix (osteoid) which is not radiopaque.

(2) Salts of calcium and phosphorus are later deposited to form true bone.

Deficiency in vitamin D results in an increase in the proportion of uncalcified osteoid present. In adults this produces a condition known as osteomalacia and in the growing skeleton of infants and children the result is rickets.

Osteomalacia (Figure 3.3)

Causes of Vitamin D deficiency in adults can be nutritional, drug-induced and secondary to chronic renal failure or due to malabsorption. Up to 30% of elderly patients presenting with a fractured neck of femur have osteomalacia [ref 2: 12]. The outcome of lack of mineralization of the bone is weakness with a tendency to deformation and pathological fractures – milkman's fractures – which are usually symmetrical. Radiographs may show linear areas of increased radiolucency – Looser's zones (*Figure 3.3*). These are particularly common in the pubic rami, inner scapular borders, neck of humerus and medial aspects of the femoral shafts. Some patients may have only a generalized decrease in bone density (which may not even be detected by radiographs), especially noticeable in the peripheral skeleton when compared with the spine. For patients with long-standing renal disease such as those on renal dialysis, *renal osteodystrophy* is a term that embraces a resultant complex of changes in the skeleton. These can include *osteomalacia* (rickets in a child), *secondary hyperparathyroidism* (see below) and *osteosclerosis*. Soft-tissue and vascular calcifications can occur. Patients undergoing renal dialysis are usually monitored for these bony changes with periodic radiographic surveys.

Rickets (Figure 3.4)

This disease is caused by low dietary intake of Vitamin D and lack of sunlight. Rickets is

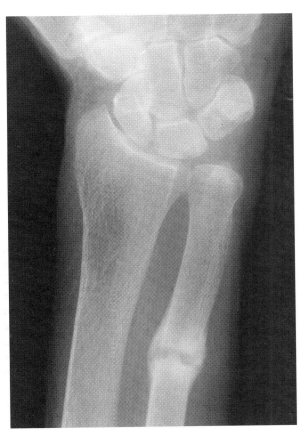

Figure 3.3 Characteristic appearance of a Looser's zone in the right ulna.

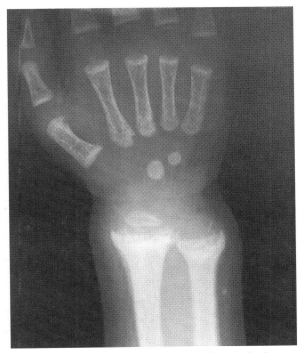

Figure 3.4 Characteristic appearance of rickets in the forearm bones of a child.

characterized by failure in the mineralization of osteoid bone and a failure of mineralization of the cartilage of the epiphyseal growth plate. Radiographs of long bones show expansion and cupping of the metaphyseal regions so that the diaphysis appears to expand into the shape of a trumpet-mouth at the metaphysis. The bone shafts lose rigidity because of the failure in mineralization. Deformities and fractures can occur.

Changes in bone due to endocrine disorders

Growth hormone oversecretion

Two conditions are the result of prolonged and excessive secretion of growth hormone which is usually caused by the presence of a tumour in the pituitary gland – *acidophil adenoma*. The lateral skull radiograph may show an increase in the size of the pituitary fossa due to the tumour.

Acromegaly *(Figure 3.5)*

This term means 'enlargement of the extremities' although other parts of the skeleton are affected. This condition occurs in an adult after the epiphyses have fused so although the bones cannot elongate they can grow thicker by periosteal ossification. There is an increase in the roughening of the surfaces of the bones and of the sites of insertion of tendons. Irregular bone growth also distorts the joint surfaces so that osteoarthritis commonly results. Changes in the skull may occur – the orbital ridges enlarge and *prognathism* (protrusion of the mandible) feature. Heel pad thickness may increase although this is no longer thought to be an infallible sign of acromegaly [**ref 5**: 1360].

Gigantism

This is a much rarer condition and occurs where there is oversecretion of growth hormone before the epiphyses have fused. There is an increased growth of the whole skeleton and this may continue for longer than normal because of delay in closure of the epiphyseal plates.

Hypothyroidism

Under-secretion of thyroid hormone may occur at any age. In adults this causes *myxoedema*. If the

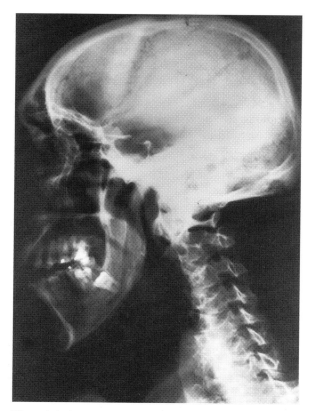

Figure 3.5 Acromegaly. Lateral radiograph of the skull and face, showing a notable increase in the size of the jaw. The pituitary fossa is also enlarged.

deficiency is present at birth then the result will be a condition called *cretinism*. The child's skeletal and mental development will be retarded. Often the earliest clue is the late appearance of secondary ossification centres in the epiphyses – for example – of the hands, lower femur or upper tibia. When they do appear growth is retarded and the centres are often fragmented.

Parathyroid hyperfunction

Blood plasma calcium ion concentrations are maintained within narrow limits (mineral homeostasis). This is necessary for normal function of muscles and nerves and for the activities of several enzymes. Normally, calcium is constantly entering the blood plasma from bone and gut; and leaving it for bone, gut or to be excreted in the urine. The principal action of parathyroid hormone (PTH) is to increase the resorption of calcium in the renal tubules. Higher concentrations of PTH in the plasma stimulate resorption of bone by osteoclasts and indirectly increase calcium absorption from the gut. Thus PTH has an important role in the regulation of plasma calcium levels.

An excess of PTH in the blood can produce symptoms associated with the action of the hormone in a condition known as *hyperparathyroidism*. Hyperparathyroidism can be classified as *primary, secondary and tertiary*. Whatever the cause of the hyperparathyroidism, one skeletal feature is common – the appearance of the surface resorption of bone by osteoclasts. These changes are called sub-periosteal erosions and may be shown by radiography of the fingers.

Primary hyperparathyroidism

In primary hyperparathyroidism there is excessive PTH secretion, which is usually due to a tumour involving one or more of the parathyroid glands. The patient may develop kidney stones, and calcium salts may be deposited in the walls of blood vessels. Radiographically, bone changes may be seen but can be difficult to detect by this method in the early stages. Over a period of time these changes can range from a generalized diminution in bone density, sub-periosteal erosions in the hand bones to cyst formation.

Secondary hyperparathyroidism

This occurs when the glands are exposed to increased stimulation to produce PTH as a compensatory reaction to *hypocalcaemia* which can occur in chronic renal failure and in untreated malabsorption syndromes.

Tertiary hyperparathyroidism

In secondary hyperparathyroidism an autonomous, usually benign parathyroid tumour may develop. If this happens then the hyperparathyroidism is no longer compensatory and is termed tertiary hyperparathyroidism.

Miscellaneous conditions of bone

Osteochondritis (osteochondroses)
(*Figure 3.6*)

This is a term used to describe a group of conditions caused by several different pathological processes

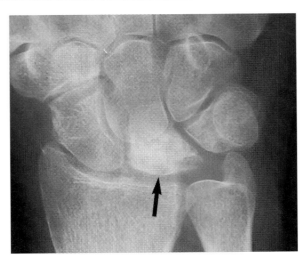

Figure 3.6 Osteochondritis of the lunate.

including an abnormality in local blood circulation. A cycle of changes can be seen and followed in serial radiographs. The avascular (bloodless) bone becomes relatively more dense than its neighbours and it then begins to crumble and collapse. Later the area becomes revascularized and its abnormal density disappears. Dead bone is removed and new bone is laid down in its place, but owing to softening the shape is now distorted.

Eponymous terms for sites affected:

(1) Femoral head – *Perthe's disease.*

(2) Lunate – *Kienböck's disease.*

(3) Navicular – *Köhler's disease.*

(4) Tibial tubercle – *Osgood-Schlatter's disease.*

(5) Head of 2nd or 3rd metatarsal – *Freiberg's disease.*

(6) Calcaneus – *Sever's disease.*

(7) Lower pole patella – *Sinding Larsens's disease.*

(8) *Scheuermann's disease* affects the ring apophysis of the thoracic vertebrae but the cause is unknown (*see* page 149).

Another aetiology for 'osteochondritis' is *traction apophysitis* where muscles attached to the apophysis (*see* Chapter 1) can pull all or part of the insertion away from the bone.

Osteochondritis dissecans

Essentially this consists of the necrosis of an area of bone adjacent to a joint surface with accompanying death of the deeper layers of its covering cartilage. Hence a segment of the articular surface may become separated and form a *loose body* inside the joint cavity (*see* – below). Areas most commonly affected are convex articular surfaces such as the medial femoral condyle knee.

As the disease usually occurs towards the end of the growing period, osteochondritis dissecans is seen predominantly in adolescents and young adults.

Osteonecrosis (avascular necrosis, aseptic necrosis)

This is a condition where a portion of bone has lost its blood supply and dies. The term aseptic may be applied as no infection is involved. Osteonecrosis may occur after injury where blood vessels are torn. Another cause is in decompression disease (*caisson disease*) where gas bubbles have occluded small blood vessels. Use of steroids and non-steroidal anti-inflammatory drugs are also associated with this condition.

MRI is the best means of detecting changes in osteonecrosis where sensitivity and specificity approach 100% [**ref 3**: 1181].

Osteoporosis *(Figure 3.7)*

This is a condition where there is a decrease in the total amount of bone present. Osteoporosis can be caused by acceleration in bone tissue resorption or a decrease in the rate of bone formation. Radiographic detection depends upon the amount of bone that has been lost; as bone mass diminishes there is a loss of bone density and radiopacity will decrease. This is radiographically described as *osteopaenia*. It should be noted that generalised (or diffuse) osteopaenia occurs in conditions other than osteoporosis – for example – in *hyperparathyroidism* [**ref 5**:1357].

Variations between individuals and variations in radiographic technique can make evaluation of bone density difficult and in general radiology is not very sensitive in this disease. Often, considerable loss of bone must occur before it is seen on the radiograph. In patients with advanced osteoporosis a fairly large decrease in exposure may be required to produce an image of relatively acceptable photographic density and contrast.

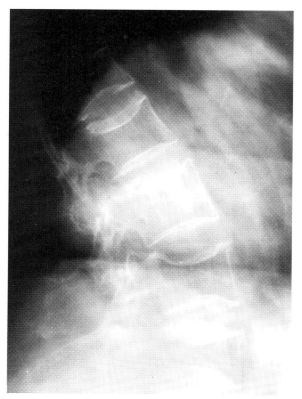

Figure 3.7 'Cod-fish' vertebrae in osteoporosis. Lack of radiographic contrast is caused by the diminution of the total amount of bone tissue present.

The radiological signs that have been attributed to osteoporosis are thinning of the cortical bone with loss of bony trabeculae. The resultant effects of reduction in bone strength may be seen in the spine. The nucleus pulposus inside the vertebral body is normally under pressure. As the bone of the vertebral body loses strength the disc tends to become more spherical. The bone collapses under the expansive force of the nucleus and this allows the discs to become biconvex with the result that biconcave vertebral bodies – cod-fish vertebrae – result (*Figure 3.7*). Weakening of bones in osteoporosis can make them more vulnerable to fractures.

The causes of osteoporosis include the following:

(1) Age-related and postmenopausal (this is mainly due to reduced physical activity). These causes are the most common.

(2) Prolonged immobilization. Bone responds to increased use by making itself better able to withstand the greater mechanical stresses. Osteoblasts build more numerous and wider trabeculae. Conversely, disuse can lead to fewer, thin and frail trabeculae as in *disuse osteoporosis*.

(3) Corticosteroid therapy. Steroids affect the trabecular bone and induce osteoporosis. Osteoporosis can also be found in *Cushing's disease*.

(4) Excess thyroid hormone – *thyrotoxicosis*. There is an increase of both resorption and bone formation but resorption exceeds formation.

Paget's disease of bone (osteitis deformans) *(Figure 3.8)*

This disease of unknown cause occurs in middle aged and elderly people, usually after the age of 40, and is more common in men than in women and more common in certain parts of the world – for example – United Kingdom, New Zealand and Australia [**ref 3**: 1192]. It is characterised by an increase in osteoclast activity with a secondary increase in osteoblast activity. The areas of the skeleton most frequently affected are the lumbar vertebrae, skull and pelvis, although limb bones may also be involved (*Figure 3.8*). The affected bone becomes larger than normal and on the radiograph the texture of the bone becomes coarsened. Deformities such as bowing of the long bones or kyphosis of the dorsal spine can occur. If the skull is affected the bones of the vault will increase in thickness, causing an increase in the size of the patient's head (*see Figure 10.7*, Chapter 10). Involvement of the base of the skull may cause nerve entrapment and deafness is not uncommon. Other complications of Paget's disease are pathological fractures, malignant changes (*Paget's sarcoma*) in the bone and heart failure because of the strain of an increased blood flow through the affected area (this may be up to twenty times the normal).

Periosteal new bone formation (periosteal reaction)

If periosteum is stimulated by trauma, inflammation or other pathology it will produce new bone. In some

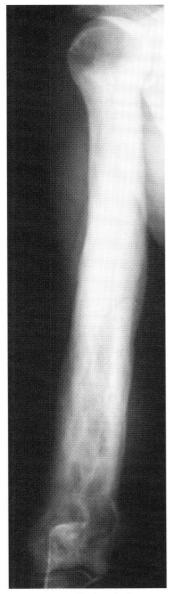

Figure 3.8 Paget's disease affecting the humerus.

conditions haemorrhage, infection or a tumour physically elevates the periosteum but generally there is a wide variety of types of periosteal reaction.

Generalised developmental abnormalities

There are many inherited disorders of bone and most are uncommon. Some may only become evident later on as growth progresses.

Achondroplasia *(Figure 3.9)*

This is the most common type of disproportionate dwarfism [**ref 3**: 1138]; a hereditary defect of 'pre-bone' cartilage in which the normal formation of cartilage cells during bone growth does not occur – hence the long bones cannot grow to their correct length. Periosteal bone formation is normal so the resulting bone is short but thick and strong. The child will have a normal trunk and short limbs. Because the vault of the skull is formed by intramembranous ossification it increases in size, whereas the base of the skull and the face are formed by enchondral ossification and do not develop to the same extent – the base of the skull tends to be flat. Spinal deformities are not uncommon and there can be a slowly progressing compression of the spinal canal

Fibrous dysplasia of bone

Fibrous dysplasia is characterized by fibrous replacement of portions of the medullary cavity of bone or bones. The fibrous tissue then undergoes varying degrees of abnormal ossification which may appear to have a cotton-wool appearance on a radiograph. The cause of the disease is unknown and it begins in young individuals, often in infancy, but because it is asymptomatic it often remains unrecognised until adulthood.

Multiple exostosis (metaphyseal aclasis)

This is a condition where there is a failure of the normal progress of remodelling of the metaphyseal region of long bones and a presence of exostoses arising from the metaphysis. The regions affected are the hips, knees, shoulders and ankles.

Osteogenesis imperfecta (fragilitas ossium) *(Figure 3.10)*

Osteogenesis imperfecta is a rare congenital disorder where there is abnormal fragility or brittleness of bones. The cortical bone is thin and defective and the patient may suffer from multiple fractures.

Osteopetrosis (marble bone disease or Albers-Schönberg disease) *(Figure 3.2)*

This is a rare inherited condition characterized by brittle bones which radiographically are shown to be excessively physically dense (with corresponding low optical density). In addition to increased brittleness, the condition causes depression of the

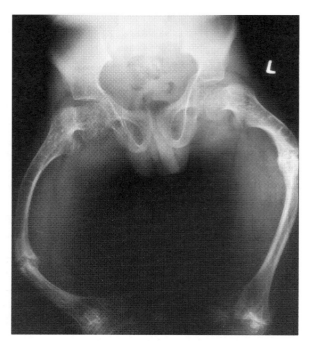

Figure 3.10 Osteogenesis imperfecta. The femora are deformed and contain healing pathological fractures.

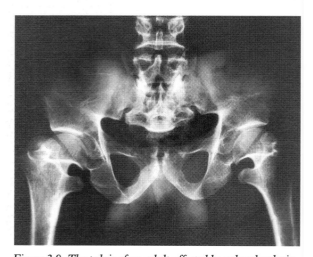

Figure 3.9 The pelvis of an adult affected by achondroplasia.

marrow function and compression of cranial nerves within the base of the skull. The spine has a characteristic striped appearance (*rugger-jersey spine*).

Infections of bone

Bone is liable to infections like any other tissue. Organisms may reach the bone either directly through a skin wound in a compound fracture, or indirectly via the bloodstream. Organisms common in bone infections are Staphylococcus aureus and salmonellae. For adults in locations where health-care services are developed, bone infections are most likely to occur following an operation such as joint replacement. Use of antibiotics takes the credit for making established bone infections relatively uncommon in the United Kingdom.

Acute haematogenous osteomyelitis

This is a bacterial infection arising in the metaphyseal region of the bone, most often a disease of children and usually affecting the bone before epiphyseal lines have closed. The infection reaches the metaphyseal region via the bloodstream from a septic focus elsewhere in the body – for example – a boil. Once established the infection spreads in various directions into the surrounding bone and neighbouring parts. A sub-periosteal abscess is formed and deprives the underlying bone of a blood supply. This segment of bone dies and eventually separates to form a *sequestrum*. As the disease progresses the elevated periosteum lays down layers of new bone, an *involucrum*. Eventually the abscess bursts through the periosteum and spreads to the surface to form a chronic sinus. *Radioisotope scintigraphy* and *MRI* may give early confirmation of the diagnosis.

Chronic osteomyelitis

This relapsing type of osteomyelitis can follow an acute attack, which suggests that the original infection has not completely responded to treatment. The causative organisms can lie dormant in certain parts of the affected area and they occasionally become reactivated. Sinus tracks may be investigated by injection of a radiopaque contrast agent in sinography. In *diabetes*, soft tissue infection may follow breaks in anaesthetic skin of the foot. This can lead to ulceration and osteomyelitis may develop in underlying bone.

Brodie's abscess

This is a persistent abscess in the metaphyseal region of a bone and appears to develop without a preceding attack. Treatment comprises opening and emptying the abscess cavity.

Tuberculosis (TB) of bone and joint
(*Figure 3.11*)

The commonest and most important type of chronic infection of bone is that due to tuberculosis. In the United Kingdom one-third of present-day patients are immigrants [**ref 3**: 1167]. The causative organism (Mycobacterium tuberculosis) reaches the bone via the bloodstream from a primary focus

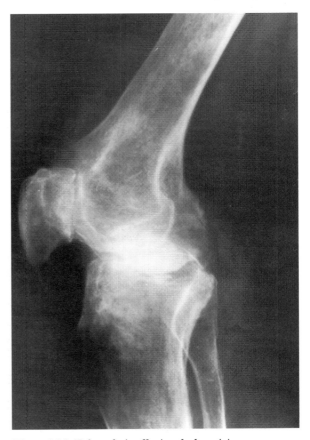

Figure 3.11 Tuberculosis affecting the knee joint.

either in the lungs or in the alimentary tract. This initial site of infection may still be active or may be healed by the time the skeletal focus is discovered. Tuberculous bacilli may infect primarily bone or synovial membrane but usually both the joint and neighbouring bones are eventually affected. TB is more common in the bodies of the vertebrae, the hip joint and the diaphyses of the metacarpals and metatarsals.

Miscellaneous joint conditions

Ankylosing spondylitis (*Figure 3.12*)

This is a progressive stiffening of the spine starting in the lumbar region and moving upwards. Ossification of the surrounding soft tissues and lateral bony bridging of the vertebrae give rise to a radiographic appearance after which the disease is sometimes named – *bamboo spine*. Stiffening of the spine/rib joints restrict the patient's breathing volume because of the limiting of chest expansion. If untreated the patient may end up with a severe

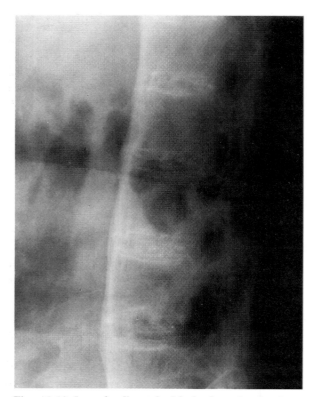

Figure 3.12 Lateral radiograph of the lumbar spine showing ankylosing spondylitis.

rigid flexion deformity of the spine and neck which is very disabling. The earliest changes in ankylosing spondylitis are seen in the sacroiliac joints; in the rest of the spine changes may not be seen until much later. In severe cases the disease may also involve the shoulders, hips, knees and occasionally the temporomandibular joints. This disease can also affect the eyes in *iritis* and other organs of the body are affected more rarely.

Loose bodies in joints

Smooth movement of a joint may be upset by the presence of a piece of bone or cartilage lying free in the joint space. The fragment has probably separated from one of the joint surfaces but its presence is not suspected until the joint suddenly locks or its range of flexion is reduced. Where there is sudden interference with its range of movement the joint may react by forming a *synovial effusion*. Loose bodies most commonly affect the knee and elbow but they can occur in the hip, ankle and shoulder and will be visible on the radiographs provided they contain an ossified or calcified portion.

Causes of loose bodies in joints include:

(1) Osteoarthritis – separation of osteophytes (*see* – below).

(2) Osteochondritis dissecans (*see* page 22).

(3) Fractures.

Osteoarthritis (degenerative arthrosis) (*Fig 3.13*)

The well-recognised term for degeneration of joints is *osteoarthritis*. In recent years *osteoarthrosis* has found some favour mainly because in this condition the joint is not necessarily inflamed, which the word-ending 'itis' would seem to suggest.

There are two main types:

(1) *Primary osteoarthritis* – where there is no known cause for the degeneration; several joints may be affected simultaneously.

(2) *Secondary osteoarthritis* – where there has been previous destruction of articular cartilage or disruption of the joint surfaces, e.g. following a fracture.

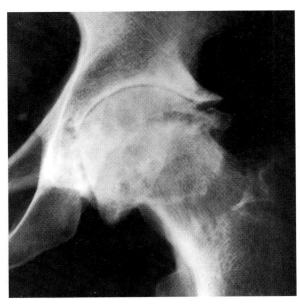

Figure 3.13 Osteoarthritis in the left hip joint.

Osteoarthritis is the commonest form of chronic joint disease and is characterized clinically by the progressive onset of joint pain and stiffness. This causes most problems when it affects the weight-bearing joints – hips, knees and ankles. The patients are usually elderly (depending on how that is defined).

The typical radiological appearances of osteoarthritis (*Figure 3.13*) are:

(1) The joint 'space' becomes narrowed and remodelled so that joint alignment alters.

(2) *Osteophytes* (bony growths) are formed at the margins of the joint and these restrict movement.

(3) *Juxta-articular sclerosis*. This is one of the cardinal radiological signs of osteoarthritis.

Degenerative joint disease can be treated surgically as follows:

Debridement – removal of osteophytes, usually where they are obstructing joint movement.

Arthrodesis – the joint is permanently stiffened. This gives complete relief of pain but may throw increased strain on other joints.

Osteotomy – cutting across the bone distal to the joint and then allowing it to unite in a slightly

altered position may relieve the pain of arthritis. The bone is fixed internally until it has united. Osteotomy can be used to correct deformities caused either by degeneration or following mal-union of a fracture.

Arthroplasty – making a new joint. There are several methods – for example – one or both bony components of the joint are excised and replaced by a metal or plastic prosthesis (substitute). The joints most commonly treated are the knee (e.g. *Freeman-Swanson* prosthesis) and the hip (*Charnley* total hip prosthesis and its variants – *see* Chapter 8). The success rate is high, but there are risks of complications such as infection and mechanical failure.

Rheumatoid disease

This is a general systemic disease which can involve many body organs. The dominant feature however is changes in the joints, i.e. *rheumatoid arthritis*. The disease tends to affect more than one joint and usually starts in the small joints of the hands and feet (*see Figure 5.8* Chapter 5) but it may also affect the larger joints such as the knee. The joints become inflamed and swollen – this often spontaneously resolves but sometimes the disease can progress leading to joint disorganization and development of deformities. Joint erosions are seen more often and earlier using *MRI* compared with plain radiography [ref 3: 1201].

Neoplastic conditions

Tumours of the locomotor system fall into two groups:

(1) Secondary or metastatic tumours – usually deposited in bone. These are the commonest tumours of the skeleton.

(2) Primary tumours. Benign tumours are relatively common and are slow-growing and do not metastasise.

Most tumours occur in young people and cease growing when skeletal maturity has been reached. Malignant tumours are rare and account for only 1% of deaths from neoplasia [ref 1: 1247]. All malignant bone tumours are neoplastic but benign tumours may include a variety of tumour-like lesions [ref 4: 1837].

Plain radiographic examination is important in the diagnosis, classification and staging of bone tumours but presence of metastatic lesions may be detected earlier by *CT, MRI* and *radioisotope scintigraphy* [**ref 1**: 1251].

New growths can provoke radical changes in the radiographic appearance of bone. Some of these lesions are *osteolytic* – producing areas of rarefaction – or *osteoblastic*, where an increase in radiopacity will occur. Pathological fractures may feature in certain types and stages of bone tumour. Certain tumours inside the cranium and face may have an effect on surrounding bony structure; some of these may be found only in this area of the body and so will be considered with the indications for radiography of the skull and face. A diagnosis may sometimes be made on the basis of X-ray evidence alone; however, some tumours may not be visible until much bone has been destroyed.

Metastatic tumours

Bone is a common site for deposition of secondary tumours. These are usually of epithelial origin and the commonest primary sites are:

(1) Breast.
(2) Bronchus.
(3) Thyroid.
(4) Kidney.
(5) Prostate.

Metastases may be blood borne and can be deposited anywhere in the skeleton, particularly in the vertebrae, flat bones, and proximal ends of femora and humerii. These areas all have a rich blood supply and correspond to sites of persistent haemopoesis in adults [**ref 1**: 1251]. Breast metastases are common in ribs, thoracic vertebrae and clavicles but can ultimately invade the entire skeleton.

Prostate metastases may reach the bone by venous spread and are common in limbs, sacral spine and pelvis. Metastases usually occur late in the development of the primary disease and sometimes a pathological fracture from – for example – carcinoma of the bronchus may be the first sign of the disease. Most secondary deposits are *osteolytic* but metastases from the prostate and very rarely from the breast are *osteoblastic*.

Primary neoplasms of bone tissue

Bones are made up of many types of tissue – bone, cartilage, fibrous tissue, marrow etc. Tumours can arise from most of these tissues as well as from associated soft tissues – muscle, fat, synovium, and blood vessels etc. – although soft-tissue tumours are comparatively rare. A simple classification is given in *Table 3.1*; note that definitive classification of primary tumours is difficult because precise tissue of origin is often uncertain, mixed cell tumours are common and different areas of a tumour may contain different types of tissue.

Table 3.1   Classification of primary neoplasms of bone

Tissue	Benign	Malignant
Bone	Osteoma	Osteosarcoma
Cartilage	Chondroma Osteochondroma	Chondrosarcoma
Marrow		Ewing's tumour, myelomatosis
Uncertain origin	Giant cell tumour	Giant cell tumour

Bone cysts

Bone cysts are tumour-like lesions that produce cyst-like cavities with thin bony walls. They are usually found in long bones.

Chondromas

These are benign tumours composed of cartilage cells found within a bone, most commonly in the finger bones of the hand. *Enchondromas* are confined within the bone cortex and *ecchondromas* protrude outside the bone cortex.

Chondrosarcoma

The tumour arises either from the ends of the major long bones or from flat bones such as the pelvis or scapula. A chondroma in a major long bone may undergo malignant change to become a chondrosarcoma. On a radiograph a chondrosarcoma appears as a bone-destroying lesion with areas of spotty calcification.

Ewing's sarcoma

This is a highly malignant tumour affecting young people, most commonly between the ages of 5 and

30 [**ref 1**: 1315]. The origin has not yet been completely clarified but most authorities accept that it arises from the endothelium of the bone marrow spaces. The shafts of femur, tibia and humerus are most commonly affected but it can also be seen in flat bones such as pelvis or ribs. Ewing's tumour metastasises early and widely to lungs, lymph nodes and skull, and sometimes to the spine, scapula and clavicle.

Giant cell tumours (osteoclastoma)

The tumour may be either benign and cause local destruction of bone or malignant in which case it may metastasise to the lungs. It occurs in the ends of the long bones, usually the lower femur, radius or upper tibia and humerus. On the radiograph, the tumour is radiolucent and adjacent bone cortex may be thinner.

Myelomatosis

Myelomatosis or multiple myeloma is a neoplastic proliferation of plasma cells or their precursors, usually confined to red bone marrow and occurring in elderly subjects. The disease is often characterized by multiple foci of bone destruction. These foci appear as small 'punched out' areas involving the 'marrow bones' (long bones of limbs; skull, sternum, pelvis and spine).

Osteoid osteomas

These are benign tumours that most commonly affect the femur or tibia. The lesion is usually located in the bone cortex and there is characteristically a reactive sclerosis around a radiolocent central area.

Osteosarcomas (Osteogenic sarcoma) (Figure 3.14)

About 25% of primary bone tumours are osteosarcomas [**ref 1**: 1216]. The tumour arises from the metaphysis of long bones and is usually found in the lower end of the femur, it is highly malignant and may metastasise to the lungs and pleurae. The tumour gives rise to new bone formation with typically raised *persiosteal reaction* (*see* page 23). Also radiologically characteristic are 'sunrise' spicules of bone. Patients with Paget's disease may develop an osteosarcoma, and a sarcoma may be induced by radiation.

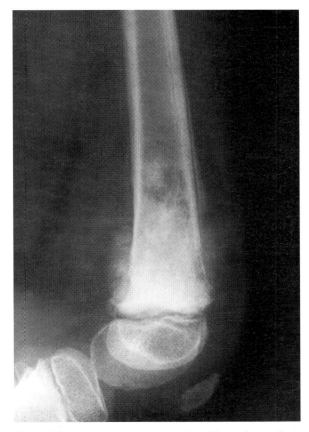

Figure 3.14 Osteogenic sarcoma in the left lower femur. On the anterior aspect of the bone the periosteum is raised and new bone is seen forming underneath it.

Soft-tissue neoplasms

Serious neoplastic disease is less common in soft tissues of the locomotor system than in bone. They may or may not cause changes in the radiographic appearances of bone. Visibility depends on the tumour's association with the proximal or surrounding bone. If it lies in muscle or fat its physical density may be sufficiently different to render it apparent; thus a tumour of high fat content may be visible because it is more radiolucent. Some soft-tissue tumours may be calcified.

Benign synovioma

These arise from the synovial tissue of joints and tendon sheaths, usually in the hand, and cause lobulated swelling.

Haemangiomas

These are probably not true tumours but a local congenital anomaly of blood vessels. Haemangiomas are more commonly found in the vertebrae, affecting a single vertebral body. Destruction of the bone may result in its eventual collapse. Large congenital haemangiomas are considered to be arteriovenous communications. They are more frequently found in the lower limb. Because they cause an increase in local blood flow they can accelerate epiphyseal growth, resulting in a discrepancy in limb length.

Lipoma

Lipomas are common tumours occurring anywhere in the body where fatty tissue is present. They are easily recognized on radiographs by their lucent nature.

Liposarcoma

Very rarely malignant changes take place in liposarcoma.

Neurilemmoma

This is an encapsulated, slowly growing tumour which arises from the neural sheath and consists mainly of Schwann cells.

Neurofibroma

Neurofibromas arise from the fibrous tissue lining of a peripheral nerve and sometimes become malignant.

Neurofibromatosis

This causes multiple neurofibromas. It is hereditary and is associated with severe kyphoscoliosis and is one of the many causes of club foot.

Rhabdomyosarcoma

True tumours of muscles and tendons are rare. Very occasionally a malignant new growth of striped muscle occurs. A rhabdomyosarcoma is highly malignant and metastasizes rapidly.

Synovial sarcoma

This is a highly malignant growth arising from synovial tissue, usually of a major joint such as the knee. It metastasizes to the lungs.

References

1. Cobby M Watt I in Sutton D (ed) (2003) *Textbook of Radiology and Imaging* Edinburgh: Churchill Livingstone

2. McRae R and Andrew W (1997) *Orthopaedics and trauma: an illustrated colour text* Edinburgh: Churchill Livingstone

3. Renton P in Sutton D (ed) (2003) *Textbook of Radiology and Imaging (Volume 2)(7th Edition)* Edinburgh: Churchill Livingstone

4. Stoker DJ and Saifuddin A in Grainger R Allison D Adam A Dixon A (eds) (2001) *Grainger and Allison's Diagnostic Radiology (Volume 3) (4th Edition)* London: Churchill Livingstone

5. Young JWR in Sutton D (ed) (2003) *Textbook of Radiology and Imaging (Volume 2) (7th Edition)* Edinburgh: Churchill Livingstone

Further Reading

1. Dandy DJ and Edwards DJ (2003) *Essential Orthopaedics and Trauma (4th Edition)* London: Churchill Livingstone

2. Manaster BJ (1997) *Handbook of Skeletal Radiology (2nd Edition)* St Louis: Mosby

3. Murray RO Jacobson HG Stoker DJ (1990) *The Radiology of Skeletal Disorders (3rd Edition)* Edinburgh: Churchill Livingstone

4. Resnick D (2000) *Diagnosis of Bone and Joint Disorders (4th Edition)* Philadelphia: Saunders

5. Taylor JAM Resnick DMD (2000) *Skeletal Imaging. Atlas of the Spine and Extremities* Philadelphia: Saunders

The radiographic examination

Whether to 'X-ray' or not

One of the key principles of radiation protection in diagnostic examinations is the justification of medical exposures. The potential value for each exposure to radiation must be assessed in advance of its performance to make sure that net benefits to the patient outweigh the risks. In other words the examination is justified if it will have a positive influence on the efficacy of diagnosis, patient management and final outcome [ref 20].

In the United Kingdom (UK), the Royal College of Radiologists (RCR) explains this process of justification and the critical roles and responsibilities of employers and various categories of personnel [ref 2]. The RCR also publish evidence-based guidelines [ref 20] to assist 'referrers' to make best use of a department of clinical radiology. A 'referrer' means a registered medical practitioner, dental practitioner or other

health professional who is entitled in accordance with the employer's procedures to refer individuals for medical exposure to a practitioner [ref 6]. These guidelines are defined as a "concept of good practice against which the needs of individual patients can be considered" [ref 20: 7]. The stated objectives are to improve clinical practice by helping (referrers) to choose the most appropriate imaging investigation or intervention for their patients. The most appropriate investigation may not be one using ionising radiation at all. The guidelines indicate which investigation (imaging modality) is best suited to the clinical or diagnostic problem, i.e. whether or not it is

- indicated
- not initially indicated
- indicated only in specific circumstances
- whether it be used as a specialised investigation.

Referral for an imaging examination

This is generally regarded as a request for an opinion from a specialist in radiology or nuclear medicine. The outcome of this request should be presented in the form of a report to assist in the management of a clinical problem [ref 20: 15]. In the UK, advanced practitioner and consultant radiographers may undertake the roles of reporting.

Optimisation of radiation protection

Once an examination has been justified and patient identity and consent (where applicable) have been confirmed, the imaging process must be *optimised*. Radiographing a person inevitably involves irradiating that person and unfortunately, even small doses carry risk. Optimisation refers to the best use of resources in reducing radiation risks so far as is reasonably achievable taking into account social and economic factors [ref 11]. This is the basis for the ALARA (as low as reasonably achievable) principle and (in part in the UK) the ALARP (as low as reasonably practicable) principle.

Practical steps for optimisation

- Choosing the appropriate radiographic technique. All imaging departments should have *protocols* for each common clinical situation. As far as plain skeletal radiography is concerned, a department will publish the protocols for radiographic examinations. These are likely to include details of which radiographic projections to use according to clinical circumstances and local conditions. Reference may be made to the RCR guidelines [ref 20] or the European guidelines [ref 4].

- Implementing department protocols for radiographing women who are or may be pregnant see [ref 20: 9]. Rules disallowing radiography of such women are generally disregarded in an emergency where the benefit from the X-ray examination outweighs the risk associated with irradiating the early pregnancy.

- Carefully applying radiographic techniques (positioning and exposure) avoiding repeating examinations or projections.

- Keeping the number of radiographic exposures within one examination to a minimum consistent with obtaining necessary diagnostic information [ref 4: 5].

- Using the most sensitive image receptor or imaging system compatible with adequate image quality.

- Limiting the size of the X-ray beam (and thus the volume of tissue irradiated) to the smallest field giving the required diagnostic information.

- Using lead equivalent protection over sensitive areas for example the lower abdomen and upper thighs for gonads in patients of reproductive capacity.

- Last – but not of least importance – adhering to statutory regulations [refs 6 and 7].

Dose reference levels and effective radiation dose

The International Commission on Radiological Protection (ICRP) does not recommend application of dose limitations to patient irradiation [ref 4: 2].

European Council Directive [ref 5] (and in the UK) IR(ME)R 2000 [ref 6] do require establishment of *dose reference levels (DRLs)* for selected examinations. These are an aid to optimisation of protection in medical exposure. Dose reference levels are expected *not* to be exceeded for standard procedures when good and normal practice is being followed. Employers are obliged to undertake reviews whenever DRLs are consistently exceeded [ref 12]. The dose reference level can be taken as a ceiling from which progress should be pursued to lower dose levels in line with the ALARA principle.

Reference to *effective radiation doses* related to natural background radiation is a useful and accessible way of explaining radiation doses for radiographic imaging to the public. The *effective radiation dose* for a radiological investigation may be defined as the sum of the doses to a number of body tissues, weighted so as to provide a value proportional to radiation-induced genetic and somatic risk even when the body is not uniformly irradiated [ref 19:

131]. Citations of *effective radiation dose* provide a single dose estimate related to the total radiation risk, no matter how the radiation dose is distributed around the body [**ref 20**: 11]. The unit used for effective dose is Jkg^{-1} with the special name *sievert*. Typical effective doses from diagnostic medical exposures and their approximate equivalent period of natural background radiation are cited in each chapter (*see* also [**ref 20**: 12 and **ref 16**]).

Terminology used in radiographic technique

What is radiographic technique?

Radiographic technique refers to a process producing suitable and accurate relative positioning of the X-ray beam, subject and image receptor. With the subject's exposure to an appropriate level of X-radiation, the emergent X-ray beam *projects* an image representative of the internal structure of the subject (*Figure 4.1*). A useful analogy is the light from an overhead projector projecting the image of the slide onto a screen.

The radiographic image is recorded by the image receptor and revealed by chemical or electronic processing. Provided the image or sets of images produced for a radiographic examination are of optimum quality (and the examination has been justified) diagnostic information obtained from the images should provide the desired positive net benefit for the patient.

The term *radiographic technique* may also be used to refer to a set of radiographic technique *parameters* that result in good imaging performance capable of meeting image quality criteria such as visibility of anatomical or pathological structures with optimum radiation dose [**ref 4**: 8]. These *parameters* are alternatively referred to as *exposure factors* or *exposure technique*. Examples include kilovolts peak (kVp), image receptor speed (sensitivity), source to image receptor distance, exposure time and nominal effective X-ray tube focal spot size. A set of optimum parameters can be cited for each projection although multiple variants of local conditions make universal standardisation difficult.

'View' or ' projection'?

The aims of using received (i.e. worthy) terminology are to help systematize the description of projections and enable accurate, safe communication. However we are reminded that scientific and technical terminology develops quickly as new activities evolve and many terms are difficult to define because they are used in different professional environments and contexts [**ref 15**: XI].

The term *projection radiography* is relatively new in common usage. It refers to the technique of radiography producing a 'flat' two-dimensional image using a range of image receptors including image intensifiers. Thus projection radiography is differentiated from the cross-sectional images produced in *computerized tomography (CT)*. CT

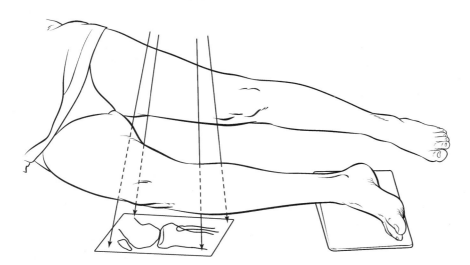

Figure 4.1 Projection radiography of the knee joint.

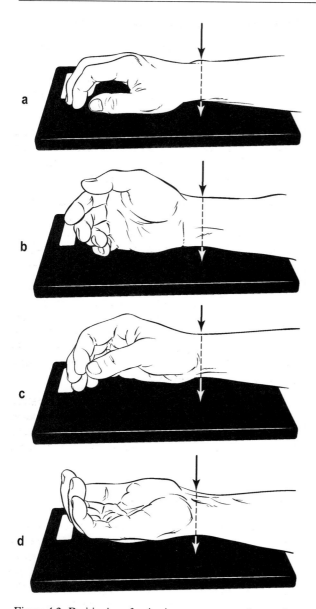

Figure 4.2 Positioning of wrist, image receptor and central ray in different projections (see text for key).

equipment can also be operated to produce projection radiographs (*scanograms*). This is generally used to display slice locations and prescribe CT slices rather than for direct diagnosis [ref 9].

This author notes the opinion that the expression *view* is not a correct positioning term in the United States [ref 4: 29]. Nevertheless in the UK, *view* is a well-known synonym for *projection* and is in constant use by health care professionals. This fact endorses the usage. *'View'* may still be deemed unworthy simply because the word lacks the scientific aura of *'projection'*.

There is more agreement about the usage of other terms for describing radiographic techniques. Many are derived from the long-established discipline of anatomy and their usage is generally deemed 'stable'. It is assumed that the reader will already be familiar with general anatomical terminology for describing the relative movements of the limbs and the aspects and planes of the body. Anatomical landmarks and planes for the head are described and illustrated in Chapter 10. Examples of some terms especially relevant to patient positioning in radiographic technique are listed in Table 4.1. Note that the word 'decubitus' simply means 'position'.

Table 4.1   Terms used for general patient position

Terms	*Description of general patient position*
Supine (dorsal decubitus)	Subject lying facing upwards
Prone (ventral decubitus)	Subject lying facing downwards
Erect	Subject standing or sitting
Lateral decubitus	Subject lying on the side
Recumbent	Subject lying down

Terminology for specific projections (views)

These are derived from the direction in which the X-ray beam passes through the subject:

Posteroanterior (PA) – The anterior or ventral aspect of the subject faces the image receptor. The X-ray beam passes through from the posterior aspect to the anterior aspect of the subject (*Figure 4.2 (a)*).

Lateral (Lat) – One side of the body or limb is next to the image receptor. For the trunk and head, the median sagittal plane lies parallel to the image receptor. For the limbs a lateral projection can also be described as mediolateral or lateromedial (*Figure 4.2 (b)*) depending on the aspect of the limb nearest the image receptor. The X-ray beam passes across the subject from side-to-side.

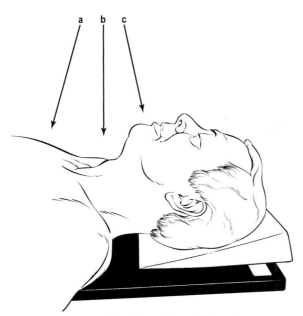

Figure 4.3 Relationship of central ray of X-ray beam to image receptor (see text for key).

Oblique (Obl) – The trunk, head or limb is placed in a position that lies somewhere between that for the AP or PA and the lateral projections (*Figure 4.2(c)*). The number of degrees rotation may be specified.

Anteroposterior (AP) – The posterior or dorsal aspect of the subject faces the image receptor. The X-ray beam passes through the subject from the anterior aspect to the posterior aspect of the subject (*Figure 4.2(d)*).

Axial projection – The X-ray beam passes through the body from above to below (or vice-versa), i.e. along the body's longitudinal axis (see as an example *Figure 7.23*, Chapter 7, page 116).

In radiography of the head, alternative terminology may be used which has been derived from the names given to local anatomical areas or aspects of the skull (*see* Chapter 10). Examples are as follows:

Occipitofrontal (OF) – The X-ray beam is directed via the occipital aspect of the head towards the frontal bone.

Occipitomental (OM) – The X-ray beam is directed through the occipital aspect of the head towards the patient's chin (*mentum*).

The direction of the X-ray beam

Central ray – This effectively represents the centre of the X-ray beam or X-ray 'field'. In radiography it is usual to refer to the direction of the central 'ray' when describing projections. Field size is adjusted around this central 'ray'.

'Centring point' – This phrase only describes the location of the point of entry of the central ray on the subject. 'Direction of central ray' includes both centring point and X-ray beam angulation.

X-ray beam angle – For the techniques described in this book, unless an X-ray tube or beam angle is specified, the central ray is usually taken to have a perpendicular relationship (i.e. *normal* or *straight*) with the cassette or image receptor (*Figure 4.3(b)*).

Cephalad or cranial X-ray beam angle (Figure 4.3(c)) – This refers to rotation of the central ray of the X-ray beam from a position where it is perpendicular to the image receptor, towards the patient's head through a specified number of degrees. An angle meter (goniometer) display on the X-ray tube housing is an aid to accuracy.

Caudad or caudal angle (Figure 4.3(a)) – This refers to rotation of the central ray of the X-ray beam from a position where it is perpendicular to the image receptor, towards the patient's feet through a specified number of degrees.

Limiting the X-ray beam size

The term *collimating* the X-ray beam commonly refers to the reduction of the X-ray field size by varying the position of the lead shutters or fixed diameter cones or diaphragms. These devices are either permanently or temporarily attached to the exit port of the X-ray tube. The term was originally used to refer to the process of 'forcing' the X-rays into a column by use of secondary radiation grids [**ref 14**: 64].

Limiting the X-ray beam size is important in optimisation and provides the additional benefit of increasing radiographic contrast. By reducing the volume of tissue irradiated less scattered radiation is produced and thus less reaches the image receptor. The X-ray beam should not fall outside the area coincident with the image receptor. In computed radiography (*CR*) care must be taken with collimation and that an appropriate area of imaging plate is covered otherwise the resultant image will require manipulation at the workstation to allow optimal viewing [**ref 13**: 99].

Terminology used in radiographic image formation and image quality

The radiographic technique and the image it produces is a system of recording information. Placing radiation protection and patient care considerations aside, the radiographer has two objectives:

(1) To select the appropriate projections for an area of the body with reference to suspected pathological or traumatic condition.

(2) To produce images that have such qualities that the person viewing the image can observe and detect the information carried.

Assuming that the criteria for (1) are satisfied the image must then have four important qualities:

(a) It must have optical density (*image blackening*).

(b) The differences between the subject densities should be apparent (*image contrast*). The amount of contrast in an image is very important when considering the effect of *noise* on an image [**ref 18**: 128].

(c) The image should have low *noise*. Noise refers to random variations of *signal* that can obscure information (*see Figure 4.4*). The *signal* arises from the processes of transmission of X-rays by the patient. Noise is a limiting factor in object detectability therefore low noise is a prerequisite to good image quality (at reasonable radiation doses) particularly when viewing small, low contrast objects.

(d) The amount of image *detail* or image *detectability* should be optimal and appropriate for the subject being radiographed. Detail related parameters include *spatial resolution* and in practical terms this refers to how much detail in an image is visible to the human eye. However, there is a *limit* to how much detail that can be resolved by any imaging system.

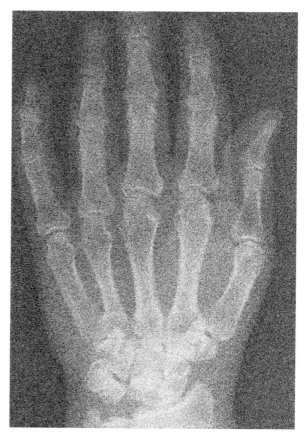

Figure 4.4 Image of hand with noise degradation.

The spatial resolution of a digital image is defined by a matrix of *pixels* (picture elements) running in horizontal rows [**ref 22**: 336] and is related (in part) to pixel size. Pixel size is a very basic measurement of the resolution capability of a system but it does give an indication of the potential *limiting resolution* of the final image [**ref 18**: 126]. *Spatial resolution* is not a reliable measure of image quality as it does not take into account noise or contrast performance

Particularly with the advent of electronic forms of radiographic imaging *detective quantum efficiency* (DQE) has emerged as the single parameter that combines noise and contrast performance of the system. This is widely accepted as the measure most representative of image quality and object detectability [**ref 10**].

Image receptors and image processing

All styles of projection radiographic image forming processes require an X-ray source, a subject and an image receptor. This has remained unchanged since Röentgen's day.

Today the choice of receptor will include:

- X-ray sensitive film in a light-tight envelope (*direct film radiography*) used almost exclusively in intra-oral dental radiography.

- Light (and X-ray) sensitive film exposed mainly by the matched colour emissions from one or two intensifying screens (*film-screen radiography*). These components are housed in a 'cassette'.

- *Computed radiography* which involves trapping electrons on photostimulated phosphor plates (imaging plates) and then reading them to generate data. Imaging plates are housed in a 'cassette'.

- *Cassetteless systems* using *digital* detectors which convert the X-rays detected into digital images within the detector itself.

In film-screen radiography, the selection of film-screen combination and characteristics of film chemical processing are crucial for image quality. Both will influence optical density, image contrast and resolution. In computed radiography and cassette-less systems, electronic image processing is aimed at creating a final image that provides the most information. The operator may make global and localised image optical density and contrast changes. The edges of objects may be sharpened or blurred. Blurring can also be applied to decrease noise in the image [**ref 8**: 33–34].

Exposure factors

The radiographer must be able to understand and thus manipulate the *exposure factors* that can affect the radiographic image. Choice of exposure factors depends upon subject type, size, composition and type of image receptor and processing system. When using film-screen imaging technology, even with automatic exposure devices the radiographer needs to take care to select appropriate exposure factors for the subject. This is because there is a relatively narrow latitude for exposure error and mistakes are rewarded with under or overexposed

films. These are images that are too 'black' or too 'pale' and lacking in contrast. A computed or digital radiography system has the ability to automatically compensate for under and overexposure and produces images where the exposure appears to be appropriate. Nevertheless these images may still have reduced diagnostic image quality that may not be obvious. Automatic compensation may become problematic if radiographers get no feedback relating to exposure selection errors. Reduction in image quality becomes accepted and consistent overexposure of patients becomes a possibility [**ref 17**]. An understanding of the exposure factors described below is easier if it is assumed that there is no facility for automatic compensation.

Exposure factors affecting optical density (image blackening)

The degree of image blackening achieved by the radiographic exposure generally depends upon the amount of radiation that has reached the image receptor.

For a particular subject, image blackening depends on:

- The X-ray tube *milliampere seconds* (*mAs*) selected. Increasing *mA* increases the intensity of the X-ray beam. Increasing the *exposure time* lengthens the duration of the exposure.

- The X-ray tube *kilovoltage peak* (*kVp*) selected. The intensity of the beam increases as the kVp increases. The beam is also more likely to reach the image receptor because it has greater penetrating power.

For a given radiographic exposure (mAs and kVp) and image receptor sensitivity, the optical density of the resultant image is also determined by:

- The *size, physical density and atomic number of the subject*. Absorption of the X-ray beam tends to bear a proportional relationship to these characteristics. The relatively high atomic number of calcium in bone increases absorption of X-rays significantly when compared with soft tissues that have a much lower average atomic number.

- For film-screen radiography – *the type of intensifying screens* used with the film – for example – 'high-speed' screens produce more film blackening for a given radiographic exposure than 'slow-speed' (detail or high-resolution) screens. In computed radiography, imaging plates may be purchased in standard or high resolution formats (determined by the size of the phosphor grains). This will theoretically determine the amount of image blackening present for a given exposure. In practice the automatically applied pre-processing algorithms and subsequent post processing will determine the degree of blackening that is apparent to the viewer.

Image contrast and grayscale

Production of radiographic images is possible because some areas of the human subject absorb fewer X-rays than others. This results in corresponding areas of the image receptor receiving more exposure compared with others. This results in variations of optical density in the final image. Where the degree of density differences is great then the image is said to have *high contrast*. If very little difference is present then the image has *low contrast (Figure 4.5 (a) and (b))*. Radiographers refer to the *optimum contrast* (Figure 4.5(c)) required in an image, rather than stating that 'good' contrast should be achieved. This is because too much (or too little) contrast can result in loss of information from the image and that information may be difficult to perceive. *Contrast performance* describes an imaging system's ability to capture and display the subject's actual contrast. *Contrast resolution* is the number of shades of grey that a 'detector' can capture and *grayscale* refers to the scale over which the grey shades in a 'black-and-white' image is spread. Computed and digital radiography have the advantage (over film-screen radiography) of having a wide *dynamic range* to permit capture of a wide range of low-to-high signal (exposure) intensities as well as very high contrast resolution to permit the display of thousands of shades of grey. Practically, this means that this newer technology can successfully image areas that might be under or over exposed on film.

Radiographic image contrast depends on the following:

- The *subject to be radiographed*. For example – bone absorbs a relatively large amount of X-rays because of its physical density and relatively

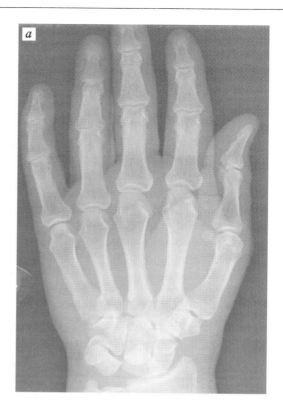

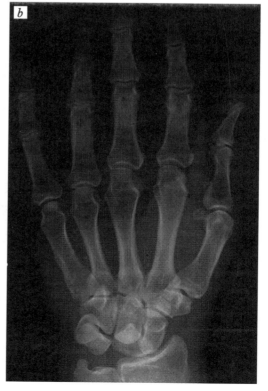

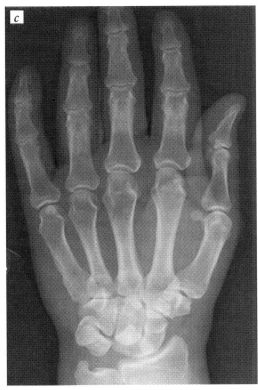

Figure 4.5 *Radiographic images with contrast variations (a) low contrast image (b) low contrast image (c) optimum contrast image.*

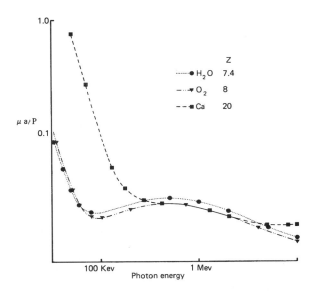

Figure 4.6 *Variance of the mass absorption coefficients ($\mu a/P$) for water (soft tissue), oxygen (air) and calcium (bone) as the energy of the X-ray beam increases. The Z number (atomic number) for each substance is also indicated.*

high atomic number compared with soft tissue which is mainly water and has low density and atomic number. On most radiographs the bones are easily seen – they look 'white' when juxtaposed with soft tissue, which is either 'black' or 'grey'. Thus a radiographic subject containing bone and soft tissue is said to have high *subject contrast*. Subject contrast can be altered by the use of *radiographic contrast agents*.

- The *differences in the amounts of radiation reaching the film*. This is called *radiation contrast* and is obviously influenced by the subject. If a radiograph is taken only of soft tissue, the X-ray beam passing through the subject will not be changed very much. Where bone lies in the path of the beam, more radiation is absorbed and hence prevented from reaching the film. The mechanism of X-ray beam absorption varies at different photon energies (*Figure 4.6*). The differential in beam absorption/attenuation between soft tissues and bone decreases as the

kilovoltage increases. This principle is exploited in high-kilovoltage technique (*see* – below).

- (i) *Amount of scattered radiation forming (Figure 4.7)*. This can be decreased by reducing the volume of tissue irradiated. Devices used are beam collimators, cones, aperture diaphragms and compression devices. (ii) *Amount of scattered radiation reaching the image receptor*. This can be decreased with the use of secondary radiation (scatter) grids or an *air-gap technique*.

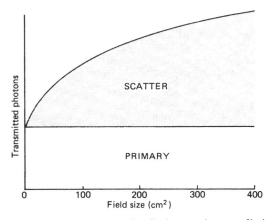

Figure 4.7 *Ratio of scattered radiation to primary radiation transmitted by the subject for a given exposure but with increasing field size.*

Movement and geometric factors degrading the radiographic image

The information content of the radiographic image can be adversely affected by factors related to the imaging system itself, i.e. image receptor and processing characteristics. Other features or circumstances of the radiographic technique may have significant importance. These features include:

- *Movement* of the patient during the exposure. This is the chief cause of radiographic image blurring (*see* – below *Figure 4.14*).

- *Distortion* is a deformity of the image so that it 'misrepresents' the original subject. For most projections the chief subject plane is positioned (so as) to attempt to maintain a parallel relationship with the image receptor plane and a perpendicular relationship with the X-ray beam (*Figure 4.8*). Alteration of these relationships can result in *elongation* (*Figure 4.9*) or *foreshortening* (*Figure 4.10*) of part or the entire image. (In some situations this effect may either be deliberately sought or it is deemed unavoidable. Some image distortion is an acceptable trade-off for further diagnostic information – for example – *see* projection (5) Chapter 7 and projection (5) Chapter 10. Note that a radiograph is a two-dimensional representation of a three-dimensional structure. It is not possible to eliminate distortion altogether as structures

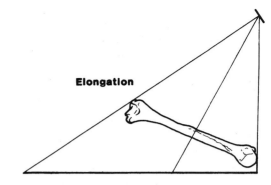

Figure 4.9 *Producing an elongated image.*

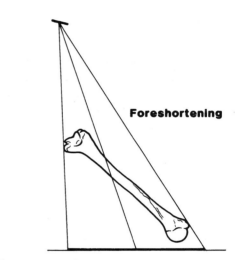

Figure 4.10 *Producing a foreshortened image.*

within the subject will exist outside of the subject plane and at only one point (i.e. at the central 'ray') is there a perpendicular relationship between X-ray beam, subject plane and image receptor plane.

- Image *magnification* is a type of image distortion although in some circumstances it may be deliberately introduced or tolerated. The X-ray source (or focus) to image receptor distance is fairly restricted because of the effects of the inverse square law that require increases in exposure as the source to image receptor distance is increased. Standard source to image receptor distance is usually 100 cm for skeletal radiography and 180 cm for posteroanterior chest radiography. If a large subject to image receptor distance is used, the diverging beam

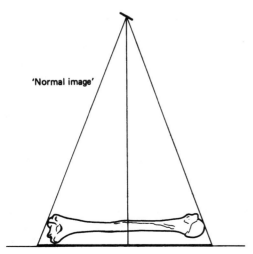

Figure 4.8 *Direction and centring of the X-ray beam for a 'normal' image.*

will project the X-ray shadow of the subject so that it covers a large area of the image receptor, i.e. it will be magnified (*Figure 4.11*). The subject should normally be positioned as close to the image receptor as possible. Where this cannot be done, in order to avoid a magnified image, the focus to image receptor distance should be increased. Magnification can be a problem in some X-ray patient tables where there is a large distance between the tabletop and image receptor.

- *Geometric factors* also play a part in image degradation because the source of the X-ray beam, i.e. at the anode target of the X-ray tube is of finite size. *Figure 4.12(a)* shows a diagram of a radiograph being taken of an object using a theoretical point source of X-rays. There is no image blurring at the edges of the object. *Figure 4.12(b)* shows the same object radiographed using a source of finite size. There is now blurring or '*penumbra*' formation at the edges of the object. Increasing the distance between the

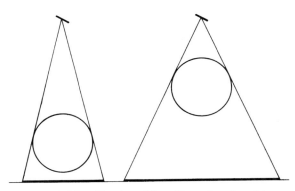

Figure 4.11 Magnification of the subject where the subject-image receptor distance is large.

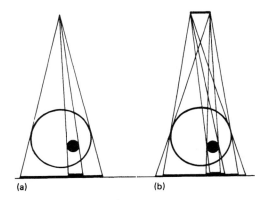

(a) (b)

Figure 4.12 Gometric unsharpness.

object and the X-ray source *or* by reducing the distance between the object and the image receptor will reduce the size of the penumbra. Reducing the X-ray source size should also reduce penumbra formation.

Guidelines for projection radiography of skeletal structures

- All radiographic examinations must be optimised to obtain maximum information with minimum radiation [**ref 20**: 8].

- The minimum number of radiographic images to be taken, with a few exceptions, is two, taken in two planes preferably at right angles to each other. A lesion may be missed if only one radiograph is taken (*Figure 4.13*). The perpendicular relationship of 'two views at right angles' is termed *orthogonal*.

- An appropriate length and breadth of the relevant anatomical area should be included on the radiograph. For a long bone or pair of long bones, i.e. radius/ulna and tibia/fibula the joints at both extremities should be included, especially where history and clinical indications suggest injury may affect the entire length of the bone and adjacent joints.

- If the subject includes a fixation device, i.e. bone screws, plates etc., the entire length of the device must be included on the radiograph.

- Supplementary projections may be needed, especially where subtle fractures or other pathology are to be demonstrated – for example – in axial projection of the patella, special views of the radial head, oblique projections of the vertebral column.

- Serial examinations may be needed to show a bony injury that is not apparent at the initial examination as – for example – in fractures of the scaphoid bone to show periodic changes in a pathological condition and to assess the outcome of a particular regimen of treatment.

- In cases of bony injury, radiography provides the basis for following the healing process, for evaluating changes in fracture fragments and for noting any problems with fixation devices [**ref 1**: 60].

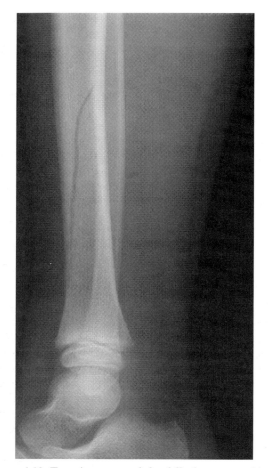 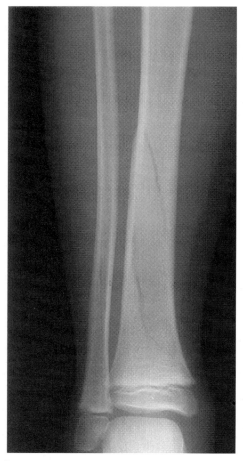

Figure 4.13 Two views are needed to fully demonstrate this tibial fracture.

- Radiographs of the other side of the body may be needed for comparison, especially in children to compare epiphyses. However in the interests of restricting radiation dose, use of comparative views may be vetoed or kept to a minimum following expert consultation.
- The body part to be examined should be unadorned or at least care should be taken that clothing or similar items do not create artefacts on the radiograph (*see* – below).

Use of anatomical markers

A marker indicating the correct anatomical side (left or right) of the patient should be placed in the primary beam so as to be imaged simultaneously with the subject. The presence of (a correct) marker must be checked along with the patient identification data. The medico-legal implications of using the incorrect marker and other identification data may be profound.

Artefacts and foreign bodies visible on radiographs

Artefacts are generally unwanted shadows produced by the presence of objects, substances or body tissues in or around the subject. Some of these artefacts are unavoidable for example the pinna of the ear may be visible on a lateral skull radiograph. Hair or retained clothing or jewellery may produce avoidable artefacts. The overlapping of soft tissues can create misleading shadows such as the visual *Mach effect* which is an optical illusion. The radiograph shows a thin dark line suggestive of a fracture (*see* page 145).

Foreign bodies are objects lying within the subject. These are likely to have been introduced during a penetrating injury. Glass and metallic foreign bodies are usually rendered visible on a radiograph but wood and plastic are unlikely to be seen. When radiographing a supected foreign body, orthogonal views should be taken with the site of entry indicated by an opaque marker.

Immobilisation of the patient

This is a very important but unfortunately sometimes neglected aspect of radiographic technique. Many repeat radiographs have been necessitated because of the movement of a badly immobilised patient (*Figure 4.14*). The radiographer should appreciate how difficult it is for even the co-operative patient to maintain a steady position for the radiographic exposure. Every reasonable step should be taken to ensure that the patient is able to remain still without undue discomfort. Attempts at

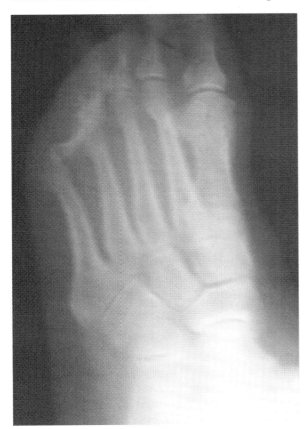

Figure 4.14 Foot radiograph with gross movement unsharpness.

immobilizing the subject for the exposure start with the simple use of correct patient posture. The patient should lie rather than sit, sit rather than stand – as appropriate for each body part. The resting of a limb or body part against the support is vital. For the upper limb up to the shoulder region in most radiographic techniques the *whole arm* should lie on the tabletop (*see Figure 5.10* Chapter 5, page 57). When examining the lower limb if the patient is seated on the table ideally he should lean against a backrest. Any ploy to increase patient comfort helps him to keep still. Special but simple immobilizing devices such as sandbags and non-opaque pads should be available for use in every examination room.

Consideration for the patient and other members of staff

Radiography is very much a medically, technically and scientifically based process taking place within a medical culture and it is easy to lose sight of the fact that the subject is a person. This is most likely to happen where pressure of workload is high and a conveyor belt mentality can emerge. Care and understanding of the needs and welfare of the patient during a radiographic examination are high on the list of priorities for the radiographer. By adapting attitude and approach the radiographer should normally fulfil these requirements. Respect for patient dignity, their comfort and physical safety are major concerns for the individual or team carrying out the examination. Communication of information about the procedure and what is to follow is valued by the patient and carers and facilitates the process.

Out of the total number of patients referred for skeletal examinations, the majority will have come to the department because they have sustained some kind of injury. This may mean that many of the patients will have some difficulty in co-operating with the radiographer. Whether or not there is trauma the radiographer should take into consideration the following:

(1) The physical and mental condition of the patient
- This may be partially evident by the appearance of the patient. The case history written on the request card may also help.

- The patient may need help in undertaking certain manoeuvres and appropriate moving and handling techniques should be applied.
- Where pain or other pathological conditions are present gentle handling and modification of technique will be needed.
- Equipment designed to aid the examination of injured patients and others with limited mobility reduces the need for the patient to be moved or lifted.

(2) *Radiography on the ward*

- For purposes of courtesy and safety, ask permission of ward staff before going to X-ray the patient.
- Consider requirements for radiation protection for other patients and staff.
- Take into account the patient's condition, need for privacy and his need for comfort.
- Special padded slide sheet envelopes for cassettes have been designed to make things easier. These are often personalised to one patient to minimise cross infection.
- Take extra care where there is equipment such as traction frames and wires, drips, oxygen and respirators in use.

(3) *Radiography of the seriously injured patient*

- Speed and accuracy of performance of examination is vital however take time to assess risks.
- Have everything to hand before you start – for example – cassettes, grids and pads.
- Using specially designed equipment such as isocentric skull units and accident table or cassette systems will reduce the need for movement and handling of the patient.
- The patient may need support – give a carer radiation protection and adequate instructions.
- When in doubt always ask for advice and assistance from the medical and nursing staff.

Other diagnostic imaging modalities and techniques

Projection radiography undertaken with standard X-ray equipment and image receptor (i.e. other than an image intensifier or CT equipment) is sometimes referred to as *plain radiography*. This term is misleading because this imaging modality – under certain circumstances – may be very demanding and anything but 'plain'.

There are a number of specialised radiographic techniques (i.e. those using X-rays that are supplementary or complementary to plain radiography. These involve the use of distinctive equipment and/or radiographic contrast agents. A specialised technique may also be characterised by manipulation of image-forming factors.

Some techniques that used to be designated 'special' may now be regarded as first line investigations – such as computerized tomography in head injury. A few of the specialised radiographic techniques listed below may be of historical interest only. Magnetic resonance imaging and ultrasound imaging do not use ionising radiation but are also included here.

In Part II occasional reference will be made to these additional techniques but a detailed description of their application is outside the scope of this book.

Angiography – A radiographic examination where radiopaque contrast agent is injected into a vessel or duct. Angiography commonly refers to imaging of blood vessels.

Arteriography – Synonym for angiography but refers especially to arteries.

Arthrography – A radiographic examination where a contrast agent is injected into a synovial joint space for study of the soft-tissue structures. Arthrography may be combined with computerized tomography. This imaging technique has become less common due to the use of *arthroscopy* and general availability of *MRI*.

Bone mineral densitometry – Dual energy X-ray absorptiometry (DXA or DEXA) is well established as one of the front-line techniques for measuring bone mineral density in clinical practice [**ref 8**:125].

Computerized tomography (CT) – A combined radiographic and electronic process that produces either transverse or longitudinal body sectional images. Information relating to X-ray absorption in the patient is processed by computer and presented visually on a television screen. CT has effectively replaced what used to be regarded as conventional tomography [**ref 8**: 49] (*see* – below). In severe trauma, the main advantage of helical and multi-slice CT is that large amounts of data may be acquired from a single breath hold [**ref 20**: 15]. A disadvantage of CT is that it imparts a high radiation dose. For musculoskeletal imaging, magnetic resonance imaging (MRI) is usually chosen, except where exact bone details are needed – for example – in tibial plateau fractures CT can provide three-dimensional image reconstructions [**ref 8**: 60]. CT is superior to plain film radiography for delineating complex anatomy as for example in the spine. CT is often able to delineate fractures that are subtle or occult [**ref 21**: 349].

Diffusion technique – A specialist radiographic technique where there is deliberate movement of part of the body so that overlying structures become blurred or diffused whilst the subject of interest remains relatively sharp. An example is the 'moving jaw' technique for demonstration of the upper cervical vertebrae in the anteroposterior plane. Diffusion techniques requires a long exposure time and are generally discouraged as it is thought that they increase radiation dose. The term *autotomography* has been applied to this technique.

High kilovoltage technique – This is the equalizing of the relative absorption of the X-ray beam by different types of tissue when a high kilovoltage is chosen. This technique is used for body areas where there is a steep difference in subject density, for example in the cervico-thoracic region of the spine. The technique allows these structures to be visualised on a single radiograph. High kilovoltage refers to kilovoltages of over 100.

In film-screen radiography and computed radiography the benefits of using a high kilovoltage will remain the same, but in *CR* a different algorithm will be required to display the image as a high kV image and to prevent pre-processing manipulating the image to appear as a traditional image. In *CR*, post-processing might be able to make a low kilovoltage appear as a high kilovoltage image but no amount of post-processing can reveal information that is not present (for example if the chosen kV was not sufficient to penetrate the heart). Also, *CR* imaging plates generally operate most effectively at around 80kVp, and thus a high kV might not give the expected image.

Because scattered radiation produced at high kilovoltages has greater energy it becomes more of a problem. Either a high ratio grid must be used or an air-gap technique is employed to prevent scatter reaching the image receptor. In this latter technique a space is left between patient and cassette – obliquely directed scattered radiation is less likely to reach the image receptor [**ref 22**: 265].

Macroradiography (magnification radiography) – A large subject-image receptor distance is used which produces magnification of the subject. For a x2 magnification, the subject is placed halfway between X-ray beam source and image receptor.

Degree of magnification

$$= \frac{\text{X-ray tube focus to image receptor distance}}{\text{X-ray tube focus to subject distance}}$$

A very small X-ray tube effective focal spot size must be used in macroradiography otherwise geometric unsharpness, due to penumbra formation, will become very significant (*Figures 4.15 (a) and (b)*).

Magnetic resonance imaging (MRI) – A generally non-invasive method of mapping the internal structure of the body that completely avoids the use of ionising radiation [**ref 8**: 63]. MRI usually provides more information than CT about intracranial, head and neck, spinal and musculoskeletal disorders because of its high soft tissue contrast sensitivity and multiplanar imaging capability [**ref 20**: 17]. MRI is acknowledged as the imaging examination of choice for assessment of internal derangements of joints especially when soft-tissue damage is the major component of injury [**ref 21**: 351].

Radioisotope scintigraphy (radionuclide imaging) – This is one of a range of 'nuclear medicine' techniques. Certain biologically active chemical substances can be injected into the patient's bloodstream and these are then taken up by bone tissue. If these substances – for example – polyphosphonate or diphosphonate, are tagged with a radioactive isotope then this uptake may be recorded. Certain gamma-emitting radionuclides – for example – technetium 99m, are suitable for this process and may be imaged by a gamma camera. The important difference between conventional radiography and scintigraphy is that where radiographs yield information about bone

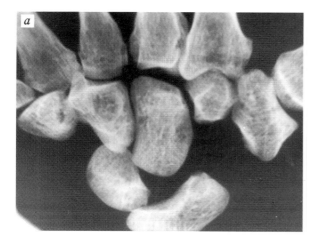

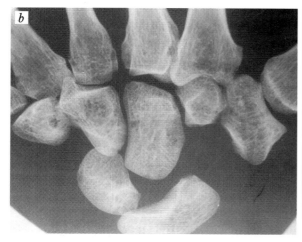

Figure 4.15 (a) Radiograph of dry bones shows geometric unsharpness because a large effective focal spot size has been used coupled with a large subject to image receptor distance (b) A smaller focal spot has been used reducing the image unsharpness.

morphology and limited disclosure of bone physiology, scintigraphy produces a poor morphological image but considerable physiological (dynamic) data.

Tomography (conventional) – The production of a radiograph of a selected layer in the body. All structures above and beneath this layer are blurred while the information contained in the layer of interest remains 'in focus'. Special equipment is required to undertake tomography. The X-ray tube and image receptor cassette are rotated around a pivot point that coincides with the level required for the 'in focus' layer. The level of this pivot point can be raised or lowered thus producing consecutive radiographic 'cuts' (*tome* – Greek for cutting) in the subject. The rule is that the greater the degree or X-ray tube/film movement the greater the degree of blurring in the subject and thinner will appear the radiographic 'cut'. Tomography has enjoyed extensive application in skeletal radiography. It was of special use in the skull and vertebral column where there is increased anatomical complexity. In countries that have access to CT, use of conventional tomography has substantially diminished.

Ultrasound imaging or sonography – This is a method of obtaining images using high-frequency sound waves. The reflected sound wave echoes are recorded and displayed as a real-time visual image. Ultrasound is an important technique for tomographic imaging of soft tissues, i.e. tendons, ligaments and muscles and also soft tissue masses.

Venography – Radiographic examination of the venous system where radiopaque contrast agent is injected into a vein.

References

1. Berquist TH (1991) *Imaging of Orthopaedic Trauma* New York: Raven Press

2. Board of the Faculty of Clinical Radiology. The Royal College of Radiologists (2000) *A Guide to Justification for Clinical Radiology* London: Royal College of Radiologists

3. Bontrager KL (2001) *Textbook of Radiographic Positioning and Related Anatomy (5ᵗʰ Edition)* St Louis: Mosby

4. Carmichael JHE Maccia C Moores BM Oestmann JW Schibilla H Teunen D Van Tiggelen R Wall B (1996) *European Guidelines on Quality Criteria for Diagnostic Radiographic Images* EUR 16260 Luxembourg: Office for Official Publications of the European Communities

5. Council Directive 97/43/Euratom of 30 June 1997 on health protection of individuals against the dangers of ionising radiation in relation to medical exposures *Official Journal of the European Community* L180 **40**: 22–29

6. Department of Health (2000) *Ionising Radiation (Medical Exposure) Regulations SI 2000/1059* London: Stationery Office

7. Department of Health (1999) *Ionising Radiations Regulations SI 1999/3232* London: Stationery Office

8. Grainger RG and Allison DJ (1997) *Grainger and Allison's Diagnostic Radiology (Volume 1) (3rd Edition)* Edinburgh: Churchill Livingstone

9. http//:www.amershamhealth.com/medcyclopaedia *Scan Projection radiography* accessed 29/06/05

10. http://www.gemedicalsystems.com *GE Medical Systems X-ray Education: Digital X-ray* accessed 10/12/03

11. International Commission on Radiological Protection (1991) 1990 Recommendations of the International Commission on Radiological Protection *ICRP Publications 60 Annals of the ICRP* **21** Nos 1–3

12. Institute of Physics and Engineering in Medicine (2004) Report 88 *Guidance on the Establishment and Use of Diagnostic Reference Levels for Medical X-ray Examinations* York: Institute of Physics and Engineering in Medicine

13. Jones T in Oakley J (ed) (2003) *Digital Imaging: A Primer for Radiographers Radiologists and Health Care Professionals* London: Greenwich Medical Media

14. Kevles BH (1997) *Naked to the Bone: Medical Imaging in the Twentieth Century* New Brunswick: Addison Wesley

15. Maccia C Moores B Padovani M R Säbel M Vanó E Schibilla H Teunen D (1999) *Multilingual Glossary of Terms Relating to Quality Assurance and Radiation Protection in Diagnostic Radiology* EUR 17538 Luxembourg: Office for Official Publications of the European Communities

16. National Radiological Protection Board (2002) *Radiation Exposure of the UK Population from Medical and Dental X-ray Examinations NRPB-W4* Didcot: NRPB

17. Oakley J (2004) Automatic compensation for over or under exposure: advantage or not? *Synergy* November pages 15–18

18. Oakley J in Oakley J (ed) (2003) *Digital Imaging: A Primer for Radiographers Radiologists and Health Care Professionals* London: Greenwich Medical Media

19. Prince JL Links JM (2006) *Medical Imaging Signals and Systems* Upper Saddle River: Pearson Prentice Hall

20. RCR Working Party (2003) *Making the Best Use of a Department of Clinical Radiology: Guidelines for Doctors (5th Edition)* London: Royal College of Radiologists

21. Rubenstein J (2003) The value of diagnostic imaging in musculoskeletal trauma *Current Orthopaedics* **17**: 346–349

22. Shephard CT (2003) *Radiographic Image Production and Manipulation* New York: McGraw-Hill

Further Reading

1. Gunn C (2002) *Radiographic Imaging (3rd Edition)* Edinburgh: Churchill Livingstone

2. Institute of Physics and Engineering in Medicine (2002) *Medical and Dental Guidance Notes* York: Institute of Physics and Engineering in Medicine

3. Soames R (2003) *Joint Motion: Clinical Measurement and Evaluation* Edinburgh: Churchill Livingstone

4. Unett EM Carver BJ (2001) The chest x-ray: centring points and central rays – can we stop confusion our students and ourselves? *Synergy* November pages 14–17 and December pages 8–9

Part II
Regional radiography and indications for examinations

The upper limb: hand to humerus

CHAPTER CONTENTS

Table of main and supplementary radiographic techniques

General anatomical area	Projection	Page	Common Indications
Hand	**1** PA (dorsipalmar) **2** PA oblique (dorsipalmar oblique) **3** Lateral **4/5** Norgaard, Brewerton	57 58 58 58–59	Injury, pathology e.g. rheumatoid arthritis. Bone age. Foreign body, dislocations. Rheumatoid arthritis.
Finger/s	**1** PA **2** Oblique **3** Lateral	57 58 58	Injury, dislocation, foreign body
Thumb	**6** Lateral **7-8** AP or PA	59 59–60	Injury, fracture-dislocation
Collective carpal bones and carpometacarpal joints	**9** PA **10** Lateral **11ii** PA oblique	60 60–61 61	Injury, dislocation, subluxation
Scaphoid	**11i** PA ulnar deviation **11i** PA oblique **11iii** AP oblique	61 61 61	Injury
Pisiform	**11iii** AP oblique	61	
Lunate	**12** PA radial deviation **10** Lateral	61 60–61	Dislocation
Trapezium	**13** PA oblique ulnar deviation	61	
Triquetral	**14** PA oblique palmar flexed	61	
Carpal tunnel	**16** Axial projection	62	Reduced tunnel volume Hook of hamate injury
Lower Radius/Ulna	**9** PA **10** Lateral	60 60–61	Injury
Radiocarpal joint	**17** PA with 25° X-ray tube angle toward elbow	64–65	
Forearm	**18** AP preferred or PA alternative **19** Lateral	65 65	Injury
Elbow	**20–21** Lateral and alternative **22–25** AP and alternatives	68–69 69–70	Injury
Head of radius	**26** Special projections	70-71	Injury
Olecranon	**27** Special projections	71	
Coronoid Process	**28** AP oblique	71	Injury
Ulnar groove	**29** Profile projection	71	Interruption syndrome
Humerus	**30** AP **31–34** Lateral and alternatives	71–72 72–73	Injury

Effective radiation dose for an extremity examination: **<0.01mSv**
Equivalent period of natural background radiation: **<1.5 days**

HAND

Essential anatomical terminology

The skeleton of the hand is made up from three distinct types of small bone:

(1) More distally are the *phalanges*, the miniature long bones of the fingers. Each digit contains three phalanges except for the thumb which has two.

(2) The palm of the hand contains the five *metacarpals*, the thumb metacarpal articulating with the trapezium at the *first carpometacarpal joint*. This is a very mobile joint and probably the most important joint in the hand as far as orthopaedics is concerned.

(3) Close to the wrist are the irregular or cuboidal *carpal bones* (carpus) arranged in a proximal and distal row of four *(Figure 5.1)*. The *scaphoid* has a key role in both carpal and *wrist (radiocarpal) joint* function.

The carpal bones are connected by a complex system of ligaments. The *transverse carpal ligament* or *flexor retinaculum* is an important accessory ligament that crosses the front of the carpus forming a gap called the *carpal tunnel*. The *flexor tendons* of the fingers and the *median nerve* pass through this tunnel. There are no muscular attachments to the proximal carpal row which relies on ligaments for stability. The hand as a unit is a complex structure and small injuries or disruptions of one area may have serious effects on the function of the entire extremity.

Indications for the X-ray examination

Injuries

Fractures of the phalanges

Various types of fracture occur. Casualty staff may strap the injured fingers together, so oblique projections may be needed in addition to posteroanterior and lateral views of the area of interest. In some circumstances it may be preferable to have dressings removed to avoid obscuring subtle injuries.

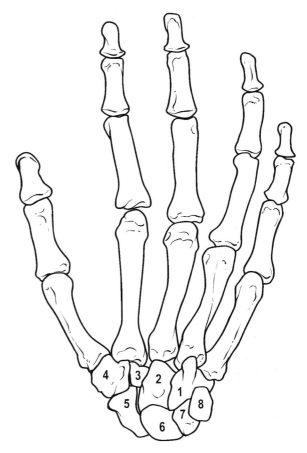

Figure 5.1 Anterior aspect of the bones of the left hand. The carpal bones are numbered.

1 *Hamate*	**2** *Captitate*
3 *Trapezoid*	**4** *Trapezium*
5 *Scaphoid*	**6** *Lunate*
7 *Triquetral*	**8** *Pisiform*

Mallet finger (baseball finger) (Figure 5.2)

This is a deformity of the distal interphalangeal joint following an injury where the extensor tendon at the base of the distal phalanx is torn away from its point of insertion by a sudden flexion violence. In 25% of cases [ref 13: 98], a small fragment of bone is avulsed by the tendon from the dorsal aspect of the terminal phalanx. The deformity may lead to significant impairment if allowed to remain untreated [ref 14: 1805]. Finger avulsion fractures can also occur at the points of insertion of a collateral ligament or volar plate.

Figure 5.2 Mallet finger, showing the torn extensor tendon.

Dislocation of finger or thumb joints

Usually caused by forced hyperextension. A phalanx is displaced backwards at its joint with a more proximal phalanx or metacarpal. Occasionally the dislocation is associated with a vertical split in the joint capsule which becomes button-holed round the metacarpal neck making open reduction necessary.

Fractures of the metacarpal shafts

If the fracture is of the transverse variety, there may be overlapping of the fragments with angular deformity. A spiral fracture of a metacarpal with rotation may need internal fixation [ref 13: 103].

Fracture of the neck of the fifth metacarpal
(Figure 5.3)

This is a common injury usually sustained in blows made with a clenched fist – hence *boxer's fracture*.

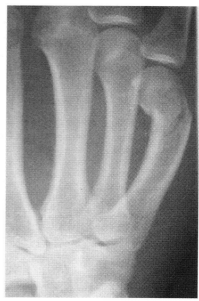

Figure 5.3 Radiograph of fractured neck of 5th metacarpal.

The head of the metacarpal is displaced anteriorly and the dorsum of the hand may appear to be deformed. Sometimes open reduction and internal fixation of the fracture are required.

Fracture of the base of the first metacarpal

The bone may be fractured transversely and the carpometacarpal joint is not involved. However, a more serious type of injury is sustained where the fracture extends into the joint. This is known as *Bennett's* fracture dislocation of the carpometacarpal joint of the thumb.

Bennett's fracture-dislocation (Figure 5.4)

In this injury a small triangular fragment of the first metacarpal remains in normal relationship to the trapezium whilst the rest of the metacarpal displaces proximally and backwards. If the surgeon cannot restore a smooth joint surface then the patient may develop osteoarthritis in this joint. Closed reduction is attempted first and the patient's forearm and hand will be enclosed in a plaster cast that is carefully moulded at the base of the metacarpal and includes the interphalangeal joint. The thumb metacarpal is held in extension at the carpometacarpal joint. The cast remains on for four weeks, during which time frequent X-rays through plaster are required to ensure that re-displacement does not occur. If closed reduction is unsatisfactory then the surgeon may have to resort to open reduction and internal fixation with Kirschner wires.

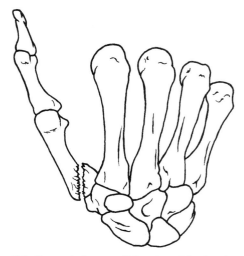

Figure 5.4 Bennett's fracture-dislocation of the thumb metacarpal.

Gamekeeper's thumb *(Figure 5.5)*

This results from a rupture of the ulnar collateral ligament of the first metacarpophalangeal joint, usually caused by forced abduction. The name of this injury originates from the trauma sustained by a method of breaking a rabbit's neck. The lesion accounts for 6% of ski injuries [**ref 16**: 979]. If untreated it will interfere with grasp function causing significant disability.

Carpometacarpal dislocations

The fourth and fifth joints are most commonly affected [**ref 13**: 102].

Fracture of the waist of scaphoid *(Figure 5.6)*

90% of carpal fractures are through the scaphoid [**ref 13**: 90]. The fracture results from a forcible radial deviation of the carpus where the scaphoid is pinched between the radial styloid and the capitate. Because of the nature of the scaphoid which has a very thin cortex and a cancellous medulla, there is sometimes no evidence of a fracture line on the initial radiograph. Radiographs taken one to two weeks later will almost certainly show a fracture because of bone resorption at the fracture line (*osteoclasis*). Complications in the healing may occur because of the interference of the blood supply to the bone. Most of the blood supply to the

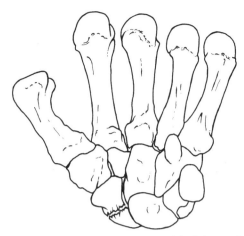

Figure 5.6 Fracture through the waist of the left carpal scaphoid.

scaphoid enters at its distal end. A fracture through the waist may cut off the circulation to the proximal fragment which may result in *avascular necrosis* (*see* Chapter 3). In time the shape of the scaphoid may become distorted and osteoarthritis could occur at the radiocarpal joint as a sequel. The diminished blood supply could alternatively cause *delayed union* of the fracture. Occult fractures are present in almost two-thirds of patients with suspected scaphoid fractures and normal first radiographs. Use of *MRI* allows an early diagnosis to be made and is regarded as the gold standard investigation [**ref 2**]

Fractures of the hook of hamate

This can occur due to direct trauma or from an avulsive force acting through the transverse carpal ligament. The fracture is seen most often as a result of a heavy golf or tennis swing [**ref 9**: 190].

Fractures of the triquetral

Violent hyperextension of the wrist can separate a flake of bone from the triquetral [**ref 4**: 221]. The triquetral is the second most commonly injured carpal bone [**ref 3**].

Fractures of the lunate

These are relatively rare and result from acute dorsiflexion strains of the wrist. In the lateral projection a flake of bone can be seen on the dorsal aspect of the carpus.

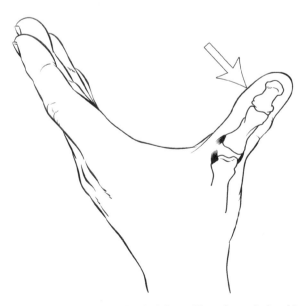

Figure 5.5 Mechanism for the injury of 'gamekeeper's thumb'.

Kienböck's disease (avascular necrosis lunate)

The lunate becomes flattened and sclerosed as a sequel to a minor injury. All patients with lunate fractures should be considered for follow up for possible development of this disease [**ref 7**] (*see* also *osteochondritis* and *Figure 3.6*, Chapter 3).

Carpal instability – perilunate dislocation

This latter term embraces a spectrum of injuries caused by hyperdorsiflexion at the wrist. Dislocations (and fracture-dislocations) are classified as 'peri' where there are undisplaced carpals in the proximal row. The condition where the carpus is pushed off the back of the radius but the lunate remains attached to the radius is termed *perilunar* dislocation.

Carpal instability – dislocation of the lunate

This is the most common carpal dislocation [**ref 11**: 206]. It is a similar injury to perilunar dislocation but the lunate is displaced forwards and tipped through 90° to lie anteriorly in the carpal canal (*Figure 5.7*). The displaced lunate may now press on the median nerve causing paraesthesias (numbness and tingling) in the thumb, index and middle fingers. Delay in diagnosis may result in the complication of avascular necrosis (*see* Chapter 3) as the widespread capsular stripping may interfere with the blood supply. The surgeon may need to excise the lunate otherwise osteoarthritis may develop.

Other conditions of interest

Carpal tunnel syndrome

This results from compression of the median nerve as it passes under the flexor retinaculum (transverse carpal ligament) of the wrist. The overall cause is fluid retention the commonest cause of that is pregnancy [**ref 4**: 369] but the condition can occur in any situation where the volume of the tunnel is reduced – for example – in a fracture of the lunate. Paraesthesias (numbness and tingling) in the thumb, index and middle finger are characteristic. Complete relief of symptoms usually follows operative division of the ligament.

Dupuytren's contracture

This is a thickening and contracture of the palmar aponeurosis and causes the fingers to be permanently flexed at the proximal interphalangeal and metacarpophalangeal joints.

Figure 5.7 The lunate, dislocated from its normal position between the capitate and radius, impinging on the median nerve of the palm (sagittal aspect).

Osteoarthritis

Following an injury or rheumatoid disease, osteoarthritis may develop in the wrist joint. *Primary osteoarthritis*, however, (i.e. that which is not a sequel to other pathology) is more common in the carpometacarpal joint of the thumb and interphalangeal joints (*see* Chapter 3).

Rheumatoid arthritis

Small joints of the fingers and the joints of the wrist are frequently the first to be affected by this disease (*see* Chapter 3). In the hand a characteristic sign of early rheumatoid arthritis is the appearance of juxta-articular erosions at the metacarpophalangeal joints (*Figure 5.8*). If the disease progresses the

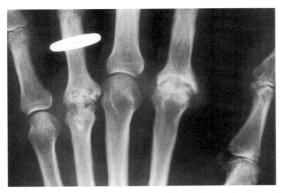

Figure 5.8 Radiograph showing changes in the fourth and second metacarpophalangeal joints characteristic of early rheumatoid arthritis.

fingers may take on a characteristic ulnar deviation at these joints, often associated with either flexion or extension deformities of the interphalangeal joints *(Figure 5.9)*. MRI is used in the early detection, staging and therapeutic planning for rheumatoid arthritis.

Radiographic techniques – hand

For the upper limb from the hand to the lower two-thirds of the humerus, most techniques can be undertaken with the patient sitting alongside the X-ray table. This general patient position is assumed for the projections described below. To help the patient feel more comfortable and to help him keep still, as much of the limb as possible should rest on the tabletop *(Figure 5.10)*. A secondary radiation grid is not normally required for the upper limb beneath shoulder level.

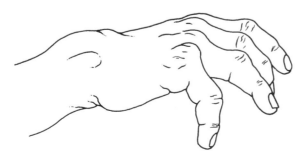

Figure 5.9 Deformity of the hand in advanced rheumatoid arthritis.

(1) Posteroanterior hand

The palmar aspect of the hand rests on the image receptor. The fingers are extended and separated slightly.

> *Central ray direction* – Perpendicular to the image receptor and centred over the head of the third metacarpal.

If both hands have to be examined, position them side by side on a single cassette.

> *Central ray direction* – Perpendicular to the image receptor and centred between the hands at the level of the head of the third metacarpal.

Individual fingers

Collimate the beam to include the distal phalanx and the metacarpal head plus adjacent fingers for orientation.

> *Central ray direction* – Perpendicular to the image receptor and centred over the proximal interphalangeal joint.

If a second fracture is suspected in the region of the metacarpal then that area should be included on the radiograph.

Injuries

The patient may not be able to extend the fingers and flatten the palm of the hand. It may be more practical to take an anteroposterior projection of the hand or individual finger.

Figure 5.10 Resting the whole limb on the table helps comfort and immobilisation. The limb position may be used for a posteroanterior wrist projection.

(2) Posteroanterior oblique hand
(Figure 5.11)

With the hand pronated, the thumb side of the hand is raised until the palm makes an angle of 45° with the image receptor. The fingers and thumb are separated and flexed slightly. The hand should be adequately supported on a non-opaque pad.

Central ray direction – Perpendicular to the image receptor and centred over the head of the third metacarpal.

(3) Lateral hand

From the prone position, the hand and wrist are rotated laterally until the palmar aspect of the hand and fingers are perpendicular to the image receptor. The fingers remain extended and the thumb is abducted and rests on a pad

Central ray direction – Perpendicular to the image receptor and centred over the head of the second metacarpal.

The lateral can be used for location of a foreign body or to determine the degree of displacement of bone fragments in transverse fractures of the metacarpals or to exclude carpometacarpal dislocations.

Individual fingers *(Figure 5.12)*

For the ring or little finger: start from the last position. Fold forwards the index and ring fingers. Separate the ring and little fingers slightly; their long axes should be parallel to the image receptor. The ring finger requires support.

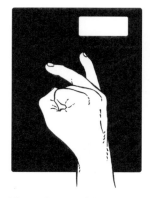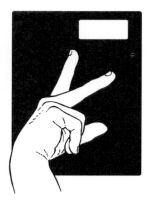

Figure 5.12 Position of the hand for lateral projections of the fingers.

Central ray direction – Perpendicular to the image receptor and centred over the proximal interphalangeal joint of the appropriate finger.

For the index and middle finger: from the prone position the hand is rotated medially 90°. The thumb, little and ring fingers are flexed palmwards out of the way of the index and middle fingers which remain straight but slightly separated. The lateral aspect of the index finger touches the image receptor.

Central ray direction – Perpendicular to the image receptor and centred over the proximal interphalangeal joint of the appropriate finger.

Where the proximal phalanx and the metacarpophalangeal joint is the area of interest, a posteroanterior oblique projection may also be necessary.

Rheumatoid arthritis

Two additional projections may be taken, as well as (1) and (2) cited above. Studies have shown that there is no significant advantages of projections (4) and (5) over the PA view [**refs 5** and **12**].

(4) Norgaard's projection
(Figure 5.13)

Both hands are placed palms upward side by side on the image receptor. They are both then rotated medially through 35° and supported on non-opaque pads. The fingers and thumb are extended and separated slightly.

Central ray direction – Perpendicular to the image receptor and centred between the hands at the level of the fifth metacarpal.

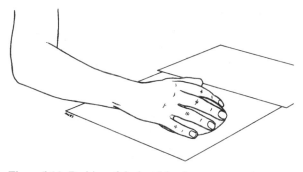

Figure 5.11 Position of the hand for the posteroanterior oblique radiograph.

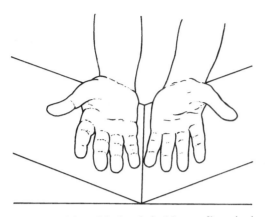

Figure 5.13 Position of the hands for Norgaard's projection.

The aim is to produce an image that avoids overlapping of the metacarpal heads and the bases of the proximal phalanges. This is an area where changes in the bone (erosions) caused by early rheumatoid arthritis may be seen but be obscured in the routine projections. The view has also been proved of value in indicating the presence of carpal erosions especially in the triquetral and pisiform.

(5) Brewerton's projection

(Figure 5.14)

With the metacarpophalangeal joints of the affected hand flexed at 60° and the thumb everted, the dorsal aspect of the fingers are placed on the image receptor.

> Central ray direction – Towards the head of the third metacarpal with the X-ray tube angled 20° from the vertical, from the ulnar side of the hand (Figure 5.15).

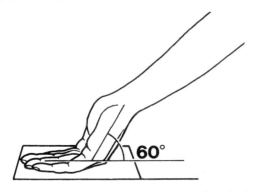

Figure 5.14 Position of the hand for Brewerton's projection.

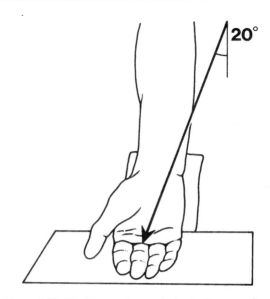

Figure 5.15 The X-ray tube angulation in Brewerton's projection.

This projection demonstrates the grooves (valleculae) on either side of the metacarpal heads and also the bases of the phalanges. Erosions in the valleculae may be dubious or invisible in routine projections but may be shown to be large in this view.

Radiographic techniques – thumb

(6) Lateral thumb

Starting with the hand prone, the fingers and the palm of the hand are raised away from the image receptor until the dorsum of the thumb is perpendicular to the image receptor. Support the raised part of the hand on a non-opaque pad.

> Central ray direction – Perpendicular to the image receptor and centred over the first metacarpophalangeal joint to include the first metacarpal and trapezium.

(7) Anteroposterior projections of the thumb

Either (i) from the prone position medially rotate the hand and arm until the dorsum of the thumb lies on the image receptor *(Figure 5.16);* or (ii) from

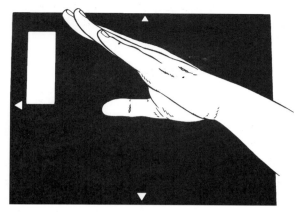

Figure 5.16 Position of thumb for anteroposterior projection 7(i).

the supine position laterally rotate the hand and arm until the dorsum of the thumb lies on the image receptor.

Central ray direction – In either case perpendicular to the image receptor and centred over the first metacarpophalangeal joint to include the first metacarpal and the trapezium.

In (i) soft tissues of the hypothenar eminence may obscure the trapezium and the carpometacarpal joint area. It may be easier if the patient sits with his back to the table and extends his arm behind him. (i) Is easier than (ii).

An innovative method of producing an anteroposterior projection is shown in *Figure 5.17* (*see* also [further reading 7]).

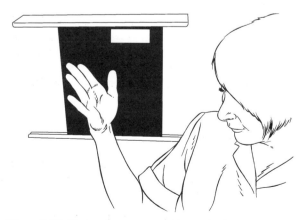

Figure 5.17 Alternative anteroposterior projection positioning.

(8) An alternative technique is to position the patient as for the lateral hand (projection (3)). Support the thumb, now in a position to produce a posteroanterior projection. This may not show the first carpometacarpal joint satisfactorily.

Central ray direction – Perpendicular to the image receptor and centred over the first metacarpophalangeal joint as before for the thumb.

Increase the X-ray source to image receptor distance by 10cm to compensate for the increased subject to image receptor distance.

Radiographic techniques – carpal bones

The distal end of the radius and ulna must be included on the radiograph.

(9) Posteroanterior wrist *(see Figure 5.10)*

The palmar aspect of the wrist rests on the image receptor. The finger joints are flexed slightly to bring the wrist in closer contact with the image receptor.

Central ray direction – Perpendicular and centred between the radial and ulnar styloid processes.

(10) Lateral wrist

From the position for the posteroanterior projection the wrist is rotated externally through 90°. The lateral aspect of the wrist and hand now rest on the image receptor. An additional backward tilt is given to the wrist to superimpose the radius on the ulna (*Figure 5.18*).

Central ray direction – Perpendicular to the image receptor and centred over the radial styloid process.

The carpal bones are superimposed in this projection. If laterals of both wrists are needed for comparison the additional backward tilt can be omitted where both wrists are exposed simultaneously.

Central ray direction – Perpendicular to the image receptor and centred between the wrists at the level of the styloid processes.

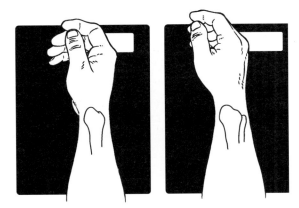

Figure 5.18 Carefully rotating the forearm externally will superimpose the radius and ulna in the lateral projection (left hand drawing).

Laterals may also be taken in flexion and extension to demonstrate range of movement.

Techniques (11–16) are additional projections where further examination of individual bones is required.

(11) Scaphoid

(i) Posteroanterior with ulnar deviation

This is often used as an alternative to projection (9) rather than as a supplementary technique. The position is the same as in (9) except that the hand is adducted (ulnar deviated) at the wrist as far as possible (*Figure 5.19*). This ulnar deviation radiographically elongates the scaphoid and helps improve the detection of subtle fractures [**ref 6**].

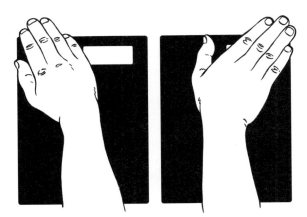

Figure 5.19 Radial deviation (left) and ulnar deviation (right) at the wrist.

A variation of this projection is to use the same patient position but angling the X-ray tube 30° to towards the elbow.

(ii) Posteroanterior oblique wrist

From the prone position the hand and wrist are externally rotated through 45° and supported.

> *Central ray direction* – Perpendicular to the image receptor and centred over the ulnar styloid process.

This is an important projection which reveals the waist of the scaphoid and its tuberosity which may more rarely be fractured. Further posteroanterior oblique projections can be taken at angles of 30° and 60°. Another alternative is a posteroanterior oblique with ulnar deviation.

(iii) Anteroposterior oblique

The wrist is placed palm upwards on the image receptor and then the radial side is raised through 45° and supported.

> *Central ray direction* – Perpendicular to the image receptor and centred over the ulnar styloid process.

(12) Lunate

Posteroanterior wrist projection (9), this time with radial deviation (*Figure 5.19*). A disclocated lunate becomes obvious on a lateral projection (10).

(13) Trapezium

Posteroanterior oblique wrist [projection (11 (ii))] with ulnar deviation. The posteroanterior oblique projection (11ii) is the only survey view that demonstrates the trapezio-trapezoid joint [**ref 7**]. The trapezium is also demonstrated on projections of the thumb.

(14) Triquetral

From the prone position the radial side of the wrist is raised and rotated through 60°. The wrist joint is palmar-flexed through 45°.

> *Central ray direction* – Perpendicular to the image receptor and centred over the triquetral.

(15) Pisiform

This sesamoid bone is demonstrated separated from the other carpal bones on the anteroposterior oblique of the wrist [projection (11(iii))].

(16) Carpal tunnel

This axial projection demonstrates bony changes causing reduction of tunnel volume resulting in the carpal tunnel syndrome. The wrist is dorsi-flexed from the anatomical position through 35°. A special angle board can be used to achieve this (*Figure 5.20*) [**ref 15**: 280]. Care must be taken with radiation protection if the X-ray beam is directed towards the patient's body.

> *Central ray direction* – Tangentially to the anterior aspect of the wrist so that the X-ray beam passes axially along the carpal tunnel.

An increase in the X-ray source to image receptor distance is necessary to offset effects of the large subject to image distance. Alternatively the wrist can be dorsi-flexed over the edge of the table (*Figure 5.21*).

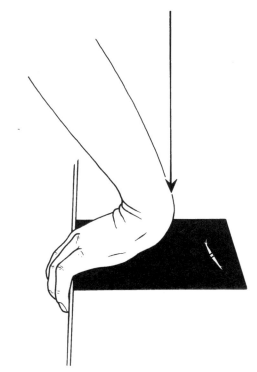

Figure 5.21 Alternative patient positioning for the axial projection of the carpal tunnel.

WRIST (RADIOCARPAL) JOINT AND FOREARM

Essential anatomical terminology (*Figure 5.22*)

The wrist joint lies between the distal radius and the proximal row of carpal bones hence its name the *radiocarpal joint*. The distal end of the ulna does not directly take part in the wrist joint as it is covered by a triangular-shaped cartilage. The distal end of the radius widens at a point around 2cm proximal to the radiocarpal joint. Distal to this point, the cortical bone thickness lessens, effectively weakening the bone and making it predispose to fractures [**ref 7**].

Between the upper and lower ends of the parallel radius and ulna are the *radioulnar joints*. Movement at these joints allows the radius to rotate around the axis of the ulna – the action of pronation and supination. This is the most significant function of the forearm and treatment of fractures must aim to maintain it.

Indications for the X-ray examination

Injuries

Wrist ligament and capsule strains

These are common sports injuries. If the patient has fallen on the outstretched hand the medical officer may have to exclude a possible fracture in the region of the wrist.

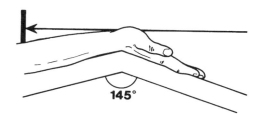

Figure 5.20 Dorsiflexion of the wrist in the axial projection of the carpal tunnel.

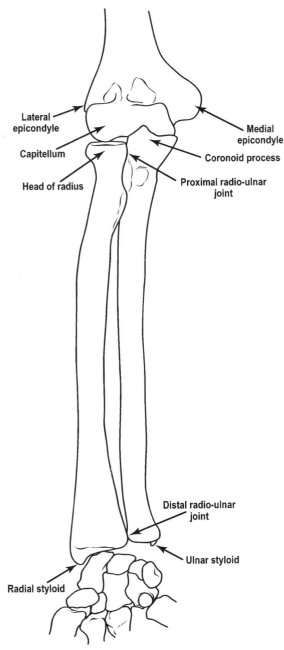

Figure 5.22 *Bony features of the forearm and elbow.*

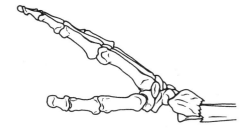

Figure 5.23 *Colles' fracture of the right radius.*

articular surface. The ulnar styloid is often avulsed as well. The distal fragment of the radius is displaced and angulated dorsally. The resultant characteristic appearance of the wrist has been termed the *'dinner fork'* deformity (*Figure 5.24*). The fracture is normally reduced under general anaesthetic and the wrist is immobilized in a 'below elbow' plaster. *Sudeck's atrophy* – a disturbance of autonomic and sensory nerve supply to bone and blood vessels [**ref 4**: 206] – is a complication of this injury if the patient is allowed to rest the hand without moving the fingers.

Smith's fracture

Like the Colles' fracture this is confined to the distal inch of the radius but the displacement and angulation of the bone fragment is reversed, i.e. towards the volar (palmar) aspect of the wrist. This fracture is comparatively uncommon.

Chauffeur's fracture and Barton's fractures

These are intra-articular fractures of the distal radius. The term 'chauffeur' is an antique name

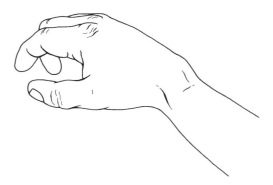

Figure 5.24 *The 'dinner fork' deformity produced by a Colles fracture.*

Colles' fracture (Figure 5.23)

The term Colles [**ref 14**: 1797] is often inappropriately used to refer to any fracture of the distal radius. However specifically: the radius is transversely fractured within an inch of its lower originating from injuries sustained from 'kick-back' from starting handles (which motor cars no longer have). This trauma could also fracture the scaphoid.

Forearm fractures

Fractures may be confined to one bone or may affect both. In adults, where both bones are involved open reduction and internal fixation may be undertaken as the fractures are difficult to reduce and immobilize by external means. Displaced children's fractures are treated by traction and attempted manipulation under general anaesthetic [**ref 10**: 82]. *Greenstick* and *torus fractures* (slight buckling of the bone cortex) of the forearm are very common in children.

Monteggia and Galeazzi fracture-dislocation complexes

Monteggia is a fracture of the upper end of the ulna and dislocation of the superior radioulnar joint. Displacement may be either forward bowing of the ulnar shaft with anterior displacement of the radial head (*Figure 5.25*) or backward bowing of the ulnar shaft with posterior dislocation of the radial head (*Figure 5.26*). The injury often requires open reduction and internal fixation of the ulnar fracture. *Galeazzi (Figure 5.27)* is fracture of the radius with dislocation of the lower radioulnar joint. The radial fracture may be internally fixed.

Radiographic techniques – wrist (lower radius and ulna)

Two projections are taken at right angles – a posteroanterior and lateral of the wrist including

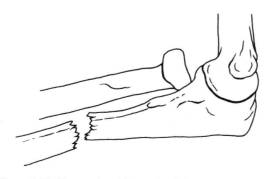

Figure 5.25 Monteggia with anterior dislocation of the radial head.

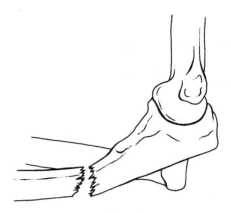

Figure 5.26 Monteggia with posterior dislocation of the radial head.

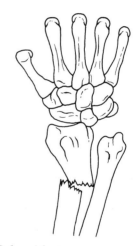

Figure 5.27 Galeazzi fracture.

the carpus and the lower third of the radius and ulna (*see* techniques 9 and 10). Where injury to the forearm bones is not obvious a posteroanterior oblique wrist [projection (11 (ii))] should be included in case of fracture of the scaphoid. If injury precludes or limits the patient's movement then a horizontal X-ray beam may be used to produce the second view. Descriptions of projections below assume that the patient is seated alongside the X-ray table.

(17) Radiocarpal joint

This is a supplementary technique that aims to demonstrate the joint space. Position as for projection (9).

Central ray direction – Central ray is angled 25–30° from the vertical towards the elbow joint and centred midway between the styloid processes.

Radiographic techniques – forearm

(18) Anteroposterior forearm *(Figure 5.28)*

This demonstrates the whole length of the forearm bones. The forearm is raised on to the table and externally rotated until the posterior surface of the limb rests on the image receptor. The styloid processes of the wrist are equidistant from the image receptor. If possible the elbow is fully extended. Place a sandbag over the fingers.

Central ray direction – Perpendicular to the image receptor and centred to the middle of the forearm.

The injured patient may find it difficult to produce and maintain the positioning. A posteroanterior projection is acceptable; however, the upper radius and ulna now overlap.

(19) Lateral forearm *(Figure 5.29)*

With the forearm pronated the radial side is raised and rotated through 90° until the dorsal aspect of the forearm is perpendicular to the image receptor. The elbow remains flexed throughout. The hand should be immobilized.

Central ray direction – Perpendicular to the image receptor and centred to the middle of the forearm.

Wrist and elbow joints should be included on both projections. After the initial examination when the

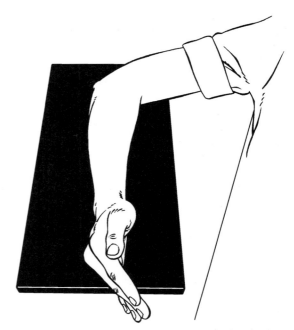

Figure 5.29 Position of the patient for a lateral forearm projection.

site of the injury is known it may be permissible to include only the joint nearest the injury on subsequent radiographs. If the patient cannot rotate his arm because of injury then the two projections may be taken at right angles to each other using a horizontal X-ray beam for the second projection.

Patients in a long arm plaster

The position of the elbow and forearm is often such that the patient cannot readily be placed in the posteroanterior or lateral position. Compensatory angulation of the X-ray beam may be required to produce satisfactory results.

ELBOW

Essential anatomical terminology *(see – Figures 5.22, 5.30 and 5.32)*

The elbow joint consists of two joints:

(1) A hinge joint between the *trochlea* of the humerus and the scoop-shaped *trochlear notch* of the ulna.

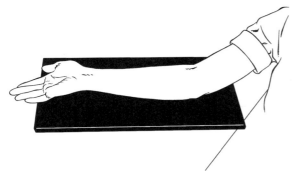

Figure 5.28 Position of the patient for an anteroposterior forearm projection.

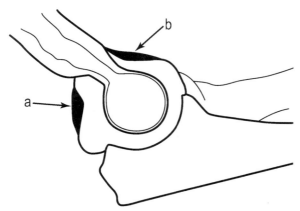

Figure 5.30 (a) posterior and (b) anterior fat pads at the elbow joint.

(2) A shallow ball and socket joint between the *capitellum* of the humerus and the head of the radius. Movement at the elbow joint is restricted to extension and flexion produced by the brachial (arm) muscles.

The distal humerus is expanded transversely and displays two bony prominences; the *medial and lateral epicondyles*. Behind the medial epicondyle lies the ulnar nerve which can be easily palpated.

When the arm is extended at the elbow and lies in the anatomical position, the long axis of the forearm is seen to make an angle with the long axis of the humerus. This is known as the *carrying angle* (average 15°) and the wrist joint lies further away from the median plane of the body than the elbow joint

Fat pads *(Figure 5.30)*

These are intracapsular but extrasynovial structure of the elbow joint. These may be visible on the radiographs, and appearances may be indicative of injury. It is quite normal to see the anterior fat pad on the lateral elbow projection. The posterior pad is obscured because of its position in the olecranon fossa. Displacement of the fat pads, and in particular the posterior pad, is indicative of an intra-articular fracture with a haemarthrosis [**ref 1**: 270]. There are other conditions producing intra-articular fluid collections that can produce a positive pad sign [**ref 8**: 1473].

Indications for the X-ray examination

Injuries

Supracondylar fractures of the humerus *(Figure 5.31)*

In children, this is usually caused by a fall on to the outstretched hand. Incidence of this injury reaches a peak around the age of eight years [**ref 11**: 146]. The fracture occurs in the lowest inch of the humerus and the lower fragment is usually displaced backwards. This fracture causes concern because there is a danger of *compartment syndrome* arising from compression of the median nerve and radial artery within the anterior compartment of the forearm. Damage to the brachial artery may lead to ischaemia of the forearm – a serious complication. There is also a possibility of injury to the median and ulnar nerves. After reduction the elbow is held in flexion by the application of a collar and cuff sling. Some surgeons also protect the limb by means of a plaster-of-Paris back-slab. A complete plaster is avoided because of the risks of swelling [**ref 11**: 149]. In adults, a supracondylar fracture line occurs more proximal than in children and comminution is common.

Capitellum fractures

This is often seen in association with injuries of the radial head [**ref 11**:157].

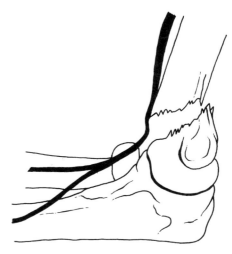

Figure 5.31 Supracondylar fracture of the humerus, the sharp upper fragment impinging on the brachial artery.

Olecranon fracture

If the triceps undergoes sudden contraction and at the same time the elbow joint is forcibly flexed then the olecranon (point of insertion for the triceps) may be snapped off the ulna and pulled posteriorly over the lower end of the humerus. This fracture requires internal fixation otherwise the hinge action of the elbow joint will be lost. Alternatively the olecranon may be fractured as a result of direct falls onto the elbow point.

Coronoid process fracture

Seldom fractured except in association with a dislocation of the elbow. If this is the case the elbow may predispose to recurrent dislocation.

Fractures of the head of the radius

This injury frequently results from a fall on the outstretched arm. The fall drives the head of the radius against the capitellum. The fracture may only be a small vertical crack; hence supplementary projections are often required to demonstrate the injury. Alternatively the whole radial head may be comminuted in which case the surgeon may excise it as treatment. Sometimes the only effect of the fall is a bruising of the cartilage covering the articular surfaces but this is not evident on the radiograph.

Dislocated elbow

The elbow is normally a stable hinge joint, so if it becomes dislocated the joint capsule may be extensively torn. The most common direction for dislocation is posterior displacement of the radius and ulna (*Figure 5.32*). A characteristic sign of a dislocated elbow is the loss of normal alignment of the olecranon process relative to the epicondyles of the humerus. After reduction under a general anaesthetic the elbow is rested in a collar and cuff sling. Although the joint is said to be stable to all forces after reduction the radiographer should nevertheless beware of attempting to extend the elbow for an anteroposterior projection. This may result in a recurrence of the dislocation. Complex patterns of elbow dislocation are likely to have associated bony injury such as radial head and coronoid process fracture.

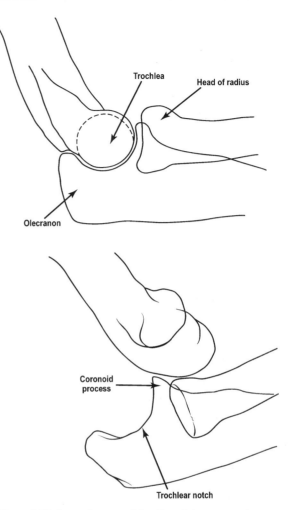

Figure 5.32 Lateral aspect of the elbow joint – normal (above) – dislocated (below).

Other conditions of interest

Cubitus varus and valgus deformities

These are the result of excessive changes in the elbow 'carrying angle' due to mal-union of either a supracondylar fracture or some other fracture at the elbow. For definitions of varus and valgus – *see* page 12.

Heterotopic ossification

This is new bone growing in soft tissues around the elbow and is a rare but serious complication of a dislocated elbow. This ossification is sometimes referred to as *myositis ossificans* (*see* Chapter 2).

Elbow tunnel syndrome (cubital tunnel syndrome)

The ulnar nerve traverses a fibrous tunnel as it passes behind the medial epicondyle. Occasionally the sheath is too tight and the nerve is compressed. This gives rise to symptoms in the area of distribution of the ulnar nerve such as numbness or a tingling sensation (paraesthesias) over the ulnar border of the hand and the ring and little fingers, plus a weakness of the hand. This compression syndrome can also be a sequel to a fracture of the lower end of the humerus.

Osteoarthritis

In the elbow, arthritis may be a sequel to an injury that produces an incongruity of the joint surfaces. Osteophytes formed may break off and form loose bodies in the joint (*see* Chapter 3).

Radiographic techniques – elbow

Descriptions of projections below assume that the patient is seated alongside the X-ray table unless otherwise stated.

(20) Lateral elbow (Figure 5.33)

This is the most critical projection [**ref 8**: 1473]. The arm is raised on to the table and the elbow is flexed to 90° if possible. The medial aspect of the elbow rests on the image receptor. The wrist, elbow and shoulder should be in the same horizontal plane – use a table with adjustable height if possible. The forearm is rotated laterally until its dorsal surface lies perpendicular to the image receptor. If this is not possible then a lateral elbow projection taken with the palm facing downwards is acceptable.

> *Central ray direction* – Perpendicular to the image receptor and centred to the lateral epicondyle of the humerus.

(21) Alternative technique – For the patient with limited shoulder and arm movement: leave the patient's arm in the sling and do not try to move it. A cassette can be placed directly behind the medial aspect of the elbow, resting between arm and the body (*Figure 5.34*).

> *Central ray direction* – Perpendicular to the image receptor and centred to the lateral epicondyle of the humerus.

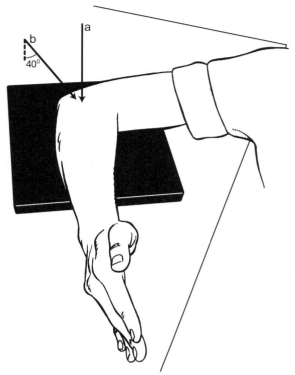

Figure 5.33 Position of the patient and direction of the X-ray beam for (a) projection (20) and (b) projection (26(iii)(d)).

Figure 5.34 Position of the patient and cassette for projection (21).

The patient remains seated or lying so the image receptor should be adequately supported against the trunk. Place lead protection between the patient and the cassette and collimate the X-ray beam.

(22) Anteroposterior elbow

The whole arm is placed on the table with the palm and anterior aspect of the elbow facing upwards. The shoulder, elbow and wrist should all be in the same horizontal plane. The posterior aspect of the elbow lies on the image receptor. Immobilize the forearm.

> *Central ray direction* – Perpendicular to the image receptor and centred 2.5 cm below the mid-point between the epicondyles.

Modified and alternative techniques – projections (23–25).

(23) For the patient who cannot straighten the arm fully, the elbow remaining slightly flexed

Choose one or more of the following three techniques according to the area of interest; image receptor and central ray orientation remain as for (22):

(i)   The patient extends the arm at the elbow as far as possible and then places the forearm down on the table. Support the upper arm. The image of the humerus will be distorted according to how great its separation from the image receptor. Increase the exposure by 5 kVp. *Centre*: 2.5 cm below the mid-point of the epicondyles.

(ii) Extend the elbow as far as possible except this time place the upper arm down on the table. Support the forearm. The distortion now occurs in the image of the radius and ulna. Increase the exposure by 5 kVp. *Centre*: Midway between the epicondyles.

(iii) Place the point of the elbow next to the image receptor. Support both the upper and the lower arm. *Centre*: To the crease of the elbow. This produces equal amounts of distortion in the image of the humerus and radius and ulna.

(24) Projection

Often a patient may be able to raise the arm on to the table for the lateral view which is relatively easy but then cannot rotate the arm laterally for an anteroposterior view. After the lateral projection has been taken the arm remains in the same position. The elbow is raised slightly on a non-opaque pad. The X-ray tube is then turned through 90° and directed so that the central ray is perpendicular to an image receptor propped behind the point of the elbow. *Centre*: To the crease of the elbow.

(25) Axial projections

For a patient with the arm fixed in extreme flexion because of injury or treatment immobilization, use either of the following:

(i) Axial elbow, inferosuperior (Figure 5.35)

With the elbow in flexion the upper arm is placed in contact with the image receptor. The palm is facing the shoulder.

> *Central ray direction* – Either centre 5 cm distal from the olecranon process with the X-ray tube perpendicular to the image receptor to show the olecranon process and the joint between the trochlear notch and trochlea of the humerus. Or centre 5 cm distal from the olecranon process with the X-ray tube angled 30° towards the shoulder to show the joint between the radial head and the capitellum.

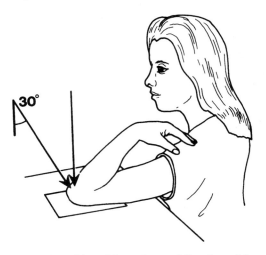

Figure 5.35 Position of the patient and directions of the central ray in projection (25(i)).

Loss of image definition and increase in magnification must be expected in more distal parts of the radius and ulna.

(ii) Axial elbow, superoinferior

The patient sits with his back against the edge of the table. With the elbow flexed the arm is extended backwards over the table. The forearm is in contact with the image receptor (*Figure 5.36*).

> *Central ray direction* – Central ray is either perpendicular to the image receptor or angled toward the shoulder, centred just above the level of the humeral epicondyles.

Patient on a stretcher

Where the arm is extended by the patient's side but cannot be moved, take two projections at right angles using a vertical and then a horizontal X-ray beam. The arm is raised on a non-opaque pad. Additional X-ray tube angulation may compensate for unsatisfactory patient position. Where the X-ray beam is directed at the patient's abdomen use lead rubber protection.

Child with a supracondylar fracture

The patient may be seated in a chair or brought to the department on a stretcher. Do not attempt to extend the elbow joint. Do the lateral projection

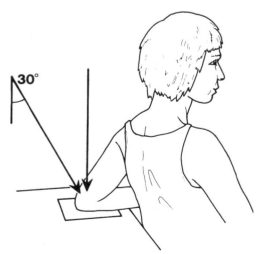

Figure 5.36 Position of the patient and directions of the central ray in projection (25(ii)).

first using (21), for example. The anteroposterior projection is taken in whatever degree of flexion happens to be present. The position of the forearm bones is largely irrelevant as what is needed is an anteroposterior view of the lower end of the humerus. If the elbow is flexed at an extreme angle, use projection (25 (i)). Where the elbow is in flexion but the angle is greater than 90° – perform an anteroposterior projection with the posterior aspect of the lower end of the humerus in contact with the image receptor, supporting the forearm. The child can be lying or sitting with the back of the arm against the image receptor, placed for example in a chest stand. Because of the scarcity of ossified cartilage, interpretation of the radiographs may be difficult. Views of the other elbow may be requested for comparison.

(26) Head of radius

This can be visualized both on routine anteroposterior and lateral projections (projections (22) and (20)). Additional views for this area are as follows:

(i) From the position for the anteroposterior projection of the elbow (projection (22)) the arm is laterally rotated to bring the head of the radius closer to the image receptor. Some separation between the upper radius and the ulna is thus achieved. This projection also demonstrates the proximal radioulnar joint.

> *Central ray direction* – Perpendicular to the image receptor and centred over the head of the radius.

(ii) Projection (23(iii)) gives an *'en-face'* view of the head of the radius.

(iii) When the forearm is moving within the action of pronation and supination the ulna provides the axis of rotation and the radius moves around the ulna. Further lateral projections of the elbow can be taken at stages of medial rotation – the radial head moving its position between each. The direction of the central ray is the same for (a) – (c), i.e. as for projection (20).

(a) Lateral elbow (projection (20)).

(b) Lateral elbow, palm facing down.

(c) Lateral elbow, forearm in full medial rotation.

(d) Lateral elbow (flexed at 90°) with the X-ray beam angled 45° towards the long axis of the humerus *(Figure 5.33)*. This projection demonstrates the capitellum (*see* [further reading **3**]).

(27) *Olecranon*

This is demonstrated in the following:

(i) Anteroposterior elbow (projection (22)).

(ii) Lateral elbow (projection (20)).

(iii) Axial elbow, inferosuperior [projection (25(i))]. If the patient cannot flex the elbow to less than 90° compensatory tube angulation towards the shoulder should be used.

(28) *Coronoid process*

This is demonstrated in the following:

(i) Anteroposterior elbow (projection (22)).

(ii) Lateral elbow (projection (20)).

(iii) From the anteroposterior position (projection (22)), medially rotate the arm raising the radial side through 45°.

Central ray direction – Perpendicular to the image receptor and centred over the coronoid process.

(29) *Ulnar groove*

A profile view. The position is the same as projection (25(ii)). The palm faces upwards and the elbow should be flexed at 45°.

Central ray direction – Perpendicular to the image receptor and centred over the ulnar groove just lateral to the medial epicondyle.

For more information on the ulnar groove and alternative projections – *see* [further reading **2**].

HUMERUS

Essential anatomical terminology

The humerus is the largest and longest bone in the upper limb. Features of the distal end are detailed above on pages 63 and 66. The upper extremity of the humerus is described in Chapter 6. A notable feature of the shaft of the humerus is the *sulcus* or *musculospiralgroove* for the *radial nerve*.

Indications for the X-ray examination

Fractures

These can occur at all levels of the bone and a spiral fracture may extend along the entire length of the bone shaft. A possible complication of a humeral shaft fracture is radial nerve palsy. This may result in a wrist-drop deformity. The humerus is a common site for metastases from a carcinoma of the breast or bronchus, and often a *pathological fracture* is the first sign of abnormality.

Radiographic techniques – humerus, lower third

An injury or pathology may involve the lower end of the bone. Two projections at right angles can be taken using similar techniques to that described for the elbow, if necessary increasing the area included in the X-ray field.

Radiographic techniques – humerus, full length

It may be necessary to demonstrate the entire length of the bone including the shoulder and elbow joints. It is usual to select an erect or where necessary, a recumbent general patient position when examining the humerus.

(30) *Anteroposterior humerus*
(Figure 5.37)

The patient faces the X-ray tube. The arm is abducted slightly from the trunk, then supinated and fully extended at the elbow joint if possible. The patient is rotated slightly towards the side of interest so that the posterior aspect of the shoulder and elbow are in contact with the cassette or table.

Central ray direction – Perpendicular to the image receptor and centred midway between the shoulder and elbow joints.

Figure 5.37 Position of the patient for an anteroposterior humerus projection (30).

The outer two-thirds of the clavicle and scapula should be included on the radiograph. If the patient cannot fully extend the elbow, position him so that the posterior aspect of the upper arm is in contact with the cassette or vertical bucky. The mid-humeral centring point provides oblique X-rays which tend to project the forearm bones downwards. Where the elbow region is of special interest, further projections of that area should be taken.

(31) Lateral humerus

This is achieved by rotating the humerus medially 90° degrees from the anteroposterior position. The elbow is flexed and the arm is abducted and internally rotated. The medial aspect of the elbow should be in contact with the cassette or table.

Central ray direction – Perpendicular to the image receptor and midway between the shoulder and elbow joints.

This approach may be unsatisfactory because:

(i) There may be difficulty obtaining sufficient internal rotation of the arm.

(ii) It may not be possible to move the arm at all.

(iii) Rotation of the arm may not give a view of the humerus that is truly at 90° to the antero-posterior projection.

(iv) The glenohumeral joint is still seen in the same plane as in the anteroposterior projection.

Alternative techniques – projections (32–34).

(32) If the patient can stand *(Figure 5.38)*

The patient faces the cassette or vertical bucky. The elbow is flexed and the forearm and hand rest on the abdomen. The arm is abducted slightly from the trunk. Turn the patient's head away from the side under examination. Raise the uninjured side away from the support so that the lateral aspect of the elbow and the anterolateral aspect of the shoulder are in contact with the cassette or vertical bucky.

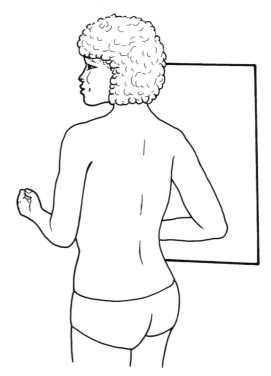

Figure 5.38 Position of the patient for projection (32).

Central ray direction – Perpendicular to the image receptor and centred midway between the shoulder and the elbow joints.

The upper third of the humerus may be obscured by the bony or soft tissues or the scapular region and thus the exposure for this upper part of the arm may have to be increased. (Further alternative projections may have to be taken.)

(33) If the patient cannot move the arm at all

(i) For lower two-thirds of humerus

A cassette can be placed between the patient's arm and thorax. Lead protection must be placed between patient and cassette. (*See* projection (21).)

Central ray direction – Perpendicular to the long axis of the bone with a horizontal or suitably angled X-ray beam and centred to the lateral aspect of the elbow and humerus.

(ii) For upper two-thirds of humerus

A cassette and grid are supported vertically against the lateral aspect of the shoulder. The opposite arm is raised over the patient's head separating the two heads of humerii. If the patient is able to stand, the positioning can take place against the vertical bucky – a grid should be used because of the large volume of body tissue the beam must traverse (*Figure 5.39*). The area covered in this projection may be extended by collimation to include most of the humerus but projections of the lower humerus via the abdomen should be avoided because of increased radiation dose to the patient. For comments on radiation protection issues *see* pages 82–83.

Central ray direction – A horizontal X-ray beam is directed through the axilla of the raised arm towards the upper third of the humerus.

The exposure is made on arrested respiration.

(34) If the patient has limited movement and cannot raise the opposite arm *(Figure 5.40)*

A cassette is propped against the lateral aspect of the upper arm. The X-ray beam is directed transversely, separating the two sides; however the

Figure 5.39 Patient position and direction of the central ray for projection 33(ii).

Figure 5.40 Position of the cassette and direction of the central ray in projection (34).

thorax will be obscured by the upper extremity of the humerus. Although not a true lateral projection this gives a second view of the humerus in the seriously injured or otherwise immobile patient.

References

1. Berquist TH (1992) *Imaging of Sports Injuries* Aspen: Gaithersburg

2. Brydie A Raby N (2003) Early MRI in the management of clinical scaphoid fractures *British Journal Radiology* **76**(912): 923

3. Cooney WP Dobyns JH Linscheid RL (1980) Complications of Colles fractures *Clinical Orthopaedics* 1980 **62**: 613–619

4. Dandy DJ and Edwards DJ (2003) *Essential Orthopaedics and Trauma (4th Edition)* Edinbugh: Churchill Livingstone

5. Edwards JC Edwards SE Huskinson EC (1983) The value of radiography in the management of rheumatoid arthritis *Clinical Radiology* **34**(4): 413–6

6. Gilula LA (1979) Carpal injuries: analytic approach and case exercises *American Journal Roentgenology* **133**: 503–517

7. Goldfarb CA Yuming Y Gilula LA Fisher MD Boyer MI (2001) Wrist Fractures: what the clinician wants to know *Radiology* **219**: 11–28

8. Grainger RG and Allison DJ (1997) *Grainger and Allison's Diagnostic Radiology (Volume 1) (3rd Edition)* Edinburgh: Churchill Livingstone

9. McRae R (1994) *Practical Fracture Treatment (3rd Edition)* Edinburgh: Churchill Livingstone

10. McRae R Andrew W (1997) *Orthopaedics and trauma: an illustrated colour text* Edinburgh: Churchill Livingstone

11. McRae R Esser M (2002) *Practical Fracture Treatment (4th Edition)* Edinburgh: Churchill Livingstone

12. Mewa AA Pui M Cockshott WP Buchanan WW (1983) Observer differences in detecting erosions in radiographs of rheumatoid arthritis. A comparison of posteroanterior, Norgaard and Brewerton views *Journal of Rheumatology* **10**(2): 216–21

13. Raby N Berman L De Lacey G (2002) *Accident and Emergency Radiology: A Survival Guide* London: Saunders

14. Sonin AH Boles CA Rogers LF in Grainger R Allison D Adam A Dixon A (eds) (2001) *Grainger and Allison's Diagnostic Radiology (Volume 3) (4th Edition)* Edinburgh: Churchill Livingstone

15. Stripp WJ (1958) Radiography of the ulnar groove and the carpal tunnel *Radiography* **26**(287): 277–280

16. Taylor JAM Resnick DMD (2000) *Skeletal Imaging. Atlas of the Spine and Extremities* Philadelphia: Saunders

Further reading

1. Bledse RE Izenstark JL (1959) Displacement of fat pads in disease and injury of the elbow: a new radiographic sign *Radiology* **73**: 717–724

2. Cooper A Vinnicombe S (1992) The ulnar groove *Radiography today* **58**(660): 11–12

3. Greenspan NA (1982) The radial head – capitellum view. A useful technique in elbow trauma *American Journal Roentgenology* **138**: 116

4. Hildebrande KA Patterson SD King GJ (1999) Acute elbow dislocations: simple and complex *Orthopaedic Clinics North America* **30**(1): 63–79

5. Marshall J Davies R (1990) Imaging of the carpal tunnel *Radiography today* **56**(633): 11–13

6. Reckling FW (1982) Unstable fracture-dislocation of the forearm (Monteggia and Galeazzi lesions) *Journal of Bone and Joint Surgery* **64A**: 857–863

7. Richmond B (1995) A comparative study of two radiographic techniques for obtaining an AP projection of the thumb *Radiography today* **61**: 696

8. Sherman GM Seitz WH (1999) Fractures and dislocations of the wrist *Current Opinions in Orthopaedics* **10**(4): 237–251

9. Thornton A Gyll C (1999) *Children's Fractures* London: WB Saunders

10. Villarin LA Belk KE Fried R (1999) Emergency department evaluation and treatment of elbow and forearm injuries *Emergency Medical Clinics of North America* **17**(4): 843–58

CHAPTER CONTENTS

Table of main and supplementary radiographic techniques

General anatomical area	Projection	Page	Common Indications
Shoulder	**1** AP general survey **3–5** Lateral (axillary) or alternatives	81 82–83	Injury, dislocation, pathology
	6 Stryker notch (*Stryker*) **7** Apical oblique (*Garth*)	84 84	Recurrent dislocation, instability
Glenohumeral joint	**2** AP profile projection (*Grashey*) **3–5** Lateral (axillary) or alternatives **7** Apical oblique (*Garth*)	82 82–83 84	Specific injury to glenoid
Rotator cuff tendon insertions			
Supraspinatus and acromial abnormalities	**8i** AP straight tube **8ii** AP 30° caudad **8iii** Supraspinatus outlet	84 84 84	Pathology, inflammation, impingement syndrome
Subscapularis	**9i** AP arm supinated **9ii** AP arm internally rotated **9iii** AP arm externally rotated **12** Bicipital groove profile	84 84 84 84–85	Pathology e.g. calcification
Infraspinatus	**10i** AP arm externally rotated **10ii** AP 25° caudad	84 84	
Teres minor	**11** AP arm full internal rotation	84	
Long head biceps	**12** Bicipital groove profile	84–85	
Scapula	**13** AP **14 or 5** Lateral or alternative	85 85	Injury
Coracoid process	**15** Special projections	86	Injury
Acromion	**16** Special projections	86	Injury
Acromioclavicular joints	**17** AP or **18** PA	86 86	Injury, dislocation, subluxation
Clavicle	**20** AP or **21** PA **22** Inferosuperior	87 87 87	Injury
Sternoclavicular joints	**23** PA **24** PA obliques **25** Lateral **26** Anteroposterior axial	87 88 88 88	Injury, pathology Dislocation
Sternum	**27** PA oblique **28** Lateral **30ii** AP chest **28** Lateral horizontal beam	90 90 91 90–91	Injury Major injury
Ribs	**29** PA chest or **30** AP chest	91 91	Moderate to major injury
	31 or 32 AP oblique	92	Not usually indicated

Effective dose for an extremity examination: < **0.01mSv**
Equivalent period of natural background radiation: **1.5 days**
Effective dose for a chest examination (single PA radiograph): **0.02 mSv**
Equivalent period of natural background radiation: **3 days**

SHOULDER GIRDLE

Essential anatomical terminology

The bones of the shoulder girdle include the head of the humerus, the clavicle and the scapula (*Figure 6.1*). The shoulder or *glenohumeral joint* is a synovial 'ball and socket joint', the rounded head of the humerus articulating with the ellipsoid *glenoid cavity* of the scapula, a bony socket made deeper by its fibrocartilaginous rim, the *glenoid labrum*. The outer aspect of the humeral head bears two bony prominences, the *greater and lesser tuberosities* into which are inserted the tendons of the *rotator cuff*. Between the tuberosities lies the *bicipital groove* that lodges the tendon of the long head of biceps muscle. The rotator cuff includes the tendons of the supraspinatus, infraspinatus, teres minor and subscapularis muscles which blend with the capsule of the shoulder joint. The muscles of the cuff originate from the blade-like scapula. Two

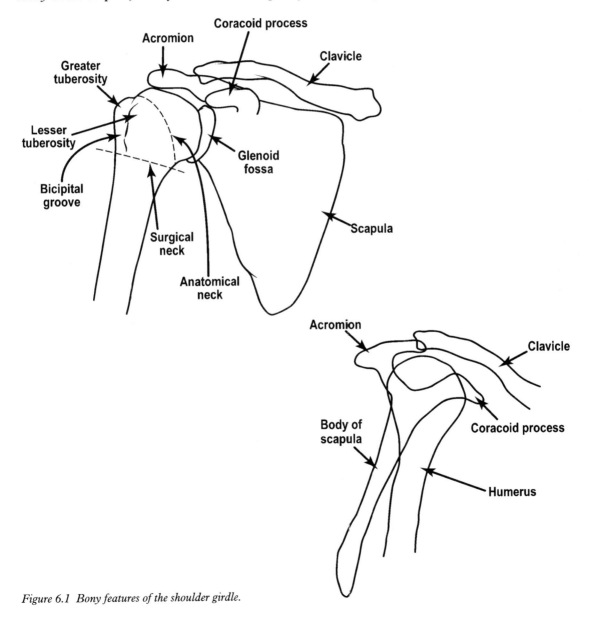

Figure 6.1 Bony features of the shoulder girdle.

important bony features of the scapula are the *acromion*, a shelf-like ridge of bone arching over the humeral head and the *coracoid process*. The function of the clavicle is to act as a 'prop' for the shoulder joint, its lateral end forming a joint with the acromion of the scapula – the *acromioclavicular* joint and its medial end articulating with the sternum forming the *sternoclavicular joint*. Extra security is given to the position of the clavicle because of its attachment to the coracoid process of the scapula and the first rib by strong ligaments.

Indications for the X-ray examination

Injuries

Fracture of the surgical neck of humerus

There are a large number of fracture patterns in the proximal humerus and these represent about 5% of all fractures [ref 2: 114]; a dislocation of the humeral head may accompany any of these fractures. In adults the most common injury is either an impacted or a moderately displaced surgical neck fracture [ref 7: 73]. In children, the corresponding injury is a *fracture separation of the epiphysis* from the upper end of the humerus and the Salter-Harris classification can be applied (*see* page 12).

Shoulder joint dislocation

The glenoid cavity of the scapula is shallow in order to allow a really wide range of movement at the shoulder. The joint depends for its stability on soft-tissue structures such as the long head of biceps, the joint capsule and the surrounding deltoid muscle. Glenohumeral joint dislocation is a very common injury in adults, they account for half of all dislocations and 97% of those in the shoulder joint are anterior dislocations [ref 2: 245]. Generally, shoulder dislocations are caused by a fall on the outstretched arm. There are three types:

(1) *Anterior dislocation (Figure 6.2)* – the humeral head is forced out of the glenoid cavity and comes to lie below the coracoid process. Because the greater tuberosity no longer holds out the deltoid muscle, which now falls as a curtain from the outer edges of the acromion, the normal curved contour of the shoulder is replaced by an acute angle or 'cut off' appearance (*Figure 6.3*). If the tip of the acromion and the lateral epicondyle can be joined by a ruler – *Hamilton's ruler sign* – then the shoulder is dislocated [ref 4: 16].

(2) *Posterior dislocation* – relatively uncommon – the head of the humerus lies behind the glenoid cavity. Examples of causes are epileptic

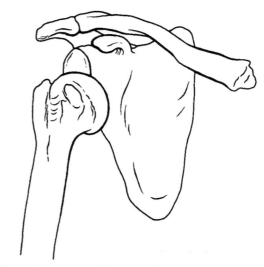

Figure 6.2 Anterior dislocation of the shoulder joint.

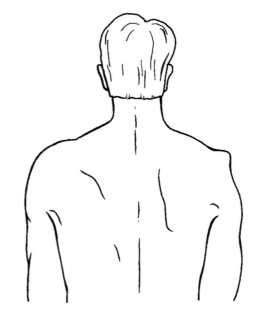

Figure 6.3 Appearance of an abnormal right shoulder in anterior dislocation.

fit or electric shock. Muscles around the shoulder joint go into spasm: the larger groups of muscles are posterior to the joint, pulling it out of the socket in that direction as they contract. Posterior dislocation may not be obvious from a single anteroposterior shoulder radiograph (*Figure 6.4*).

(3) *Inferior dislocation (luxatio erecta)* – also rare. The head of the humerus lies beneath the glenoid cavity.

Recurrent instability of the shoulder joint
(Figure 6.5)

If the patient has a history of traumatic dislocation of the shoulder a situation may subsequently develop where the joint may repeatedly dislocate. This is usually due to the presence of an unhealed tear in the attachment of the glenoid labrum to the anterior margin of the glenoid cavity (*Bankart lesion*). This rent allows the capsule to balloon forward so that the humeral head can pass over the rim of the glenoid cavity. Recurrent dislocation can

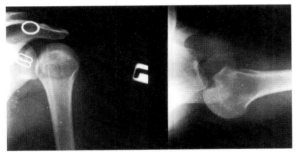

Figure 6.4 Anteroposterior and lateral (axillary) radiographs of the left shoulder. The patient has a posterior dislocation of the humeral head.

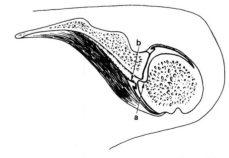

Figure 6.5 Transverse section through a left shoulder joint affected by recurrent anterior dislocation . (a) Notch formed on the head of the humerus. (b) Tear in the capsular ligament.

occur with a progressively smaller amount of force and after some time the joint becomes very lax. It may then dislocate on very mild external rotation of the shoulder, for example on opening a newspaper. As the humeral head dislocates, the postero-lateral aspect of the humeral head comes in contact with the glenoid rim and this may result in an associated impaction fracture – the *Hill Sachs deformity* [**ref 7**].

Treatment of recurrent dislocation is by surgical repair. This is usually recommended by the time of the fourth dislocation [**ref 7**: 73]. *Arthrography* (with or without *CT*), *ultrasound* and *MRI* may all be used in the diagnosis [**ref 12**: 46].

Fractures of the greater tuberosity

These may be caused by a direct blow to the shoulder or may occur in association with dislocation of the shoulder joint.

Ruptures of the rotator cuff

These usually result from chronic impingement (*see* – below) and attrition [**ref 7**: 67] worsened by trauma. In a fall, if the abducted arm is forcefully brought to the side, the rotator cuff may be extensively torn. This usually involves mainly the supraspinatus tendon, which is normally subjected to the greatest mechanical strains. If the tendon is torn, the patient will be unable to initiate abduction of the shoulder – the action of the supraspinatus. Bony evidence is usually absent in rotator cuff tears which are investigated using *arthrography*, *ultrasound* and *MRI* [**ref 12**: 46].

Shoulder impingement syndromes

This painful condition may occur if part of the rotator cuff (the supraspinatus tendon) is compressed between the humeral head and the acromion, the acromioclavicular joint and the coracoclavicular ligament [**ref 7**: 66]. Clinical features include painful arcs of shoulder abduction movement. *Arthrography*, *ultrasound* and *MRI* may help to confirm the diagnosis.

Rupture of the long head of biceps tendon

An injury of elderly patients often occurring spontaneously and associated with attrition of the tendon as it passes through the bicipital groove, the surface of which may be roughened.

Fractures of the scapula

These are caused by direct blows to the bone. They are uncommon, usually affecting either the neck or the body of the scapula. As the bone is an important site for muscular origins, the surgeon will be more concerned about soft tissue than bony injury.

Fractures of the glenoid are usually associated with dislocations. Fractures of the acromion are usually due to a direct blow from above. Fractures of the coracoid process may be due to direct trauma or avulsion. Repeated trauma in clay pigeon shooting may result in a coracoid stress fracture [**ref 2**: 253].

Fractures of the clavicle

This bone is usually fractured at the junction of its middle and outer thirds. The lateral fragment is usually displaced downwards and medially. Applying traction along the line of the bone may reduce the fracture and this is achieved by 'bracing the shoulders back' with a special 'figure of eight' bandage or clavicular brace. If there is no displacement then a broad-arm sling is used. Non-union of clavicular fractures is extremely rare [**ref 7**: 70] and internal fixation is not usually needed.

Acromioclavicular joint injuries

Dislocation (*Figure 6.6*) is rare but subluxation is more common, resulting from a blow on the shoulder forcing the acromion downwards. The joint capsule will be torn but the joint cannot be displaced unless the strong coracoclavicular ligament has been torn.

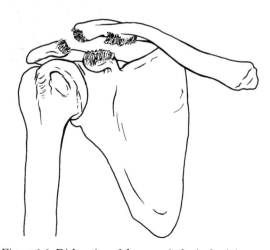

Figure 6.6 Dislocation of the acromioclavicular joint.

Sternoclavicular joint injuries

The joint may rarely be dislocated, although fracture of the clavicle is far more likely. If the medial end of the affected clavicle is depressed it may impinge upon the great vessels. Plain radiographs can be very difficult to interpret. Use of *CT* may help to confirm the plane and extent of displacement [**ref 7**: 71].

Other conditions of interest

Rheumatoid arthritis

The shoulder joint is commonly affected in rheumatoid disease but usually in association with other joints. Two-thirds of rheumatoid patients will have some degree of shoulder involvement [**ref 8**: 68]. Tears of the rotator cuff occur more commonly in patients with rheumatoid disease. The sternoclavicular joints can also become affected by *rheumatoid arthritis*. Destruction of the cartilage and the articular ends of the bones occurs in the same manner as in other joints.

Osteoarthritis

Osteoarthritis is rare because the shoulder is not a weight-bearing joint. When it occurs it is usually secondary to trauma. If the patient is affected and also suffers from osteoarthritis in joints of the lower limb then this could be very disabling because he may not be able to make use of crutches. Osteoarthritic changes may sometimes occur in the acromioclavicular joints. Some severe degenerative problems of the shoulder may require replacement of the painful joint with a prosthesis in arthroplasty (*see Figure 6.7*).

Calcific tendinitis

Calcification in the shoulder joint is most commonly due to calcific deposits within the tendons of the rotator cuff. The insertion of the supraspinatus is the most frequently involved.

Supraspinatus tendinitis

This inflammatory condition is usually localized to the upper part of the rotator cuff region of the capsule of the shoulder joint. The condition may progress to spontaneous rupture of the supraspinatus tendon. The radiographs may show calcification just above the greater tuberosity.

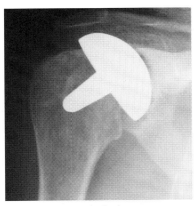

Figure 6.7 Shoulder joint prosthesis.

Frozen shoulder (adhesive capsulitis)

This is characterized by pain and stiffness in the shoulder joint where all shoulder movements are restricted.

Sprengel's shoulder

A rare congenital condition where the scapula is smaller and higher than normal (*see* Klippel-Feil syndrome, page 143). The deformity is due to failure of the shoulder girdle to descend from its embryonic position in the neck [**ref 15**: 2].

Craniocleidodysostosis (Figure 6.8)

This is a failure in the development of membrane bone in the skull, clavicle and pubic bones. The clavicles are either absent or the outer halves of the bones are missing (*see* also page 169).

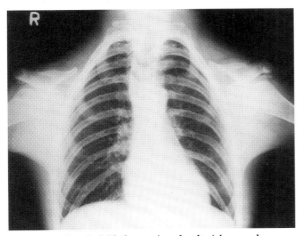

Figure 6.8 Craniocleidodysostosis – the clavicles are absent.

Radiographic techniques – Shoulder

In shoulder radiography the usual rules apply for use of secondary radiation grids, i.e. the volume of tissue dictates choice of grid or non-grid technique. There are discussions amongst users of computed radiography as to whether application of grids help or hinder visualisation in shoulder radiography.

(1) Anteroposterior shoulder (general survey projection)

The patient faces the X-ray tube. The image receptor is behind the shoulder. If the patient is erect the elbow should be flexed and supported. If the patient is recumbent the arm is extended and abducted slightly if possible. Rotate the patient slightly towards the side under examination so that the posterior aspect of the shoulder and humerus lie against the cassette or table (*Figure 6.9*).

Central ray direction – Perpendicular to the image receptor and centred to the head of the humerus.

The radiograph should include the whole of the clavicle, scapula and upper third of humerus.

Figure 6.9 Position of the shoulder for projection (1) and (20).

(2) Glenohumeral joint (Grashey)

In order to obtain a profile view of the glenoid cavity the patient must be rotated up to 45° towards the affected side from the position used in (1). The arm should be abducted slightly and the elbow flexed, the hand resting on the abdomen.

Central ray direction – Perpendicular to the image receptor and centred to the head of the humerus.

The clavicle will be considerably foreshortened in this projection.

The eponymous term for this projection is *Grashey* [**ref 14**: 1788].

(3) Lateral shoulder (axillary projection)

This projection is the only true lateral projection of the shoulder. The patient needs to be able to abduct the affected arm. The patient is seated alongside the table. A cassette is placed under the axilla using a pad for support. The arm is extended over the cassette and the elbow is flexed for support. The neck is flexed and moved away from the side under examination (*Figure 6.10*).

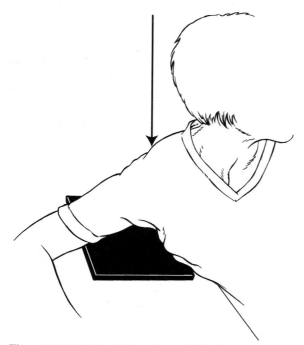

Figure 6.10 Position of the patient and direction of the central ray for projection (3).

Central ray direction – From above towards the head of the humerus.

Difficulty may be experienced with this technique due to the following:

(i) Inability of the patient to extend the arm adequately.

(ii) It may not be possible to position the cassette far enough into the axilla to include the glenoid of the scapula on the radiograph.

Positioning of the cassette is aided by placing a non-opaque pad underneath it. Angling the cassette slightly towards the thorax and angling the X-ray beam approximately 10° distally along the axis of the arm may help to solve these problems.

Alternative techniques – projections [(4(i)), (4(ii)), (4(iii)) and 5]

(4) Where the patient has limited movement

(i) An *inferosuperior axillary* projection. With the patient recumbent a cassette is placed above the shoulder joint and supported. The X-ray tube surface of the cassette faces the superior aspect of the shoulder. The arm is abducted to 90° *if possible*, however a diagnosis can be obtained with only a 10° – 15° abduction [**ref 6**: 1468].

Central ray direction – From below the axilla towards the head of the humerus.

(ii) An *inferosuperior axillary* projection. Here, the arm of the side under examination remains at the patient's side. The patient can be seated or standing (provided that there is adequate immobilization). A cassette is supported above the patient's shoulder (and can be held by the patient). The X-ray beam is directed from below the axilla and from behind the patient towards the shoulder joint. To avoid the trunk the X-ray tube can be angled forwards and the cassette angled appropriately to be perpendicular to the central ray (*Figure 6.11*). This projection is a modification of the *Stripp axial – see* [further reading **3**].

(iii) A '*transthoracic lateral*' projection may be taken (*see* projection (33(ii)), page 73 and (*Figure 5.39*, Chapter 5). Although it is not recommended

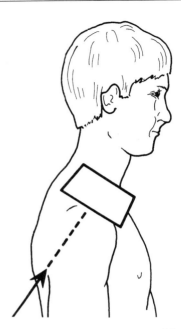

Figure 6.11 Cassette position and direction of the central ray for projection (4 (ii)).

Figure 6.12 Patient position for projection (5).

because of radiation dose it may be considered useful for evaluation of proximal humerus fractures [**ref 14**: 1789].

(5) *Posteroanterior oblique shoulder ('Y' projection)*

The patient stands with the affected side facing a cassette. The affected arm lies across the trunk or hand of affected side placed so fingers touch the opposite shoulder. The trunk is rotated so that the blade of the scapula is 90° to the cassette (*Figure 6.12*).

Central ray direction – Perpendicular to the image receptor and centred along the medial border of the scapula.

This results in a 'Y' configuration of the scapula where the glenoid cavity is seen 'en face' (*See Figure 6.1*). An alternative approach to producing a 'Y' projection is to position the patient facing the X-ray tube for an anteroposterior oblique.

Dislocation of the shoulder

If an anterior dislocation is present then it will be readily identified on the anteroposterior radiograph

and certified by clinical examination. A posterior dislocation (*see Figure 6.4*) is not so obvious and the anteroposterior radiograph may look 'normal' or the head of humerus may appear 'light-bulb' shaped [**ref 11**: 62]. The relationship between the head of humerus and glenoid needs to be demonstrated radiographically. Follow up radiographs for reduced dislocations need to be scrutinised for fractures of the glenoid cavity [**ref 11**: 60]. Projection (7) may be a useful supplementary technique. Detection of glenoid fractures is vital because, if displaced they lead to secondary arthritis [**ref 2**: 253].

Recurrent dislocation (instability) of the shoulder

In chronic shoulder instability, a number of projections (including (6) and (7)) have been developed to show bony and calcific reaction or fractures of the anterior glenoid rim or a *Hill Sachs lesion* [**ref 2**: 227]. Further anteroposterior and axillary projections of the shoulder [projections (1), (4(i))] can be taken with the arm in varying degrees of internal and external rotation. The relationship between the humerus and glenoid cavity alters, revealing different aspects of the humeral head.

For radiographic demonstration of recurrent transient *subluxation* see the discussion in [further reading **4**].

(6) Stryker notch projection

This is intended to disclose a *Hill Sachs lesion*. With the patient supine the arm is raised and the palm of the hand is placed adjacent to or on top of the head. The arm is also rotated medially so the elbow faces in a forward direction [**ref 2**: 63]. The image receptor is behind the shoulder.

> *Central ray direction* – Central ray is angled 10° cephalad from the vertical and centred over the coracoid process.

This projection was developed by Stryker and is described in [further reading **2**].

(7) Apical oblique shoulder (Garth)

This projection provides a coronal view of the glenohumeral joint that is ideal for revealing intra-articular fractures, dislocations, instability, *Hill Sachs* deformities and glenoid injuries [**ref 5**].

The patient is seated or lies supine with the posterior surface of the injured shoulder placed against the image receptor. The opposite shoulder is rotated forwards through 45°.

> *Central ray direction* – Central ray is angled 45° caudad from the vertical and centred over the coracoid process.

The eponymous term for this projection is *Garth*.

Calcification of rotator cuff tendon sheaths

The following are profile projections (8–12) of the regions of the tendinous insertions. It is sometimes difficult to localize precisely calcifications in *infraspinatus* and *teres minor* because of the high mobility of the shoulder joint. Lesions may also occur in the bone at the points of insertion. The patient should be recumbent to aid immobilization. Exposure technique should aim to demonstrate soft tissue as well as bony detail.

(8) Supraspinatus and acromial abnormalities

Position as for anteroposterior projection (1) with (8(i)) a 'straight' X-ray tube; or (8(ii)) the X-ray tube angled 30° caudad; or undertake both. The second projection demonstrates the space between acromion and head of humerus.

(8(iii)) is a 'Y' projection, (*see* projection (5)) using a 5° caudad angle may also record acromial changes. This latter has been termed the *supraspinatus outlet view* [**ref 2**: 230]. For more information – *see* [further reading 5 and 8].

(9) Subscapularis

Position as for anteroposterior projection (1) but with (9(i)) the patient's arm supinated; and (9(ii)) in internal rotation; and (9(iii)) in external rotation. If the calcification is in the subscapularis tendon it will appear to displace medially on internal rotation whereas calcification in the supraspinatus tendon will lie in a relatively constant position.

A profile projection of the *bicipital groove* (12) shows the calcification towards the medial margin of the groove (insertion into the lesser tuberosity). An inferosuperior projection (4(i)) with the arm abducted to 90° demonstrates the calcification over the lesser tuberosity.

(10) Infraspinatus

Position as for anteroposterior projection (1) with (10(i)) the patient's arm in external rotation and (10(ii)) the X-ray tube is angled 25° caudad.

(11) Teres minor

Anteroposterior (1) with patient's arm in full internal rotation.

(12) Bicipital groove

A *profile* projection and is best done with the patient supine for immobilization. The arm lies by the patient's side with the elbow extended. The arm is then abducted about 20°. A cassette is propped upright above the head of the humerus and the central ray needs to be directed along the axis of the bicipital groove. When the arm is in the anatomical position, the groove is positioned approximately 15° lateral to the mid-portion of the anterior aspect of the humeral head.

Central ray direction – Central ray is angled 10°
from the horizontal towards the long axis of the
humerus and centred to the anterior surface of the
head of humerus and tip of the acromion.

For an alternative projection see [further reading
1].

Radiographic techniques – scapula

Exposures for the scapula should be made on
arrested respiration.

(13) Anteroposterior scapula

This can be taken with the patient supine but in
cases of injury erect positioning may be easier. The
patient faces the X-ray tube and the image receptor
is behind the shoulder. Rotate the patient slightly
towards the side under examination so that the
body of the scapula is parallel to the image receptor.
The elbow of the affected side is flexed and the
forearm is supported.

> *Central ray direction* – Perpendicular to the image
> receptor and centred over the head of the
> humerus.

The rationale for using this centring point is that it
is laterally placed in relation to the scapula and the
oblique X-rays project the ribs towards the
vertebral border of the bone thus revealing a
greater proportion of the scapular body. Off-
centring the X-ray beam in this instance does not
involve unnecessary irradiation of the patient. The
clavicle and upper third of the humerus should be
included on the radiograph.

Inferior angle of the scapula

Use position for projection (15(iii)) but in addition
the affected side is raised slightly away from the
image receptor to separate the lateral border of the
scapula from the rib cage.

> *Central ray direction* – Perpendicular to the image
> receptor and centred over the axilla.

(14) Lateral scapula

The aim is to produce a profile projection of the
scapular body, superimposing it upon the scapular

neck, head and glenoid cavity. The head and
possibly the upper one-third of the humerus will
obscure part of the scapula in the lateral projection,
the degree of obscurity will depend on how far the
patient can flex or extend the arm at the shoulder
joint thus moving the humeral shaft away from the
scapula. Assuming a normal relationship, the
humeral head is inevitably superimposed on the
glenoid cavity.

Choose the following technique if the patient can
co-operate fully. The patient faces the vertical
bucky. The head is turned away from the side
under examination. The arm of the affected side is
extended behind the body (by 40° from the
vertical), the elbow is flexed and the wrist rests on
the iliac crest of the affected side. Raising the
unaffected side away from the table bucky the body
is rotated through about 25° (*Figure 6.13*).

> *Central ray direction* – Perpendicular to the image
> receptor and centred along the medial border of
> the scapula.

Alternative technique for a patient with limited
movement – projection (5).

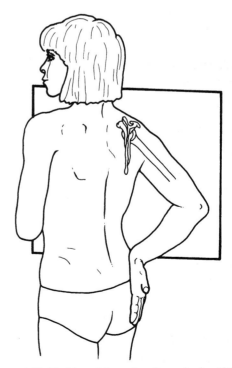

Figure 6.13 Position of the patient for projection (14).

(15) Coracoid process

This may be demonstrated using the following projections:

(i)   Lateral scapula (projections (14) or (5)).

(ii)   Axillary projections of shoulder [(3), (4 (i) or (ii))].

(iii)   Anteroposterior shoulder (projection (1)) with arm raised and hand resting on head.

Central ray direction – With a 30° cephalad tilt and centered immediately below the outer third of the clavicle.

(16) Acromion

This is demonstrated with the following projections:

(i)   Anteroposterior shoulder (projection (1)).

(ii)   Axillary projection of shoulder [projections (3), (4 (i) or (ii))]. The process will be superimposed on the upper part of the humeral head.

(iii)   Lateral scapula (projection (14).

(iv)   Lateral scapula for acromion. The patient sits or stands in the general lateral position with the median sagittal plane parallel to the image receptor. The injured side is nearest the image receptor and the arm of the *affected* side is raised and folded over the head. Rotate the patient's trunk so the unaffected side moves forward through 20–30° to show the scapula in profile.

Central ray direction – Perpendicular to the image receptor and centred to the medial border of the scapula at the level of the scapular spine.

Radiographic techniques – acromioclavicular joints

The value and veracity of taking radiographs of both acromioclavicular joints for comparison and that of weight-bearing projections is disputed (*see* [ref 18] and [ref 8:119]).

(17) Anteroposterior acromioclavicular joints

Position as for anteroposterior shoulder (projection (1)).

Central ray direction – Perpendicular to the image receptor and centred just above the head of humerus using a collimated X-ray beam.

Because of superficial position of the joint in the shoulder, the exposure should be reduced from that given to a routine anteroposterior shoulder projection. This projection usually results in the lateral end of the clavicle being superimposed on the acromion. To avoid this use the same patient position but angle the X-ray tube cephalad by 15–25°. The degree of tube angle will vary from subject to subject. An eponymous term for the projection using a 10° X-ray beam tilt is *Zanca* [ref 20]. The Zanca projection has been cited for use in acromial arthritis [ref 9].

(18) Alternative technique

This can be useful if the patient is round-shouldered; the radiograph is taken with the patient facing the image receptor. A caudal X-ray tube angle may be required.

Subluxation

It has been recommended that weighted views should be done at the discretion of the treating surgeon (*see* [ref 18]). For radiography, the patient should be standing erect. Both joints are radiographed and then the examination is repeated with the patient holding a heavy weight – for example – a sandbag in each hand, e.g. between 6 – 9 kg [ref 14: 1791]. The joint space of the affected side may be seen to widen when placed under this additional stress.

Radiographic techniques – clavicle

The clavicle can be examined using either anteroposterior or posteroanterior projections. Both techniques have advantages and disadvantages. Usually only one projection is required.

(20) *Anteroposterior clavicle*

This is easier for injured patients although there is an increase in subject to image receptor distance. The patient is erect or horizontal facing the X-ray tube, otherwise use the same positioning as for projection (1) (*see Figure 6.9*).

Central ray direction – Perpendicular to the image receptor centred to the middle of the clavicle.

Alternative technique – projection (21).

(21) *Posteroanterior clavicle*

Placing the clavicle next to the image receptor reduces magnification and geometric unsharpness.

Patient positioning may be recumbent but erect is more convenient. The patient sits or stands facing the image receptor. The head is turned away from the affected side. With a cassette placed in contact with the anterior aspect of the shoulder, better subject to image receptor contact can be achieved than with positioning against a vertical bucky especially if the patient's arm is in a sling.

Central ray direction – Horizontal and centred to the superior angle of the scapula.

(The sternoclavicular joint is located at the level of the fourth thoracic vertebra.)

For the accurate assessment of shortening of the fractured clavicle a posteroanterior projection with a 15° caudad angle is recommended [**ref 13**].

(22) *Inferosuperior clavicle*

This provides a second view of the bone and may be required to demonstrate displacement of fracture fragments or the state of fracture union.

The patient lies supine. The affected shoulder is raised slightly from the table on a non-opaque pad. The arm rests by the patient's side. A cassette is propped behind the affected shoulder and angled backwards 25–35° from the vertical (*Figure 6.14*). The head is turned and the neck angled away from the affected side; the medial border of the cassette is placed well into the neck.

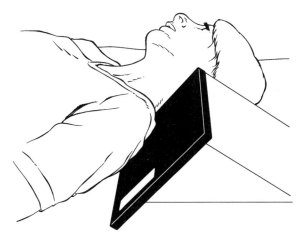

Figure 6.14 Position of patient and cassette for projection (22).

Central ray direction – Centre 2.5 cm from the sternal end of the clavicle with the X-ray tube is angled 35° from the horizontal towards the vertical (to be almost perpendicular to the image receptor) and 15 ° from the median plane towards the shoulder.

The second lateral angulation projects the sternoclavicular joint away from the vertebral column.

Radiographic techniques – sternoclavicular joints

Both joints should be examined for comparison. The joints are sometimes difficult to demonstrate with plain radiography. In the absence of *CT*, *conventional tomography* would be an important additional examination.

(23) *Posteroanterior sternoclavicular joints*

The patient stands facing the image receptor, leaning slightly forward to bring the upper end of the sternum in contact with it. Both shoulders are eased forwards slightly. Make sure the patient is not rotated, i.e. that the shoulders are equidistant from the image receptor.

Central ray direction – Horizontal and centred over the third thoracic vertebra.

The X-ray source to image receptor distance is increased to 180 cm. This projection does not demonstrate the joints clearly but it may give information about the symmetry of the medial ends of the clavicles.

(24) *Posteroanterior oblique sternoclavicular joints*

The patient is erect or horizontal facing the bucky table. For the right joint – the left side is raised away from the table and rotated through 45°. For the left joint – the right side is raised away from the table and rotated through 45°. If the patient is horizontal the raised side must be adequately supported.

> *Central ray direction* – Perpendicular to the image receptor and centred at the level of the fourth thoracic vertebra, over the raised side 10 cm from the mid-line.

Each side in radiographed in turn. The medial end of the clavicle of the raised side tends to be overshadowed by the sternum.

(25) *Lateral sternoclavicular joints*

The patient stands with the affected side against the vertical bucky and the median sagittal plane is parallel to the image receptor. The patient then places his forearms behind his back and grasps each elbow pulling the shoulders well back.

> *Central ray direction* – Horizontal and centred over the sternoclavicular joints.

The subject to image receptor distance is significant therefore the X-ray source to image receptor distance is extended from standard 100cm to 180 cm to reduce image magnification.

Dislocation

The following projection may be beneficial in suspected sterno-clavicular dislocation [ref 10]. The resultant image will show either neutral, anterior (elevated) or posterior (depressed) positions of the medial ends of the clavicles.

(26) *Anteroposterior axial*

The patient lies supine with the arms resting at the sides of the body. A cassette is placed carefully beneath the head and shoulders. The X-ray source to image receptor distance is extended to from standard 100cm to 150cm.

> *Central ray direction* – Central ray is angled 40° cephalad from the horizontal and centred to the manubrium

This projection is attributed to Rockwood [ref 17] who cheerfully named it the *serendipity* technique.

BONY THORAX

Essential anatomical terminology

The walls of the bony thorax are made up of the *ribs* supported anteriorly by the *sternum* and articulating posteriorly with the *dorsal (thoracic) vertebrae*. The functions of the thorax are to protect its vulnerable contents and to assist in the provision of the respiratory movements. Separating the trunk from the abdomen is the diaphragm which is attached to the lower ribs and costal cartilages. During breathing the actions of the intercostal muscles and diaphragm produce alteration in the volume of the thorax. This is possible because the posterior end of each rib forms a pair of articulations with the dorsal vertebrae known as the *costotransverse* and *costovertebral joints*. Movement at these joints allows the rib cage to expand.

Indications and radiographic techniques for ribs and sternum ae given below; for thoracic vertebrae – *see* Chapter 9.

Indications for the X-ray examination

Injuries

Fractures of the ribs

Ribs are most frequently fractured as the consequence of compression of the thorax and this is most likely to occur during a road-traffic accident or fall. In elderly people, a fit of violent coughing may result in a single rib fracture [ref 4: 161]. Ribs can bend under stress but if too much force is exerted then they will break. A fracture is usually located in the weakest area of the rib in front of the angle. In compression injuries the middle ribs are most commonly involved and rib fractures may be single, multiple, one-sided or bilateral and the fragments may or may not be displaced. Quite often rib fractures have no serious consequences for the patient because the ribs are largely splinted by the intercostal muscles; but where there is involvement of internal viscera then the injury is more serious. About half of traffic deaths result directly or indirectly from chest injury [**ref 3**]. Note that intrathoracic damage may have occurred without bony injury to the walls of the chest (which includes the sternum and spine).

The following serious medical conditions may arise as a result of injury to the chest:

Pneumothorax – Lacerations of the pleurae allow air into the pleural space and there is a collapse of underlying lung tissue which may vary in severity.

Haemothorax – Bleeding into the pleural space largely from lacerated intercostal vessels. If this bleeding is considerable then the patient may require a thoracotomy.

Traumatic emphysema *(Figure 6.15)*

Air enters the chest wall through a break in the pleura and distends the subcutaneous tissue. Tears in the pleura can be the result of either the rib fracture or be caused by the shearing force of the trauma.

Flail chest

Where there are several adjacent ribs fractured in two places or bilaterally a flail segment is formed. This segment is free to move independently and is sucked in during inspiration and pushed out during expiration. This is known as paradoxical breathing and normal ventilation may be severely impaired. A common cause of a flail segments is a direct blow to the chest. A kick from a horse's hoof can produce a flail segment 15cm across, i.e. hoof-size. Another well-known cause is a blow to the sternum from a steering wheel. This can fracture all of the ribs to produce a section that includes the mediastinum [**ref 4**: 162].

Lower rib fractures

There may be associated injury to the diaphragm and upper abdominal organs – for example – liver, kidney and spleen.

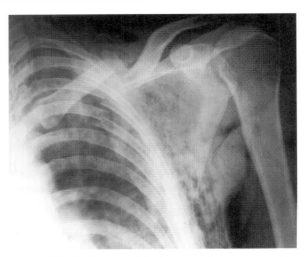

Figure 6.15 Radiograph of the left upper thorax and shoulder girdle showing rib fractures and traumatic emphysema. Note also the fractured clavicle.

First and second rib fractures

These are relatively uncommon and may follow a severe downward blow that would also involve the clavicle. An isolated fracture of the first or second rib may be a stress fracture, caused for example by building site hod-carrying.

Sternal fractures

These are comparatively rare and often the result of direct violence to the chest such as a steering-wheel injury. There is apparently a high mortality rate because violence severe enough to fracture the sternum may also cause serious intrathoracic injuries – for example – rupture of the aorta. Most fractures occur in the body of the sternum or near its junction with the manubrium, and they are frequently of the transverse type.

Other conditions of interest

New growths

Metastases may occur in the ribs from a primary tumour in the breast (*see* Chapter 3). Ribs may also be destroyed by tumour infiltration from a lung carcinoma. New growths in the sternum are usually of a metastatic nature.

Other pathology of ribs

Ribs may be involved in any disease process of bone tissue, for example *Paget's disease*.

Evidence of previous thoracotomy

A rib may be displaced or become irregular, usually the 4th, 5th or 6th. This may be the only indication on the radiograph that there has been surgery.

Rib notching

Indentations may be present on the inferior border of the posterior third of the ribs. The most frequent cause of this is *coarctation* of the aortic arch and the notching is due to dilatation of the intercostal arteries.

Congenital anomalies of ribs

The anterior end of a rib may be bifid or a rib may be absent. Ribs may articulate with or touch their neighbours. One or a pair of ribs may be present at the seventh cervical vertebra – *cervical rib* (*see* page 142). Abnormal curvatures of the spine such as *kyphosis* and *scoliosis* will affect the spacing and direction of the ribs. In *kyphosis* the posterior parts of the ribs are crowded together in scoliosis the ribs are more vertically inclined on the concave part of the spine (*see* Chapter 9).

Congenital depressed sternum

This is a malformation that is not in itself an indication for radiography but the appearances of the posteroanterior chest radiograph are characteristic. The posterior ends of the ribs are horizontal, and the anterior ends slope down and inwards. The silhouette of the heart is altered due mainly to rotation about its vertical axis. The changes in the heart appearance may be misinterpreted as indicative of heart or lung disease.

Radiographic techniques – sternum

Posterior to the sternum lie the mediastinum and vertebral column. The patient must be positioned so that although relatively close contact is maintained between sternum and X-ray table, there is minimal overlapping of the bone by these dense thoracic structures.

(27) Right posteroanterior oblique sternum

The patient stands erect or lies horizontal, facing the bucky table. The left side is raised and rotated through approximately 30°. If the patient is horizontal, the raised side is supported on a non-opaque pad.

> *Central ray direction* – Perpendicular to the image receptor and centred 10 cm to the left of the fifth thoracic vertebra.

If the obliquity of the patient is excessive (over 40°) then the width of the sternum is forshortened to an unacceptable degree [**ref 1**: 160]. For an alternative technique – *see* [further reading 7].

Diffusion technique

The sternum is a thin bone and being superimposed by lung tissue it has relatively low *subject contrast*. Confusing lung markings makes it is difficult to see on the radiograph. A diffusion exposure technique can be used to improve the demonstration of the sternum. The aim is to deliberately induce movement blurring in the lung tissue whilst the sternum's position remains static. Immobilization of the wall of the thorax is vital; breathing will be mainly diaphragmatic. Horizontal positioning must be used and for added patient immobilization a broad bucky band is placed across the patient's chest. The patient breathes gently whilst a long exposure – for example – 5 seconds, is used. The milliamperage is reduced accordingly.

Conventional tomography

If using linear tomography, the long axis of the sternum would not be positioned parallel to the direction of the X-ray tube travel. Ensuring that it is not parallel reduces the effect of 'trailing shadows' produced by an overlying spine.

(28) Lateral sternum

The patient stands or sits in the general lateral position, i.e. the median sagittal plane of the body is parallel to the image receptor and the transverse axis of the sternum is perpendicular to the support. The shoulders are pulled well back.

> *Central ray direction* – Perpendicular to the image receptor and centred to the sternal angle.

The X-ray source to image receptor distance should be increased from the standard 100cm to 180 cm because of the large subject to image receptor distance. Expose the radiograph on arrested inspiration.

Major sternal injuries

Where a patient has sustained serious thoracic injuries that may include a fractured and/or depressed sternum, the lateral projection has the greatest significance in diagnosis.

A radiographic examination of such a case could include:

(i) An anteroposterior chest radiograph.

(ii) A lateral sternum radiograph taken with a horizontal X-ray beam. Where possible the patient's arms are raised above his head to accommodate a shorter subject to image receptor distance. A grid should be used. Imaging of the thoracic spine may also be required.

Radiographic techniques – ribs

Radiography of the ribs in minor chest trauma is not routinely recommended. This is because the demonstration of a rib fracture does not alter medical management [ref 12: 109]. Nevertheless for completeness, the radiographic techniques for chest *and* ribs are given below.

In moderate to serious trauma, chest radiographs aimed at demonstrating potential pneumothorax, fluid or lung contusion have overriding importance.

(29) Posteroanterior whole chest

The patient stands or sits facing the image receptor. The chin is raised to rest on the top of the image receptor which must be high enough to include the first ribs and lung apices. The shoulders are pressed forwards and the patient's elbows are flexed and the backs of the hands rest against the buttocks. Alternatively the arms can be internally rotated and rest at the sides of the image receptor and its support. The rationale for these manoeuvres is to rotate the scapulae away from the lung fields. Check that the patient is not rotated, i.e. the coronal plane should be parallel to the image receptor.

Central ray direction – Perpendicular to the image receptor and centred to the mid-chest or eighth thoracic vertebra.

Exposure is made on arrested full inspiration. A longer X-ray source to image receptor distance (180 cm) reduces magnification of the posterior sections of the ribs. Because of high inherent subject contrast, the desire for a short exposure time to reduce movement blurring and the large source to image receptor distance, it is not usual to use a secondary radiation grid.

This projection will demonstrate the lung fields and the outline of the mediastinum and the ribs above the diaphragm. The number of ribs shown may depend upon the degree of diaphragmatic excursion on inspiration.

Alternative techniques – projections (30(i)) and (30(ii)).

(30) Anteroposterior whole chest

(i) For a patient who can sit upright on a trolley but cannot support himself. The back of the trolley is raised and a covered cassette is placed behind the patient's back. The arms should be extended in front and internally rotated. The patient may hold the cot sides for support. The cassette should be high enough to include the first ribs and lung apices. Caudal angulation of the X-ray beam to cater for a patient position less than upright should be avoided where fluid levels are to be demonstrated.

Central ray direction – Perpendicular to the image receptor and centred to the middle of the thorax.

As for projection (29) use an 180cm X-ray source to image receptor distance.

(ii) If the patient cannot sit up it may be possible to place a protected cassette behind his back if he can be gently lifted, otherwise a cassette may be placed in the table or trolley tray and no patient movement is required. A larger subject to image receptor distance is produced when using the table tray therefore an extended X-ray source to image receptor distance is recommended to avoid projecting the thoracic wall off the radiograph by the effect of magnification.

Pneumothorax

Where a pneumothorax is suspected but where it may be small, then a second radiograph should be taken on expiration. Under-exposure of the chest walls is a fault that may result in a small pneumothorax remaining undetected.

(31) Anteroposterior oblique ribs (ribs 1–10)

In the anteroposterior or posteroanterior chest projection there is overlapping of the ribs in the axillary line. Fractures tend to occur in this region. The anteroposterior oblique ribs projection demonstrates the full length of the ribs on the side nearest the image receptor. As the ribs slope downward an image receptor of sufficient size should be used to include their upper and lower extremities. It is important to include a range of the adjacent ribs as a fracture may also affect neighbouring bones.

The patient is erect or horizontal facing the X-ray tube and the image receptor lies behind the chest. Rotate the patient 45° on to side of interest, raising the uninjured side. If the patient is lying horizontal the raised side must be supported. The patient's arms are raised and forearms should be folded over the head.

> *Central ray direction* – Perpendicular to the image receptor and centred through the mid-point of the subject.

Expose on arrested full inspiration.

(32) Anteroposterior oblique ribs (ribs 9–12)

Because of the dome-like structure of the diaphragm the lower ribs are closely related to abdominal tissues. This situation is increased when the patient breathes out because of upward excursion of the diaphragm. Although ribs 9 and 10 in part or whole can be demonstrated by projection (31) where they are overshadowed by less dense lung tissue, a second radiograph may have to be taken *adapting exposure technique* for abdominal conditions. This second radiograph will also show ribs 11 and 12.

Patient positioning is the same as for projection (31). Horizontal positioning may be preferable as abdominal contents tend to push the diaphragm to a higher level. The exposure is made on full *expiration* and a grid must be used. The lower border of the image receptor is placed at the level of the lower costal margin.

> *Central ray direction* – Centre over the mid-line at the level of lower costal margin. Start with the X-ray beam perpendicular to the image receptor and then angle it cephelad to be coincident with the centre of the image receptor.

Lead rubber radiation protection should be used for the adjacent part of the abdomen.

First and second ribs

In the posteroanterior chest radiograph (projection (29)) the upper two ribs tend to overlap. They are more clearly demonstrated if the patient is horizontal. The patient is positioned as for the clavicle (projections (20) or (21)) to demonstrate clearly the posterior and anterior extremities of the ribs, respectively.

Major thoracic injuries

Where damage to the lungs, pleurae or mediastinal structures has been sustained (this may have occurred *without* any bony injury) then the situation is potentially more life threatening to the patient when compared with the problems arising from simple rib fractures.

Assuming that the patient cannot be moved, the anteroposterior chest radiograph [projection (30(ii))] is likely to show rib fractures but should also demonstrate (if present) haemothorax, pneumothorax, any associated shifts in the mediastinum and also changes in the normal pattern of the lung markings. The projection will not, however, demonstrate *fluid levels* although this demonstration may not be of prime importance at this stage.

It is not usual or often possible to attempt oblique projections of the ribs in these cases, and the patient will be a clear candidate for *CT*; however, if this is required and the patient cannot be turned then an oblique view of the ribs can be taken by angulation of the X-ray beam across the patient. If a grid is used in this instance then it must be turned so that the grid lines run transversely in the direction of the tube angulation.

The bony thoracic walls are partly formed by the sternum and spine. In major thoracic injuries these will also probably require examination. In some cases air infiltrates the tissues of the thoracic wall either because of the injury – *traumatic emphysema* – or after the insertion of a drain into the thoracic cavity during treatment – *surgical emphysema*. The amount of air present can vary but its presence has an effect on the radiopacity of the subject and exposures for the chest radiograph may have to be lowered.

Abdominal injuries involving lower rib fractures

Lower ribs can be demonstrated by projection (32). If the patient is suspected of having abdominal injuries then the whole abdomen (and pelvis) will require examination.

References

1. Arnold M Mills P (1988) The oblique sternum: an alternative projection *Radiography* **54**(616): 160

2. Berquist TH (1992) *Imaging of Sports Injuries* Aspen: Gaithersburg

3. Cohn R (1972) Non-penetrating wounds of the lungs and bronchi *Surgical Clinics North America* 52: 585 – 95

4. Dandy DJ and Edwards DJ (2003) *Essential Orthopaedics and Trauma (4th Edition)* Edinburgh: Churchill Livingstone

5. Garth WP Slappey CE Ochs CW (1984) Roentgen demonstration of instability of the shoulder: the apical oblique projection *Journal of Bone and Joint Surgery* **66A**: 1450 – 1453

6. Grainger RG and Allison DJ (1997) *Grainger and Allison's Diagnostic Radiology (Vol 1) (3rd Edition)* London: Churchill Livingstone

7. McRae R Andrew W (1997) *Orthopaedics and trauma: an illustrated colour text* Edinburgh: Churchill Livingstone

8. McRae R Esser M (2002) *Practical Fracture Treatment (4th Edition)* Edinburgh: Churchill Livingstone

9. Miller MD (2000) *Review of Orthopaedics (3rd Edition)* London: WB Saunders

10. Moore T Watkins G (1991) Radiographic demonstration of the dislocated SC joint *Radiography today* 57(650): 13 – 14

11. Raby N Berman L De Lacey G (2002) *Accident and Emergency Radiology: A Survival Guide* London: Saunders

12. RCR Working Party (2003) *Making the Best Use of a Department of Clinical Radiology: Guidelines for Doctors (Fifth Edition)* London: The Royal College of Radiologists

13. Sharr JRP and Mohammed KD (2003) Optimizing the radiographic technique in clavicular fractures *Journal of Shoulder and Elbow Surgery* 12: 170–2

14. Sonin AH Boles CA Rogers LF in Grainger RG Allison DJ Adam A Dixon A (eds) (2001) *Grainger and Allison's Diagnostic Radiology (Volume 3) (4th Edition)* London: Churchill Livingstone

15. Sutton D (ed) (1998) *Textbook of Radiology and Imaging (Sixth Edition)* London: Churchill Livingstone

16. Reeves PJ (2003) Radiography of the acromioclavicular joints: a review *Radiography* 9: 169–172

17. Rockwood CA Green DP (eds) (1984) *Fractures in adults (Volume 1) (2nd Edition)* Philadelphia: Lippincott

18. Yap JJL Curl LA Kvitne RS McFarland EG (1999) The value of weighted views of the acromioclavicular joint *American Journal of Sports Medicine* **17** (1): 20–4

19. Hill AA Sachs MD (1940) The grooved defect of the humeral head – a frequently unrecognised complication of dislocations of the shoulder joint *Radiology* 35: 690

20. Zanca P (1971) Shoulder pain; involvement of the acromioclavicular joint (analysis of 1000) cases *American Journal Roentgenology* **112** (3): 493–506

Further reading

1. Fisk C (1965) Adaptation of the technique for radiography of the bicipital groove *Radiologic Technology* **37**: 47 – 50

2. Hall RH Isaac F Booth CR (1959) Dislocation of the shoulder with special reference to accompanying small fractures *Journal of Bone and Joint Surgery American* **41**: 489 – 493

3. Horsfield D Jones SN (1987) A useful projection in the radiography of the shoulder *Journal of Bone and Joint Surgery* **69B**: 388

4. Horsfield D Phillips RR (1990) The zero projection *Radiography today* **56** (635): 14–16

5. Neer CS (1987) Supraspinatus outlet *Ortho Trans* **11**: 234

6. Rubin SA Gray RL Green WR (1974) The scapular 'Y': a diagnostic aid in shoulder trauma *Radiology* **110**: 725 – 736

7. Stripp WJ (1956) Special views in orthopaedics *Radiography* **22**: 650 – 75

8. Truelove P (2000) Impingement and the outlet view *Synergy* March pages 10 – 11

The lower limb: foot to knee

CHAPTER CONTENTS

Table of main and supplementary radiographic techniques

General anatomical area	Projection	Page	Common Indications
Foot	1 DP (dorsiplantar) 2 DP Oblique (dorsiplantar oblique) 3 Lateral	101 101–102 102	Fracture, dislocation, subluxation, pathology Bony alignment, FB
Toes	1 DP (dorsiplantar) 2 DP (dorsiplantar oblique)	101 101–102	Injury
Calcaneus	4 Lateral 5 Axial ('*Harris*')	103 103	Injury
Talus	3–4, 14 Lateral 11 AP	102–103, 107–108 107	Injury
Subtalar Joints	4, 14 Lateral 6 DP Oblique 7 Medial oblique axial (*Brodén*) 8 Lateral oblique axial (*Brodén*) 9 Posterior tangential (*Harris, Beath*) 10 Cobey's posterior view (*Cobey*)	103, 107–108 104 104 104 104–105 105	Injury, pathology Bony alignment Bony alignment
Ankle	11 AP 12 Internal oblique 45° 13 External oblique 45° 14–15 Lateral	107 107 107 107–108	Injury
Tibia and Fibula	16 AP 17–18 Lateral	112 112	Injury
Knee	20, 22 AP 21 AP obliques 45° 19 Proximal tibiofibular joint 23 PA 45° knee flexion (*Rosenberg*) 24 Lateral	112–113 113 112 113 113	Injury, pathology
Intercondylar notch	25i, 25ii Special projections	114–115	Pathology
Patella	26 PA 27 AP 28 Lateral 29 Inferosuperior (axial) 30 PA oblique	115 115 115 115–116 115	Injury

Effective radiation dose for an extremity examination: **<0.01mSv**
Equivalent period of natural background radiation: **<1.5 days**

FOOT

Essential anatomical terminology

The skeleton of the foot (Figure 7.1) can be divided into three regions – the navicular, cuboid and cunieiform bones which form the central portion or *midfoot*. All the bones distal to these – the five metatarsals (*MTs*) and five sets of *phalanges* – form the *forefoot*. The big (great) toe is sometimes termed the *hallux*. Posterior to the midfoot section is the *hindfoot* consisting of the calcaneus and talus.

The *midtarsal joint* is a compound joint (formed by the *talonavicular joint* along with the *calcaneocuboid joint*) which divides the midfoot from the hindfoot. This joint is also called the *transverse tarsal joint* or *Joint of Chopart*. The joints between the forefoot and the midfoot may be termed the *Lisfranc joints*.

The *subtalar joint* (*Figure 7.2*) lies below the talus and may be divided into three facets and two joints. The middle and anterior facets form a common cavity with the *talonavicular joint* and together this is called the *talocalcaneonavicular joint*. The large posterior facet is a separate joint cavity otherwise know as the *talocalcanean joint*. This latter joint transmits about half of the force of weight during walking. The area in front of the posterior facet is called the *sinus tarsi*. The *sustentaculum tali* of the calcaneus is a rectangular medial projection of the calcaneus which supports the middle facet.

The forefoot and midfoot incline backwards and upwards, meeting the hindfoot at an angle and forming the *longitudinal arch* (*see Figure 7.12*, page 105). This arch is high on the medial side but almost in contact with the ground on the lateral side. The metatarsal heads form a second arch; the *transverse*

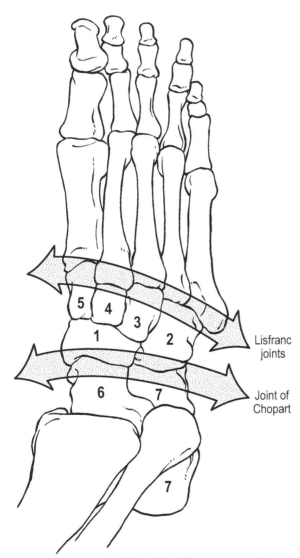

Figure 7.1 *Bones of right foot. Tarsal bones are named:*
1 *Navicular* **2** *Cuboid*
3 *Lateral cuneiform* **4** *Intermediate cuneiform*
5 *Medial cuneiform* **6** *Talus*
7 *Calcaneus.*

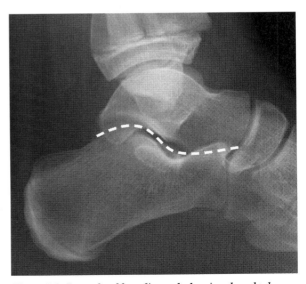

Figure 7.2 *Lateral ankle radiograph showing the subtalar joints (marked with dotted line).*

arch. This arch is present only at rest and tends to disappear when the foot is weight bearing. The bony arches of the foot are maintained by the actions of muscles, tendons and ligaments. The arches have a significant role to play in shock absorption and energy conservation during the activities of walking, running and jumping [**ref 11**:140].

The tarsal bones each ossify from a single centre. Sometimes the posterior process of the talus is ossified from an independent centre and remains separated as an accessory ossicle, in this case known as an *os trigonum*. In all there are twenty-nine different locations for accessory ossicles in the foot and they are not always present bi-laterally. For a map of the ossicles in the foot – *see* [**ref 10**].

Indications for the X-ray examination

Injuries – forefoot and midfoot

Fractures and dislocations of the phalanges

These may occur as the result of a crushing injury or 'stubbing' or twisting injury.

Fractures of the metatarsal shafts

These are usually due to direct violence such as from a heavy object falling on the foot. Twisting injuries of the forefoot may cause spiral fractures of more than one metatarsal. These fractures may sometimes be accompanied by dislocation of the tarsometatarsal joints [**ref 5**: 269].

March fractures

These are stress fractures that affect the neck or shaft of a metatarsal bone, usually the second through fourth. They occur where there is a flattening of the transverse metatarsal arch so that the heads of these bones take an excessive amount of body weight. It is common for most of these injuries to show some periosteal reaction (new bone formation) [**ref 14**: 180].

Fracture of the base of the fifth metatarsal

A common type of fracture affects the tuberosity. A piece of bone is avulsed from the base of the metatarsal by the tendon of the peroneus brevis muscle, which is inserted into it. This injury may

occur when the foot is forcefully inverted. The accessory ossicles *os peroneum* in the peroneus longus tendon and *os vesalianum* in the peroneus brevis tendon may be misinterpreted as fractures.

Metatarsophalangeal (MP) dislocations

Toe dislocations may be single or muliple and generally occur at the MP joints.

Tarsometatarsal (TM) dislocations

Dislocation of one or more of the TM joints can be caused by a variety of mechanisms. A dislocation of the forefoot across the TM joints may be termed a *Lisfranc dislocation*. Fractures of the second metatarsal or the cuneiforms are commonly associated with Lisfranc dislocations [**ref 4**: 79].

Injuries – hindfoot

Fractures of the talus

Fractures vary in severity. Minor fractures such as a small chip or flake of bone (avulsion fractures) are most common. More seriously the neck of the talus may be fractured resulting in a disruption of the blood supply to the proximal fragment. This may lead to *avascular necrosis* of this part of the bone with subsequent development of arthritis of the ankle subtalar and calcaneocuboid (midtarsal) joints (*see* Chapter 3). Neck fractures may occur in car accidents when a foot pedal impacts against the foot forcing the talar neck against the margin of the tibia. Dome fractures occur where a part of the upper articular surface of the talus becomes detached as a result of a shearing force injury [**ref 12**: 393]

Fractures of the calcaneus

The commonest cause is a fall from a height on to the feet. Minor fractures are usually just isolated cracks in the region of the tuberosity. In severe trauma the bone can be crushed and flattened – the degree of loss of the calcaneal angle – *Böhler's salient angle* – gives an indication of the severity of the injury (*Figures 7.3 and 7.4*). The angle should be no less than 20° [**ref 4**: 68]. Major calcaneal fractures destroy the subtalar joint and cause stiffness of the subtalar and midtarsal joints [**ref 5**: 268]. A fracture of the calcaneus may be accompanied by bony injuries elsewhere as the causative force is

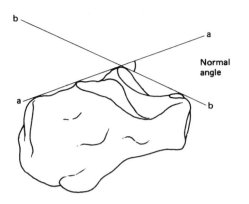

Figure 7.3 The lateral aspect of the right calcaneus showing the normal calcaneal angle

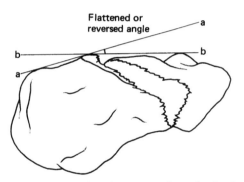

Figure 7.4 Fracture of the calcaneus causing reduction in Böhler's angle.

transmitted through the axial skeleton. The patient may also have a crush fracture of a vertebral body. A fracture at the dorsolumbar junction is present in 5% of calcaneal fractures [**ref 12**: 395]. Because of its complex anatomy the calcaneus is difficult to image with conventional projection techniques. *CT* often shows comminution of fractures not evident on plain radiographs.

CT is routinely used for pre-operative planning [**ref 4**: 69].

Midtarsal dislocation

The midtarsal joint lies between the talus and the calcaneus posteriorly and navicular and cuboid anteriorly. Dislocation of elements of the midtarsal joint may be accompanied by fractures of any of the component bones.

Peritalar dislocation

This term refers to a subtalar joint or talonavicular joint dislocation. The talus remains within the ankle mortise.

Other conditions of interest

Hallux valgus

This is a common deformity of the foot, often hereditary. The big toe deviates laterally at the metatarsophalangeal joint and the prominent head of the first metatarsal bone becomes painful owing to rubbing of the shoe – a *bursa* (*bunion*) is formed between the bony angle and the skin (*Figure7.5*).

Metatarsalgia

This is pain under the metatarsal heads usually in overweight people. The pain is due to chronic strain of the ligaments supporting the arches of the foot.

Pes planus (flat foot)

If the heel tilts into valgus (eversion), the medial side of the foot is lowered, leading to flattening of the longitudinal arch [**ref 11**: 140]. *Genu valgum*

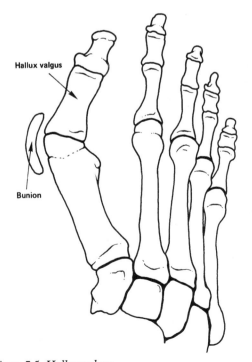

Figure 7.5 Hallux valgus

(knock knee) is a common cause. Flat foot can be hereditary in which case it is considered a normal variant [**ref 15**].

Pes cavus

The medial side of the foot becomes abnormally high-arched. The condition is a result of imbalance in muscles associated with the formation and maintenance of the longitudinal arches.

Congenital foot deformities

There are a number of deformities possible. These deformities are always described in terms of the mal-alignment of the distal bone or part of the body relative to the proximal point of reference.

In *talipes equinovarus* (*Figure 7.6*) there are three major abnormalities. Relative to the lower leg or ankle:

(1) The forefoot is in varus (deviated in the coronal plane towards the body midline)

(2) The foot is inverted (sole turned inwards)

(3) The foot is in equines (plantar flexed)

Treatment is by manipulation and splinting of the foot and ankle; and later, if necessary, by surgery.

Osteochondritis (*see Chapter 3*)

Osteochondritis affecting the foot includes:

(1) *Köhler's disease* affects the navicular. It usually occurs in children; the navicular becomes flattened and sclerosed so that it appears like a disc. Later, even without treatment, the bone reverts to its normal shape.

(2) *Freiberg's disease* affects a metatarsal epiphysis (the distal end), usually the second or third metatarsal.

(3) *Sever's disease* affects the traction apophysis of the calcaneum at the insertion of the Achilles tendon. An *apophysis* is a secondary centre of ossification taking no part in the formation of a joint – in this case of the posterior surface of the calcaneus.

Rheumatoid arthritis

Joints of the foot and ankle can be affected by rheumatoid arthritis, often early in the course of the disease. The MP joints of the toes are most commonly affected [**ref 11**: 145]. Gradual erosion and destruction of the joint surfaces leads to pain on weight bearing and the forefoot and toes can become severely deformed and subluxated (*see* Chapter 3).

The 'high-risk' foot

Patients with diabetes, peripheral vascular disease or a peripheral neuropathy carry the risk of skin ulceration. This can lead to infection spreading to underlying bone as osteomyelitis (*see* Chapter 3).

Another foot condition closely linked to diabetes is *Charcot neuropathy* (*Figure 7.7*). This is fragmentation, destruction and remodelling of bones of the foot. If this is left untreated then a characteristic pattern of deformity is likely to develop, including the collapse of the foot arches.

Gout

This is caused by a deposition of uric acid crystals within a joint. The hallux metatarsophalangeal joint is often the first to be affected. Radiographic findings include bone erosion.

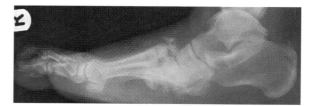

Figure 7.7 Lateral projection of Charcot foot. Note deformity of longitudinal arch.

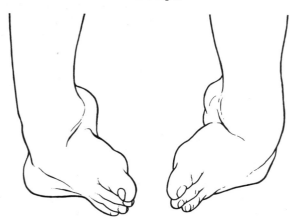

Figure 7.6 Talipes equinovarus.

Sesamoiditis

This is inflammation of the sesamoid bones – often those behind the first metatarsophalangeal joint.

Congenital fusions (coalition)

Fusion of certain tarsal bones can cause pain and deformity of the foot. Important fusions are:

(1) *Calcaneonavicular bar (synostosis)* is seen in the oblique projections of the foot. If untreated it will cause flat feet.

(2) *Talocalcaneal fusion* seen in the axial projection of the calcaneus.

Exostosis

This is a bony outgrowth relatively common in the big toe – usually from the terminal phalanx.

Spurs

A spur is a bony outgrowth which usually represents nothing more than a proliferative change due to stress from a tendon as in the case of an *Achilles spur* or at the origin of the flexor digitorum brevis – a *plantar (calcaneal) spur* [**ref 17**]. Spurs can be seen in profile on the lateral projection of the calcaneus.

Radiographic techniques – foot

An exposure technique using a secondary radiation grid is generally unnecessary for radiography of the lower leg but owing to the greater volume of soft and bony tissue in the thigh, use of a grid is usually advisable for the femur and the hip depending on the subject size and type. Use of computed radiography may reduce the need for a grid.

(1) Dorsiplantar foot *(Figure 7.8)*

The patient is lying or seated on the table with his back adequately supported. Flex the knee and hip of the affected side and place the plantar aspect of the foot on the image receptor. The opposite leg can act as a support.

> *Central ray direction* – 90° to long axis of first MT bone and centred to a point midway between the navicular tuberosity and base of the fifth MT bone.

Both feet can be exposed on the same radiograph where comparison is required. It is difficult to demonstrate toes to hindfoot with a single radiographic exposure because of the steep

Figure 7.8 Patient position for (left) projection (1) dorsiplantar foot and (right) projection (2(ii)) dosiplantar oblique foot.

differences in subject density. In conventional film/screen radiography, subject densities can be flattened using a wedge filter or high kilovoltage technique. In computerised radiography, image manipulation will form the convenient alternative.

Individual toes

Collimate X-ray beam size to include the affected toe and one (or both) of its neighbours. The metatarsophalangeal joint should be included.

Forefoot

The beam can simply be collimated to include only this area.

Surgical, biomechanical assessment and bone alignment

Examine both feet exposed together on the same radiograph (or individual feet) with the patient standing so the effects of weight bearing will be seen. Collimate the X-ray beam to include only the forefeet and centre between the heads of the first metatarsals. The central ray is angled from the vertical to be 90° to the long axis of the first MT bone. If the patient cannot stand safely then resting views may suffice.

(2) Dorsiplantar oblique

There are two approaches to this:

(i) Position as for projection (1). The knee is then allowed to lean medially about 30° from the vertical, the sole of the foot remaining flat on the image receptor.

Central ray direction – As for projection (1)

(ii) Position as for projection (1). The foot and leg are then tilted medially so that the sole of the foot makes an angle of 45° with the image receptor (*Figure 7.8*). Support the foot on non-opaque pads. Crim [**ref 4:** 21] suggests 30° foot rotation.

Central ray direction – As for projection (1).

Both projections produce similar appearances – the tarsometatarsal articulations are more clearly seen in projection (2) compared to projection (1).

Individual toes

Because the toes are not as mobile as the fingers they are difficult to demonstrate separately in a lateral projection. It is usually more convenient to use a dorsiplantar oblique projection to produce the second view of a toe or toes. This also allows for the proximal phalanx and metatarsophalangeal joint to be shown without being obscured by neighbouring bones.

Use the technique as for projection (2(ii)). Separate the toes if possible and if necessary with some non-opaque material. The sole of the foot must be adequately supported.

Central ray direction – Perpendicular to the long axis of the relevant phalanx and centred to a point over the first metatarsophalangeal joint for the great toe or over the relevant proximal interphalangeal joint for the other toes.

(3) Lateral foot

The patient lies on the affected side with the hip and knee slightly flexed and supported. The lateral aspect of the foot lies on the image receptor. The sole should be perpendicular to the image receptor so that the MT bones are superimposed.

Central ray direction – Parallel to the sole of the foot and centred over the navicular tuberosity.

This view gives further information in cases of tarsometatarsal dislocation and localization of foreign bodies. The posterior and middle facets of the subtalar joint are seen on this projection.

Biomechanical assessment and bone alignment

A lateral projection of each foot may be taken with the patient standing using a horizontal X-ray beam. Make sure the patient is capable of this manoeuvre and that he is safely supported. A special cassette holder is used for this purpose. The ankle joint may be included on the radiograph.

Central ray direction – Perpendicular to the image receptor and centred towards the lateral aspect of the foot.

Sesamoid bones

The sesamoid bones behind the first metatarsophalangeal joint can be seen on the lateral projection of the foot (projection (3)), and superimposed on the head of the first metatarsal bone in the dorsiplantar projection (1). A third view can be obtained if the great toe is dorsiflexed at this joint and the central ray directed tangentially to the posterior surface of the head of the first metatarsal (*Figure 7.9*). The sesamoids should be shown separated from the metatarsal. An alternative approach is to lay the patient prone with the toes dorsiflexed against the image receptor (on the table top).

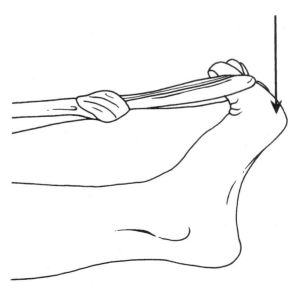

Figure 7.9 Position of the patient and direction of the central ray for demonstration of the sesamoid bones behind the big toe joint in the axial plane.

Radiographic techniques – calcaneus

(4) Lateral calcaneus

Position as for projection (3). The sole of the foot should be perpendicular to the image receptor.

Central ray direction – Perpendicular to the image receptor and centred to a point immediately distal to the medial malleolus.

(5) Axial calcaneus ('Harris')

There are several ways of producing this projection of the bone but the following two seem to be the most useful:

(i) The patient is seated on the table with both limbs extended. The foot of the affected side should be dorsiflexed so the toes point straight upwards. To achieve this, place a bandage sling around the forefoot and ask the patient to pull gently, thus maintaining the position. The sling also helps immobilization. The lower border of the image receptor should correspond to the lower border of the heel (*Figure 7.10*).

Central ray direction – Central ray is angled 40° cephalad or 45° cephalad for a Harris projection [ref 4: 21] and centred to the plantar aspect of the heel.

(ii) As an alternative – The patient lies on the affected side. The unaffected limb is moved out of the way in front of the affected limb. Place a small pad under the lower leg of the affected side raising it slightly from the table. The image receptor is supported vertically against the sole of the heel.

Central ray direction – Horizontal, making an angle of 60° with the image receptor and directed towards the back of the heel (Figure 7.11).

The sole of the foot should be at 90° to the lower leg in either technique. This may not always be possible and sometimes a compensatory change in X-ray tube angulation can be made. Sources vary as to what should be the standard angulation. For a version of projection (5(ii)) with the patient standing – *see* projection (9).

Radiographic techniques – talus and subtalar joints

The talus is demonstrated in a lateral projection of the foot, hindfoot or ankle (projections 3, 4 and 14) and the trochlear surface of the talus can be seen on the routine anteroposterior projection of the ankle (projection (11)). If an *os trigonum* is present in a case of injury a comparative lateral projection may be taken of the other foot.

Although one aspect of the talocalcanean joints can be seen on projections (3) or (4), further projections may be required to demonstrate them more fully. For some illustrative radiographs – *see* [further reading 5: 101–103]. Overall, the subtalar joints

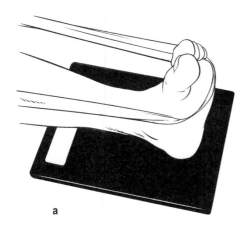

a

b

*Figure 7.10 (a) Patient positioning for projection (5 (i)) axial calcaneus
(b) Main bony structures shown by this projection are:*
1 *anterior subtalar joint*
2 *sustentaculum tali*
3 *posterior subtalar joint (talocalcanean joint)*
4 *'pillar of heel'*

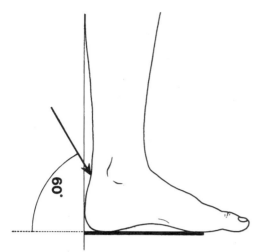

Figure 7.11 Position of the cassette and direction of the central ray in projection (5(ii)) axial calcaneus.

have a very complex multifaceted surface that makes evaluation with plain radiography and conventional tomography difficult [**ref 8**]. This area is therefore a viable candidate for *CT*.

(6) Dorsiplantar oblique

This demonstrates the *anterior (talocalcaneonavicular) joint*. Same position as projection (2(ii)).

Central ray direction – Vertical and centred to a point 2.5 cm below and anterior to the lateral malleolus.

(7) Medial oblique axial (Brodén)

This demonstrates the *middle facets* and also gives a tangential view of the convexity of the *posterior facets (talocalcanean joint)*.

The patient sits on the table with the legs extended. The affected foot is 90° dorsiflexed. The leg is now rotated medially through 45° and the foot is supported on a non-opaque pad.

Central ray direction – Central ray is angled 10° cephalad from the vertical and centred to a point 2.5 cm below and anterior to the lateral malleolus.

The posterior talar articular surface (talocalcanean joint) is convex, therefore a series of radiographs with central ray cephalad angulations of 10°, 20°, 30° and 40° will render a full demonstration.

The radiograph taken with the X-ray tube angled 40° shows the anterior part of the talocalcanean joint, the radiograph taken with the X-ray tube angled 10° reproducing the posterior part. Some of the radiographs (generally those with the X-ray tube angled 30° or 20°) make the articulation between the sustentaculum and the talus visible [**ref 2**: 90].

(8) Lateral oblique axial (Brodén)

Brodén considered that the anatomy of the *talocalcaean joint* was best radiographically examined using projections in two planes perpendicular to one another [**ref 2**: 90].

For this second profile view of the *posterior facets* – the patient sits on the table with the legs extended. The affected foot is 90° dorsiflexed. The leg is now rotated laterally through 45° and rested on a non-opaque pad.

Central ray direction – Central ray is angled 15° cephalad from the vertical and centred to a point 2 cm below and in front of the medial malleolus.

(9) Harris, Beath posterior tangential projection

This is 'weight-bearing' projection demonstrates the *posterior* and *middle facets*. Harris and Beath used this projection to demonstrate talocalcaneal bridge (coalition) [**ref 7**].

The patient stands on the image receptor (placed in an appropriate holder) and leans forward placing their hands on the table for support. The ankles are dorsi-flexed as far as possible.

Central ray direction – Central ray is directed first vertically and then approximately 45° from behind the patient towards the front of the foot passing through the Achilles tendon.

Where the intention is to project the central ray through the posterior subtalar joint then the exact X-ray tube angulation may be determined by examination of a weight-bearing horizontal ray lateral projection of the foot. The angle of declination of the joint can be determined from this radiograph (*see* [**ref 18**: 7]). The resulting

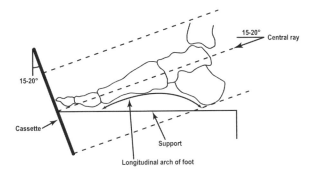

Figure 7.12 Position of foot, cassette and direction of central ray in Cobey's posterior view.

image is a distorted radiographic view of the hindfoot as the image receptor is not perpendicular to the central ray (*see* projection (10)).

(10) Cobey's posterior view *(Figure 7.12)*

This projection enables visualisation of the precise relation of the calcaneus to the ankle joint and the longitudinal axis of the tibia. This view also allows the study of the subtalar joint motion when the tibia is rotated externally and internally. It gives a third radiographic dimension of the weight-bearing heel to complement weight-bearing dorsiplantar and lateral projections [**ref 3**]. An angled X-ray beam is used because if an attempt is made to use a horizontal X-ray beam, the metatarsals and toes become superimposed upon the hindfoot and this makes interpretation impossible.

The patient stands on a radiolucent suface with the toes touching the image receptor. The alignment of the foot is standardised by placing the second metatarsal perpendicular to the image receptor in both horizontal and perpendicular planes. The X-ray source to image receptor distance is increased from the standard 100cm to 110cm.

Central ray direction – Central ray is angled caudad and from behind to be parallel to the axis of the forefoot. This angle is usually between 15 and 20° (downwards) from the horizontal.

ANKLE

Essential anatomical terminology

The ankle or talocrural joint lies between the rounded upper surface of the body of the *talus* – the trochlear surface of the talar dome – and the 'socket' or mortise formed by the distal end of the *tibia* and *fibula*. Medially lies the distal end of the fibula. The horizontal articular surface of the tibia is termed the *plafond* (*see Figure 7.13*). The ankle is sometimes referred to as a *mortise* joint because it is analogous in form to a mortise and tenon joint in woodwork. A fibrous capsule supported by strong *collateral ligaments* surrounds the joint. The active movements at the ankle joint include dorsiflexion and plantar flexion. In dorsiflexion the angle between the front of the leg and the dorsum of the

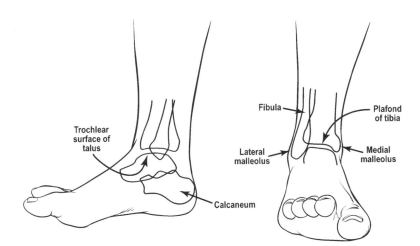

Figure 7.13 Outline of appearance of projections (14) lateral ankle and (11) anteroposterior ankle (mortise)
The tibia, fibula and talus form the talocrural or ankle joint.

foot becomes diminished, in plantar flexion the angle is increased. It should be noted that inversion and eversion of the foot are brought about chiefly by movements at the intertarsal joints and not at the ankle joint. The lateral collateral ligament prevents inversion at the ankle and is the most frequently injured [**ref 4**: 1]. The medial collateral ligament limits eversion of the foot. The fibrous joint between the distal fibula and the tibia is called the *tibiofibular syndesmosis*. This maintains the fibula within the peroneal groove of the tibia.

Indications for the X-ray examination

Injuries

Sprained ankle

This is an injury sustained when the foot is forcefully inverted, the patient 'going over' on the outside of the foot. This may result in tearing of the lateral ligament of the ankle. The lateral ligament is in three parts:

(1) The anterior talofibular segment.

(2) The calcaneofibular portion directed downwards.

(3) The posterior talofibular segment directed posteriorly.

The first of these three parts of the lateral ligament is most likely to be torn and this injury is known as a sprained ankle. Often associated with this is a fracture of the fifth metatarsal base (necessitating radiography), although no bony injury is seen at the ankle. In more severe injuries the whole ligament may be torn.

Fractures of the ankle region

The range of combinations of ankle injury is large. Most involve fractures of the malleoli, with or without ligament damage. Some injuries are associated with a degree of subluxation or dislocation of the joint surfaces. Generally the function of the ankle mortise is threatened if the malleoli are fractured or the tibiofibular ligaments torn. The stability of the talus may also be reduced by rupture of one or other collateral ligaments. There have been several attempts to classify these

injuries and most of these classifications are based on the mechanism by which the injury has been caused for example adduction or external rotation. To simplify the subject, the joint can be injured on either the lateral or medial side, or on both sides. In the most severe injuries both sides may be injured together with the posterior lip of the lower end of the tibia (*Figure 7.14*). This structure is often called the 'third malleolus' or posterior malleolus. In some external rotation injuries the interosseous ligament of the inferior tibiofibular joint is ruptured with separation of the two bones. This is known as a *diastasis*. The fibula may also be fractured at a higher level – for example – at the neck. This combination may be termed *Maissoneuve fracture*. The term *Pott's fracture* is loosely applied to any fracture-dislocation of the ankle. This is confusing because the type of fracture Pott [**ref 13**] described is quite rare [**ref 5**: 260]. A *pilon fracture* is the result of an axial landing – for example – when a standing person falls from a height.

Accessory ossicles (*see* page 6) adjacent to the tips of the medial or lateral malleoli are common and need to be distinguished from a fracture.

Other conditions of interest

Footballer's ankle

Repeated forced plantar flexion may lead to tears in the anterior joint capsule of the ankle giving rise to tibial or talar osteophyte formation and limitation of dorsiflexion [**ref 12**: 383].

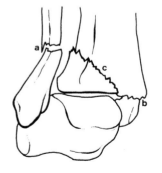

Figure 7.14 A trimalleolar fracture. The posterior and lateral aspects of the left ankle shows fractures through: (a) the lateral malleolus (b) the medial malleolus and (c) the posterior malleolus.

Radiographic techniques – ankle

(11) Anteroposterior ankle (mortise view) (*Figures 7.13 and 7.15*)

With the patient seated or lying the leg is extended with the toes pointing upwards. The back of the heel and ankle are placed on the image receptor. The foot ideally makes an angle of 90° to the lower leg. To help achieve this a 45° non-opaque pad and sandbag are placed against the sole of the foot. The foot is rotated medially until the malleoli tips are equidistant from the image receptor (*Figure 7.15*).

> *Central ray direction* – Perpendicular to the image receptor and centred to a point midway between the malleoli.

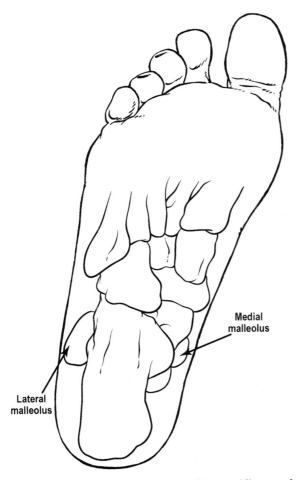

Figure 7.15 Positioning of the foot to achieve equidistance of malleoli.

Because of the reciprocally curved surfaces of talus and tibia it will not be possible to demonstrate the talocrural joint space completely. The space between the talar margins, medial malleolus and between the plafond and lateral malleolus should be equal. Talar asymmetry is a likely indicator of the presence of injury.

Ligament injuries

Damage to the joint ligaments can produce instability of the talus within the ankle mortise. Clinical rather than radiological evaluation is likely to be used to produce a diagnosis. However, stress views can be used to diagnose ligament disruption. A mortise projection radiograph is taken of the ankle and then repeated with the surgeon forcefully inverting the foot on the ankle joint (for the lateral ligaments). The talus will tilt outwards if the joint is unstable. The procedure may have to be repeated with the other ankle for comparison. If the talar tilt of the injured ankle is 10° greater than that of the normal side it generally indicates both anterior talofibular and calcaneofibular ligaments on the lateral side of the ankle are torn [**ref 1**: 178].

(12) Distal tibiofibular joint

Further information about the joint and the lower end of the fibula may be obtained by repeating projection (11) but with the leg rotated internally through 45 °.

> *Central ray direction* – Perpendicular to the image receptor and centred to the lateral malleolus.

(13) External oblique ankle

As for (11) but rotating the leg externally through 45°. This is recommended for demonstration of subtle posterior tibial fractures [**ref 1**].

(14) Mediolateral ankle (*Figure 7.13*)

The aim is to produce a projection that demonstrates the joint space between the trochlear surface of the talus and the inferior surface of the tibia. The medial malleolus will be superimposed on the lower end of the fibula. The patient is rotated on to the affected side and the lateral surface of the ankle is placed on the image receptor.

Keep the affected leg straight at the knee. The unaffected leg lies behind the affected leg. The foot is dorsiflexed so that it is at 90° to the lower leg. *Avoid* any inversion of the foot. The tibia should be parallel to the image receptor. With the lateral aspect of the foot touching the image receptor, medially rotate the leg slightly by about 15 °. This rotation superimposes the malleoli. The lateral aspect of the foot must now be supported on a pad.

Central ray direction – Perpendicular to the image receptor and centred to the medial malleolus.

Alternative technique – projection (15).

(15) *Lateromedial ankle*

This technique is said to produce a better demonstration of the joint space and gives a different perspective of the talar neck. The patient lies on the unaffected side. Bring the affected limb forward to lie on the table in front of the unaffected limb. The medial aspect of the foot and ankle lie on the image receptor. Place a pad underneath the knee of the affected side for support.

Central ray direction – Perpendicular to the image receptor and centred to the lateral malleolus.

Injuries

Modifications to technique may be necessary because the patient cannot move to facilitate the two basic views. Two projections must be taken at right angles to each other and the radiographer should at least attempt to produce an anteroposterior and lateral projection. If the patient cannot rotate the leg and body then the X-ray tube must be rotated around the axis of the leg accordingly.

With some patients it may sometimes be more convenient to take a conventional anteroposterior view and then turn the X-ray tube through 90 ° for a lateromedial view. The cassette can be propped vertically against the medial aspect of the foot and ankle while the ankle is raised slightly on a non-opaque pad.

MID TO PROXIMAL TIBIA, FIBULA AND KNEE JOINT

Essential anatomical terminology

The shaft of the tibia is triangular in section with a subcutaneous *anterior border*. Its proximal extremity is expanded into two *condyles* and forms the knee joint with the femur (*Figure 7.16*). The tibia transmits the body weight to the ankle joint – a role in which its lateral partner bone – the fibula – plays little part. The head of the fibula forms a *synovial plane joint* with the lateral condyle of the tibia. The *crural interosseous membrane* connects the interosseous borders of the tibia and fibula and forms in part, a base for muscle attachments.

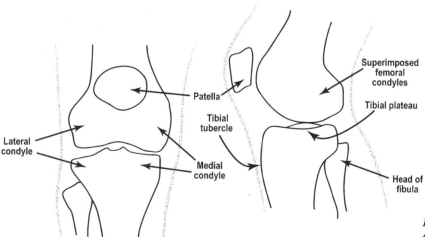

Figure 7.16 Outline appearance of projections (20) anteroposterior knee projection and (24) lateral knee.

The knee joint is the largest joint in the body and is notable for its complex intra-articular structures. The distal extremity of the femur is expanded into two *condyles* forming the knee joint with the tibia. A deep notch lies posteriorly between the two femoral condyles – the *intercondylar notch*. Lying between the articular condyles of the femur and tibia are the two radiolucent semilunar cartilages (*menisci*). Two *cruciate ligaments* – anterior and posterior – lie in the central part of the joint and the *collateral ligaments* lie on either side of the joint help to stabilize and strengthen it. The prime movements made by the knee joint are those of flexion and extension. As the knee moves, a third bone – the sesamoid *patella* – glides up and down the patellar surface of the femur. The patella lies in the tendon of the *quadriceps muscle* and is linked to the tibia via the *patellar tendon*. Occasionally a patella may ossify from two bony centres instead of the usual one and the centres fail to merge. This is termed a *bipartite patella*. Characteristically this normal variant is located in the upper outer quadrant of the patella [**ref 14**: 154]. A sesamoid bone may also be present in the outer head of the gastrocnemius muscle – the *fabella* – and is most easily seen on the lateral knee radiograph. The synovial membrane of the knee joint forms a large pouch above the knee. This is the *suprapatellar bursa* and is regarded, for practical purposes as an extension of the knee joint [**ref 19**: 484].

Indications for the X-ray examination

Injuries

Fractures of the shafts of tibia and fibula

The tibia and fibula are vulnerable to twisting stresses, from direct blows and from forces transmitted through the feet. Isolated fractures of either bone from direct blows are comparatively uncommon [**ref 12**: 346]. A large proportion of tibial shaft fractures are compound because about one-third of the bone is only covered by skin and subcutaneous tissue. Because the bone is triangular in shape and because of the frequency of injuries caused by torsion, oblique and spiral fractures are common (*see* [**ref 12**: 346] and *Figure 2.5*). Damage to the tibial arteries sometimes occurs and this may have to be assessed using *arteriography* if either

resection of the arteries or amputation of the limb is deemed necessary. The fractured tibia is often treated by open reduction and internal fixation. Sometimes there may be difficulty in union of these fractures because the tibial shaft has a poor blood supply particularly to its lower third. Treatment of *delayed union* is by bone grafting and internal fixation. Sometimes the healed fibula acts as a 'prop' keeping the tibial fragments apart so the surgeon may excise a short length of the fibular shaft to prevent this.

Fractures of the tibial plateau (tibial table, tibial condyles)

These usually occur as a result of a road traffic accident or fall. The knee is forced into *valgus* or *varus* and as a result one side of the tibial plateau may become fractured and depressed below the level of surrounding surfaces. Ligament damage may also accompany this injury. If the depressed fracture is not corrected, *secondary arthritis* will follow. *CT* or *conventional tomography* may be used to define the position of fragments and the degree of articular involvement.

Isolated fractures of the neck and head of the fibula

These are uncommon and are often associated with other knee injuries.

Fracture of the femoral condyles

The fracture may involve one or both of the condyles. There is also a severe T-shaped fracture of the lower end of the femur that results in both femoral condyles being separated from each other and from the lower end of the shaft of the femur.

Lipohaemarthrosis and haemarthrosis

Lipohaemarthrosis is defined as a joint abnormality characterised by synovial fluid containing both fat droplets and blood (*see Figure 7.20*, page 114). A lipohaemarthrosis in the suprapatellar bursa should be regarded as indicating an intra-articular fracture – even if the fracture is not seen [**ref 14**: 150]. A haemarthrosis involves only blood in synovial fluid. Tears of the anterior cruciate ligament will cause haemarthrosis in 75% of patients [**ref 1**: 75].

Fractures of the patella

There are two forms of fracture of the patella. The first is caused by a direct blow to the kneecap when the patella may break into several pieces. This is known as a *stellate fracture* but because the soft-tissue structures around the patella remain intact the fragments tend not to become separated (*Figure 7.17*). The second form is the *transverse fracture* of the patella (*Figure 7.18*) and is caused by sudden violent contraction of the quadriceps muscle. This can occur in attempting to preserve the balance after stumbling. The enormous muscle pull causes the bone to fracture transversely about its midpoint accompanied by tearing of the fibrous tissues (the patellar retinaculum) on either side of the bone. Wide separation of the two fragments usually occurs. In some individuals a similar force may result in rupture of the quadriceps or patellar tendon instead of a fracture.

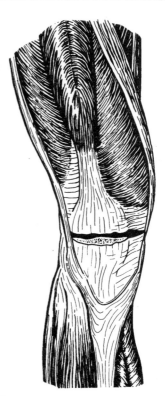

Figure 7.18 Transverse fracture of the patella with tearing of the patella retinaculum.

Dislocation of the patella

The patella can be dislocated from its groove on the femoral surface by trauma. Road accidents or sports injuries provide the usual cause and the patella is displaced either medially or laterally. In some patients, *recurrent lateral dislocation* of the patella can occur. It is thought that this condition is caused by certain inherent structural anomalies such as a shallow intercondylar groove and a small, highly placed patella.

Dislocation of the knee

A rare traumatic condition where there is a loss of alignment between the femur and tibia.

Ligament injuries

A tear of the *medial collateral ligament* is caused by a stress that abducts the tibia on the femur. The joint is momentarily subluxated but when the patient is examined in the casualty department the subluxation has nearly always been reduced

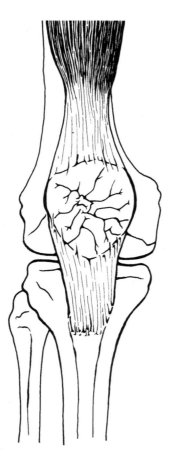

Figure 7.17 Stellate fracture of the patella.

spontaneously. Whether or not the rupture is complete can sometimes be determined by taking anteroposterior radiographs while an abduction strain is deliberately applied to the tibia. If the tear is complete the knee joint space will widen at the medial side. Very wide abduction of the tibia on the femur cannot occur unless the *cruciate ligaments* and the *joint capsule* are torn as well. A tear of the *lateral collateral ligament* is much less common than that of the medial, and isolated tears of the cruciate ligaments are apparently quite rare. A sequel to a torn medial ligament is its calcification near the upper attachment; this is known as *Pellegrini-Steida's* disease.

Meniscus injuries

The menisci or semilunar cartilages are the remains of the complete cartilaginous discs which in foetal life separate the articular surfaces of the tibia and the femur. In the vertical section they are both triangular but they differ on the two sides in that the medial meniscus is *crescentic* in shape whilst the lateral meniscus is more circular. Owing to the width of the pelvis, the femur normally makes a small angle with the tibia in the coronal plane. Most of the body weight passes through the lateral side of the joint and during rotation the lateral femoral condyle pivots on the outer side of the tibial plateau whilst the medial femoral condyle moves across the inner side. It is partly because of this relatively greater degree of movement that the medial meniscus is more likely to be injured than the lateral meniscus. This can occur when the knee is weight bearing, semi-flexed and the body is rotated. The semilunar cartilages are placed under a stress which could result in a tearing injury. The menisci are radiolucent so they cannot be seen on 'plain' radiographs with the exception of the older patient who may have early osteoarthritic changes [ref 1: 127]. A damaged meniscus may need excision – *meniscectomy.*

Other conditions of interest

Osteoarthritis

The knee is the largest joint in the body and is subject to great mechanical stress therefore it is frequently affected by osteoarthritis. The degeneration is quite often secondary to some underlying cause – such as a fracture and the arthritis develops in the half of the joint bearing the greatest weight. Sometimes operative treatment is carried out and this may involve *arthroplasty* (*see* Chapter 3).

Loose bodies in the knee joint

For the description and causes of loose bodies refer to Chapter 3. Intercondylar notch projections of the knee joint may be required. Non-opaque loose bodies can be investigated by *arthrography*.

Rheumatoid arthritis

The knee is the commonest of the large joints to be affected by this disease. The patient complains of pain and stiffness in the joint and as the disease progresses the articular cartilage becomes damaged and this leads to a *secondary osteoarthritis* (*see* Chapter 3).

Osgood-Schlatter disease

The tibial tubercle is the commonest site for *osteochondritis* (*see* Chapter 3); both knees may be affected.

Genu varum (bow legs) and genu valgum (knock knees)

The distance between the hip joints is normally greater than that between the knees when the legs are together. Also, the femur usually makes an angle with the tibia in the coronal plane. Alterations in this angle are common and are usually termed knock-knees or bow legs. These deformities can result from a disease producing weakening of the bones. Examples are *rickets*, *osteomalacia* and *Paget's disease* (*see* Chapter 3). Changes in the joint ligaments have an effect on the bony relationships at the knee. Long continued stretching of the lateral side of the capsule accounts for the horseman's bow legs.

Radiographic techniques – tibia and fibula

The whole length of the two bones should be included on the radiograph. This may mean that two separate exposures may be required for each projection. In subsequent follow-up examinations it may be permissible to include only the joint nearest the lesion.

(16) Anteroposterior tibia and fibula

The patient lies supine with the limb extended. The affected leg is placed on the image receptor and rotated medially so that the malleoli are equidistant from the image receptor. Immobilize the limb.

Central ray direction – Perpendicular to the image receptor and to the long axis of the tibia; centre at mid-shaft level.

The ankle and knee joints should be included on the radiograph. If two separate cassettes have to be used their positioning should overlap. After the initial examination, further radiological information may be gained by undertaking anteroposterior oblique projections of the lower leg. From the position for the anteroposterior projection the leg is rotated either medially or laterally by the required degree.

(17) Lateral tibia and fibula

From the position for the anteroposterior projection the patient is rotated on to the affected side. Flex the hip and knee slightly. The unaffected limb lies behind the affected limb. Make sure the patient has adequate support. The transverse axis of the patella should be 90° to the image receptor and the malleoli at the ankle are superimposed.

Central ray direction – Perpendicular to the image receptor and to the long axis of the tibia; centre at mid-shaft level.

(18) Lateral fibula

The patient lies on the affected side with the unaffected hip and knee flexed. The patient rolls forward until the heel is raised by 45°.

Central ray direction – Perpendicular to the image receptor and to the long axis of the fibula; centre at mid-shaft level.

Injuries

Two projections must be taken at right angles to each other. Where a serious injury such as a compound tibial fracture has occurred, the limb tends to be externally rotated below the fracture. It is commonplace for orthopaedic surgeons to require projections (for one joint) that are in

appearance close to conventional projections. This is to allow assessment of the degree of fracture fragment rotation (for example).

Use an appropriate angled beam for the first projection. Great care must be taken if a cassette has to be placed underneath the leg. It is preferable to use an accident trolley system avoiding moving the patient. For the second projection, rotate the X-ray tube through 90° and direct the central ray from an orthogonal aspect. The cassette is supported against the appropriate limb aspect. Always seek medical advice and assistance if you consider it needed.

(19) Proximal tibiofibular joint, head of fibula

This joint lies on the posterolateral aspect of the upper tibia. The limb must be rotated out from a standard anteroposterior or lateral 'position' for the joint and head of fibula to be clearly demonstrated. There are two techniques:

(i) With the limb outstretched at the knee and the toes pointing upwards, medially rotate the leg through about 35°.

Central ray direction – Perpendicular to the image receptor and centred to the head of the fibula.

(ii) Position the patient as for projection (16). Now rotate the leg further laterally until the lateral border of the patella touches the cassette.

Central ray direction – Perpendicular to the image receptor and centred to the head of the fibula.

In this projection the head of the fibula is closer to the image receptor.

Radiographic techniques – knee

(20) Anteroposterior single knee
(see Figure 7.16)

The patient is seated or lying on the X-ray table with the leg outstretched and the toes pointing upwards. The image receptor lies behind the knee. Medially rotate the leg slightly to centralize the patella over the lower femur. Immobilize the leg with sandbags.

Central ray direction – Perpendicular to the image receptor and to the long axis of the tibia, centred at a point 2.5 cm below the lower border of the patella.

Make sure an adequate exposure is used. Underexposure of this projection is a common fault. If the patient cannot fully extend the knee an 18 x 24 cm cassette can be placed with its long axis cross-wise, the cassette being supported on a pad behind the flexed knee. Although the length of bone shown is limited because the cassette is small, this method gives improved subject to image receptor contact.

(21) Anteroposterior oblique 45° knee

The knee may be radiographed whilst in external or internal rotation. The latter provides further information on the medial tibial plateau and femoral condyle. The former provides further information on the lateral femoral condyle.

(22) Anteroposterior both knees

With the patient seated or lying, both knees can be examined with a single exposure on one cassette. Placing a rigid piece of lead rubber vertically between the knees will prevent a lot of scattered radiation from reaching the image receptor. This markedly improves radiographic contrast.

Knee replacement prosthesis (arthroplasty)

Include the full length of the 'implant' on the radiograph.

Weight-bearing anteroposterior knees

This is for orthopaedic assessment of the femorotibial joint. Where visualization of the alignment of the tibiae and femora is required a projection of the knees is taken with the patient standing weight bearing with both feet (provided it is safe for the patient to do so). Take radiographs of either single or both knees together. Patients who are unsteady on their feet may be positioned facing the image receptor for a posteroanterior projection where they can hold on to the support.

If more of the limb bones are required on the radiograph simply use a bigger image receptor – for example – a 35 × 43 cm cassette placed lengthwise.

(23) Posteroanterior 45° flexion knees (Rosenberg)

This projection has been found to be more accurate than conventional 'leg extended' weight-bearing views for evaluating cartilage lesions [**ref 16**]. The patient stands facing a cassette placed in a vertical holder. Weight is distributed evenly on each foot and toes pointed anteriorly. The knees are bent slowly until they rest anteriorly against the cassette. The angle between the femur and tibia is 135°. The patient must be safe and stable and thus adequately supported in this position.

Central ray direction – Central ray is angled caudad 10° from the horizontal and centred through the knee joint.

The intercondylar notch ('tunnel') is also visualised [**ref 9**: 10].

(24) Lateral knee (see Figure 7.16 and 7.19)

From the anteroposterior position (projection (20)) the patient is turned on to the affected side; the unaffected limb lies behind the affected limb. Flex the knee under examination to approximately 30° and flex the hip slightly. The transverse axis of the patella is 90° to the image receptor. The heel should be raised on a narrow wedge pad.

Central ray direction – Central ray is angled 5° cephalad from the vertical and centred over the medial condyle of the tibia.

The 5° angle prevents the magnified medial condyle from obscuring the joint space. For a rationale for the 30° knee flexion *see* [**ref 9**:11].

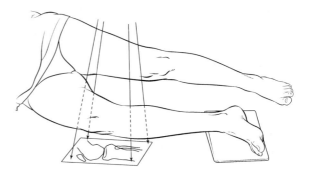

Figure 7.19 Patient and cassette positioning for projection (24) lateral knee

Weight-bearing lateral knees

Place a cassette in a vertical holder. The patient stands with the lateral aspect of the knee next to the cassette. Flex the hip and knee of the unaffected leg and move it forward out of the way. The toes of the unaffected leg should rest on some immobile object but most of the body weight should be directed through the leg under examination. Make sure the patient is safely supported.

Central ray direction – Perpendicular to the image receptor and centred over the medial tibial condyle.

Osgood-Schlatter's disease

Standard lateral projections of both knees may be required for comparison, centring over the tibial tubercle but generally radiography is not recommended for this condition.

Injuries and patients with limited movement

With the patient lying supine carefully place a 45° non-opaque pad under the knee and prop a cassette vertically against the medial aspect of the knee so it is parallel to the tibia. A 'rule of thumb' for foot positioning in horizontal beam lateral projections is that the right foot should be at an 11 o'clock position and the left foot at 1 o'clock [**ref 9**:11].

Central ray direction – Perpendicular to the image receptor and centred over the lateral tibial condyle.

In injuries a *lipohaemarthrosis* (Figure 7.20) indicates a fracture involving the joint. A horizontal X-ray beam is essential to potentially demonstrate less dense fat that floats on blood and forms a radiographically visible fluid level. It is recommended that the patient lies supine for ten minutes prior to exposure to allow level formation and visualisation. An *effusion* may be detected on the lateral view – the patella may be displaced more anteriorly than usual in relationship to the femur.

(25) Intercondylar notch

These projections visualise the tibial spines and detect osteochondral fragments in the joint space.

(i) The patient sits on the table with the leg in the position for the anteroposterior projection. Flex the knee over a curved cassette *or* use a flat 18 × 24cm cassette placed transversely. Two separate radiographs are exposed.

Central ray direction – Just below the lower border of the patella (Figure7.21) with the X-ray tube directed:

(a) To make an angle of 90° to the tibia. This shows the posterior part of the notch.

(b) To make an angle of 110° to the tibia to show the anterior part of the notch. (*See* [further reading 5: 116]).

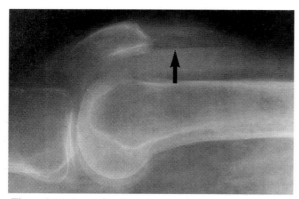

Figure 7.20 Lateral radiograph of the knee taken with a horizontal X-ray beam. A lipohaemarthrosis can be seen proximal to the patella.

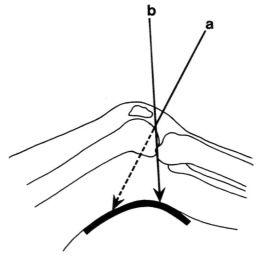

Figure 7.21 Position of the cassette and direction of the central ray for projection (25(i)) intercondylar notch. The illustration shows a curved cassette however a flat 18 × 24 cm cassette would do just as well.

(ii) The following technique can be used as an alternative to projection (25(i)). The patient lies prone. Raise the lower leg off the table and flex the knee through 40° – 45° and support. Place a cassette underneath the knee (*Figure 7.22*).

Central ray direction – Central ray is angled caudad 40° – 45° from the vertical and centred to a point 2.5 cm below the crease of the knee [ref 1: 112]. The beam is directed along the axis of the notch.

For alternative approaches *see* [further reading **3** (*Homblad*)] and also [further reading **1**: 236 (*Camp Coventry*)].

Radiographic techniques – patella

The patella is often examined in cases of trauma and care should be taken to avoid undue flexion of the knee as this may exacerbate an injury such as a transverse fracture of the bone.

(26) Posteroanterior patella

The patient lies prone if this is tolerable. The image receptor is placed under the knee. The leg is rotated so that the patella is centralized under the lower end of the femur. Place a pad underneath the ankle for support. (Include the whole knee on the radiograph).

Central ray direction – Vertical and to the crease of the knee.

Alternative technique – projection (27).

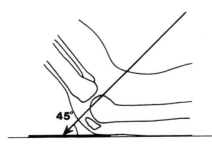

Figure 7.22 Position of the patient, direction of the central ray and position of the cassette for projection (25(ii)) intercondylar notch.

(27) Anteroposterior patella

Same position as in projection (20). The patella is several centimetres from the image receptor therefore the source to image receptor distance should be increased from the standard 100cm to 120 cm to reduce geometric unsharpness and magnification of the patella. (Include the whole knee on the radiograph).

Central ray direction – Perpendicular to the image receptor and centred over the patella.

(28) Lateral patella

From the anteroposterior position the patient turns to lie on the unaffected side. Position as for projection (24). This position is more easily maintained if the knee is flexed slightly. The transverse axis of the patella is 90° to the cassette. Include the whole knee joint on the radiograph. Note that with the knee straight the patella lies higher on the femoral patellar surface than when the joint is flexed.

Central ray direction – Perpendicular to the image receptor and centred over the medial border of the patella.

Injuries

The lateral projection should be taken with a horizontal X-ray beam as in the case of knee injuries.

In patella dislocations it will be impossible to produce a true lateral projection of the bone. Where a patella is *bipartite* a radiograph should be taken of the other side for comparison.

(29) Inferosuperior (axial) patella

Radiographers like to term this a 'skyline' projection. It is a supplementary technique where additional information is required about the bone and its sellar joint with the femur for example in osteoarthritis or instability. The patient must be able to bend his knee. This projection is not attempted in injury. Sit the patient upright on the table and support his back if possible. Flex the knee to about 150°. The patient holds the cassette, resting on a pad, at an angle behind the knee

(*Figure 7.23*) and at 90° to the central ray which is directed upwards along the vertical axis of the joint between the patella and femur.

> *Central ray direction* – With a 15° angle to the long axis of the tibia and centred to the apex of the patella. (See [ref 9] and [ref 6 (Ficat)]).

Where axials of both patellae are required, a larger cassette is placed behind both knees which are exposed simultaneously, the centre lying between the knees. If the patient is not able to hold the cassette himself then a special cassette support should be used.

For a review of alternative approaches – *see* [further reading 4 (*Merchant*)].

(30) *Posteroanterior obliques of the patella*

From the prone position (projection (26)) the leg is rotated 45° first laterally and then medially. The knee should be flexed slightly. Support the foot on a pad.

> *Central ray direction* – Perpendicular to the image receptor and centred over the femoral condyle of the raised side – each side in turn.

The medial or lateral side of the patella is projected clear of the femur.

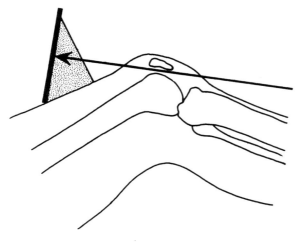

Figure 7.23 Position of the knee, direction of the central ray and position of the cassette in projection (29) axial patella.

References

1. Berquist TH (1991) *Imaging of Orthopaedic Trauma* New York: Raven Press

2. Brodén B (1949) Roentgen examination of the subtalar joint in fractures of the calcaneus *Acta Radiologica* 57: 85–91

3. Cobey JC (1976) Posterior roentgenogram of the foot *Clinical Orthopaedics and Related Research* 118: 202–207

4. Crim JR (1996) *Imaging of the Foot and Ankle* London: Martin Dunitz

5. Dandy DJ and Edwards DJ (2003) *Essential Orthopaedics and Trauma (4th Edition)* Edfinburgh: Churchill Livingstone

6. Ficat P Phillipe J Bizou H (1970) Le défilé fémoro-patellaire *Toulouse Medical Review* 6: 241–244

7. Harris RI Beath T (1948) Etiology of peroneal spastic flat foot *Journal of Bone and Joint Surgery* 30: 624–634

8. Hellman AE Braley WG Bishop JO (1990) An anatomic study of subtalar instability *Foot and Ankle* 10(4): 224–228

9. Hussain M (2001) Back to basics orthopaedic positioning of the knee *Synergy* June p8–13

10. Keats TE Anderson MW (2001) *Atlas of Normal Roentgen Variants that may Simulate Disease (7th Edition)* St Louis: Mosby

11. McRae R Andrew W (1997) *Orthopaedics and trauma: an illustrated colour text* Edinburgh: Churchill Livingstone

12. McRae R Esser M (2002) *Practical Fracture Treatment (4th Edition)* Edinburgh: Churchill Livingstone

13. Pott P (1769) *Some Few General Remarks on Fractures and Dislocations* London: Howes

14. Raby N Berman L De Lacey G (2002) *Accident and Emergency Radiology: A Survival Guide* London: Saunders

15. Ritchie GW Keim HA (1968) Major foot deformities. Their classification and X-ray analysis *J Can Assoc Radiol* 19: 155–66

16. Rosenberg TD Paulos LE Porter RD Coward DB Scott SM (1988) The 45° posteroanterior flexion weight-bearing radiograph of the knee *Journal Bone and Joint Surgery American* **70**: 1479–1482

17. Tanz SS (1963) Heel pain *Clinical Orthopaedics* **28**: 169–75

18. Stelmach D (2003) The appearance and significance of the talar beak in adults *Synergy* February p4–8

19. Williams P Warwick R (eds) (1980) *Gray's Anatomy (36th Edition)* Edinburgh: Churchill Livingstone

Further Reading

1. Bontrager KL (2001) *Textbook of Radiographic Positioning and Related Anatomy (5th Edition)* St Louis: Mosby

2. Foster SC Foster R (1976) Lisfranc's tarsometatarsal fracture-dislocation *Radiology* **120**: 79–85

3. Homblad EC (1937) Posteroanterior X-ray of the knee in flexion *Journal of Bone and Joint Surgery American* **109**: 1196–1197

4. Merchant AC Mercer RL Jacobsen RH Cool CR (1974) Roentgenographic analysis of patellofemoral congruence *Journal of Bone and Joint Surgery American* **56**: 1391–6

5. Swallow RA NaylorE Roebuck EJ Whitley AS (1986) *Clark's Positioning in Radiography (11th Edition)* London: Heinemann

The femur, hip joint and pelvis: the innominate bones

CHAPTER CONTENTS

Table of main and supplementary radiographic techniques

General anatomical area	Projection	Page	Common Indications
Femur	**1** AP	125–126	Injury, pathology
	2 Lateral	126	
Hip	**3** AP single hip	126	Injury, pathology
	4 AP both hips	126–127	
	5 'Turned lateral' single hip	127	Pathology or 'follow up post treatment'
	6 Lateral both hips ('frog's')	127	
	7i–iv Lateral 'neck of femur'	127–128	Injury
Pelvis	**8** AP	131	Injury, pathology
	9 Pelvic inlet	132	Injury
	10 Pelvic outlet	132	Injury
	11 Lateral	132	
	12 External (iliac) oblique	132	
	13 Internal (obturator) oblique	132	
Pubic bones, pubic symphysis	**14** Localised projections	132	Pathology, injury
	15 'Flamingo views'	133	Instability

Typical effective radiation dose for a limb (below hip) examination: **<0.01mSv**
Approximate equivalent period of natural background radiation: **<1.5 days**
Typical effective radiation dose for a single hip examination: **0.4mSv**
Approximate equivalent period of natural background radiation: **2 months**
Typical effective radiation dose for a pelvis radiograph: **0.7 mSv**
Approximate equivalent period of natural background radiation: **4 months**

FEMUR AND HIP

Essential anatomical terminology

The femur is the longest bone in the body, and because its shaft has a very thick cortex, it is also the strongest. For a description of features of the distal end of the femur–*see* page 109. In the standing position, the femoral shaft normally inclines medially 10° (*Figure 8.1*). Within the context of trauma, structurally, the femur is able to resist angulatory forces but its tubular design is not optimal for resisting tortional forces [**ref 1**: 99]. The proximal end of the femur is characterized by the bony prominences – the *trochanters*. Directed medially and upwards from between the trochanters is the *femoral neck* with its rounded *head*. The head together with the bowl-like *acetabulum* (*Figure 8.13, page 129*) of the *innominate bone* form the hip joint. The *capsule* of the joint is attached above to the margins of the acetabulum and below close to the base of the femoral neck. The ligament of the head of the femur (*ligamentum teres*) carries a relatively small blood supply to the femoral head. This has significance for the process of neck of femur fracture healing and treatment.

Indications for the X-ray examination

Injuries

Fractures of the femoral shaft

Because of the inherent strength of the bone, considerable force must be applied to it in order for it to break. A fracture of the femoral shaft tends to occur in road traffic accidents and a patient with a fractured femur will probably have injuries elsewhere (some individuals may also have a *dislocated hip* on the affected side). The patient is likely to be severely shocked and in great pain, and despite the surrounding bulk of thigh muscles femoral fractures are often open (compound). The blood loss from a fractured femur (whether open or

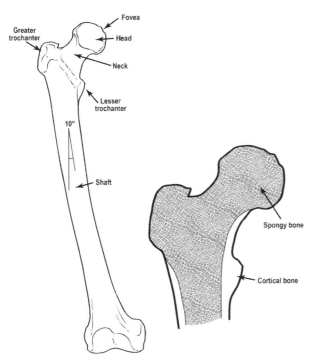

Figure 8.1 The right femur, anterior aspect. The smaller diagram shows a section through the upper extremity. The head and neck consists of mainly cancellous (spongy) bone with a criss-cross trabecular architecture which is able to withstand compressional forces. The shaft has a thickened wall of cortical (compact) bone.

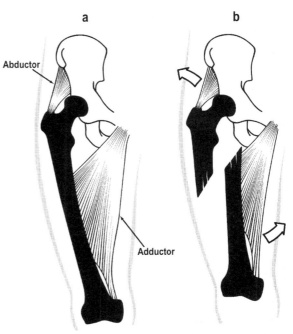

Figure 8.2 In fractures of the femoral shaft the hip abductors muscles will act in an opposite direction to the hip adductor muscles. The two fracture fragments will separate.

closed) is one to two litres. A fracture of the femoral shaft is most likely to be of the transverse type, and because there is no splinting action of a second parallel bone and because of the powerful muscles that span the bone, there is a characteristic angulation and overlapping of the two fragments (*Figure 8.2* and *Figure 2.1*, Chapter 2). This displacement of the ends of the bone can produce a considerable degree of shortening of the leg, and the correction of this shortening is one of the main problems in the treatment of femoral factures. There are different methods of treating this type of fracture. A common approach is to use *internal fixation* with an intramedullary nail. The use of a locking nail can control rotational displacement.

Supracondylar fractures of the femur (Figure 8.3)
Supracondylar fractures are commonest in older patients who have soft porotic bone [ref 2: 244].

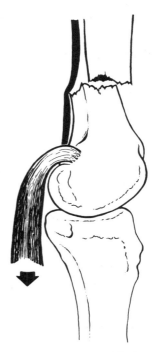

Figure 8.3 Supracondylar fracture of the femur. The gastrocnemius muscle causes displacement of the distal fragment.

Treatment is either by traction reduction or internal fixation. The lower fragment is displaced posteriorly because of the pulling force exerted by the gastrocnemius muscle. The popliteal nerves or femoral blood vessels may be damaged at the fracture site.

Fractures of the neck and trochanteric region of the femur

Elderly patients tend to be most prone to fractures in the upper end of the femur. Although the term 'neck of femur' fracture is applied to most of these injuries there are in fact several distinct types of fracture grouped according to the level at which they occur. The exact site of the fracture and whether there is displacement have some bearing on how treatment will be carried out. The affected leg may be shortened and externally rotated because the shaft of the femur can move independently of the hip joint. The action of the iliopsoas muscle and gravity can now rotate the femur externally [**ref 2**: 232].

Fractures, however, may be missed – for example impacted fractures where there is only small displacement [**ref 6**]. *MRI* is sensitive to both stress and occult fractures [**ref 9**] and may be recommended for patients with indeterminate radiographs and suspected fractures. *CT* is useful for assessing comminuted fractures.

(1) *Intracapsular high transcervical fractures* – where the neck of the femur joins the head. This type seems to be common in women over 60 years of age. There could be a combination of factors accounting for this – the bone may be weakened by senile osteoporosis, which tends to be more marked in post-menopausal women, also the angle between neck and shaft of femur is more acute in women, thereby throwing more severe strains on the femoral neck. Treatment of these fractures – where there is displacement – is nearly always by internal fixation. In order to obtain union of the fracture, perfect immobilization would be required and this is unlikely to be achieved by external splinting. Another important reason for not choosing extended immobilization of the patient is the risk to life from subsequent development of bedsores or pneumonia. The advantage of 'hip pinning' by some variety of

dynamic or compression screw is that it allows the patient to become ambulant fairly soon after the injury, thus avoiding these complications and accelerating healing. A problem with intracapsular fractures is that the blood supply to the head of the femur may be disrupted by the fracture (*Figure 8.4*). The supply via ligamentum teres is insignificant, and there is a possibility of subsequent development of *avascular (aseptic) necrosis* in the femoral head (*see* Chapter 3 and also hip joint dislocation, *below*). Even after internal fixation, the fracture will fail to unite; the head of the femur may collapse, often causing the fixator to protrude into the acetabulum. To avoid this the femoral head is excised and replaced by a prosthesis – for example – Austin-Moore prosthesis (*Figure 8.5*).

(2) *Extracapsular basal fractures* – these are less difficult because the blood supply is not seriously interrupted. Nevertheless, non-union and avascular necrosis may still occur.

(3) *Fractures around the trochanters – pertrochanteric –* means through the trochanters. *Intertrochanteric* – means between the trochanters. Unlike fractures of the neck which can occur with little or no injury, trochanteric fractures are usually

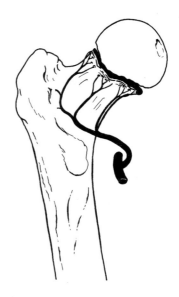

Figure 8.4 Disruption of the blood supply to the head of the femur as a result of a fracture through the femoral neck.

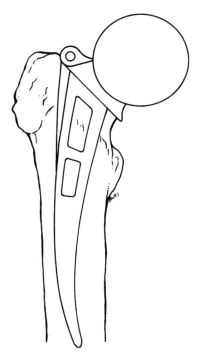

Figure 8.5 The Austin – Moore type femoral prosthesis.

caused by a sharp twisting injury. Inter-trochanteric fractures are often *comminuted*, are very unstable and mal-union is almost inevitable without internal fixation (*see Figure 2.7*, Chapter 2).

(4) *Subtrochanteric fractures* – fractures of the upper third of femoral shaft. These are comparatively uncommon unless the bone at this site is abnormal, for example where a secondary (metastatic) deposit from a carcinoma has caused a *pathological fracture*.

Hip joint dislocation

Anatomists often make comparisons between the hip and shoulder joints because they are both of the ball and socket variety. The hip joint, however, is much less frequently dislocated, because the acetabulum is much deeper than the glenoid cavity.

There are two types of hip dislocation:

(1) *Posterior dislocation*. The head of the femur can be driven out of the acetabulum backwards if a force is applied along the axis of the bone when the hip is flexed and also slightly abducted. As this is the position a car driver adopts, a posterior hip dislocation is often the result of a traffic accident such as a head-on car collision.

(2) *Anterior dislocation*. The head of the femur will lie in front of the acetabulum. This type of dislocation is not so common.

To allow for the abnormal position of the femoral head both the joint capsule and the ligamentum teres must be torn. As these form the major route for blood vessels supplying the femoral head *avascular necrosis* may develop in this part of the bone (*see* Chapter 3). Radiographs are often taken of the hip at intervals for several months following such an injury so that any changes in the femoral head can be detected early, and *MRI* or *radioisotope scintigraphy* has also been used to confirm the presence of avascular necrosis. A dislocated hip can also be complicated by injury to the sciatic nerve which passes behind the femoral neck. The incidence of *sciatic nerve palsy* is about one in ten for posterior hip dislocations [**ref** 5: 114].

Other conditions of interest

Osteoarthritis

The hip is the joint most commonly affected by osteoarthritis. Apart from the expected radiological changes of osteoarthritis (*see* Chapter 3) there may also be a disturbance of Shenton's line (*see* page 124) on the affected side or sides. The degree of severity of the symptoms tends to influence the choice of treatment. If a surgical method is chosen then there are several techniques that include *arthrodesis, osteotomy* or *arthroplasty* (*see* Chapter 3). The last of these where both joint surfaces are replaced is the most popular. In total hip replacement the acetabulum is reamed out to take a cup. The femoral head is replaced by a metal ball attached to a stem inserted into the femoral shaft. *Charnley* contributed much to this field and his low-friction arthroplasty is the one of the best known [**ref** 2: 376]. There are several others types of arthroplasty based on the Charnley pattern (*Figure 8.6*). Charnley also pioneered the use of a separate operating enclosure to reduce the hazard of sepsis which remains a major complication of the operation.

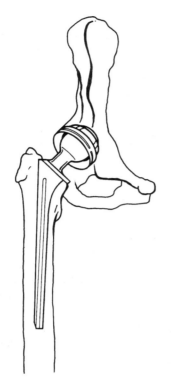

Figure 8.6 A total hip joint prosthesis.

Rheumatoid arthritis

The hip joint can be involved – usually relatively late in the course of rheumatoid arthritis (*see* Chapter 3).

New growths

See Chapter 3, especially osteosarcoma (page 29).

Tuberculosis of the hip

Tuberculosis of the hip usually commences from a bony focus, either in the femoral neck or acetabulum, from which it spreads to invade the joint cavity. The disease usually affects children who are often quite young. Early cases are treated by immobilizing the hip and by giving the patient appropriate antibiotics. If the disease remains untreated, destruction both of the bones and of the joint will result (*see* Chapter 3). About 25% of all cases of bone and joint TB affect the hip [**ref 5:** 106].

Congenital dislocation of the hip

This term is used to embrace a range of conditions where movement and stability of the hip joint are affected. True congenital dislocation of the hip – where the femoral head is displaced up out of the acetabulum at birth – is quite rare. Alternatively the hip may dislocate within the first few post-natal months. The cause of the condition is not known but diagnosis is very important because success in its treatment depends on early recognition. If treatment is not started and if instability persists the development of the acetabulum and the femoral head and neck will be affected. X-ray examination of the suspect hips is of limited value for children under three months [**ref 5:** 102].

One radiological method of gauging the position of the femoral head is to refer to *Shenton's lines* (*Figure 8.7*). If the child's legs are held together and the hips are extended when the anteroposterior radiograph is taken, it is possible on the radiograph to trace the line of the under-surface of the neck which when continued in the form or an arc is continuous with the under-surface of the superior pubic ramus. In the early stages, however, paediatricians rely mainly on clinical tests to determine the presence and degree of congenital dislocation of the hip rather than on radiographic examination. After about four to six months the femoral head epiphysis becomes visible and diagnosis from radiographs is more easily made. Treatment initially consists of splinting the child's legs in abduction and there are many different

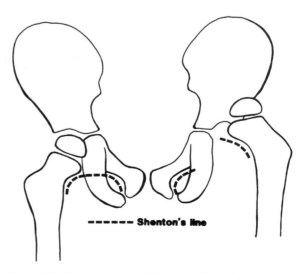

Figure 8.7 The application of Shenton's lines when comparing both hips.

types of splint. For older children traction followed by splinting may be used. Frequently osteotomy is required to correct anteversion of the femoral neck or to deepen the acetabulum.

Perthe's disease

This is *osteochondritis* of the epiphysis of the femoral head resulting from a disturbance of the blood supply. Plain radiographs can be used to judge and grade the severity of the case. *Arthrography, MRI* and *radioisotope* scans are complementary modalities.

Slipping of the upper femoral epiphysis (Figure 8.8)

In adolescents, this is a change in the relationship between the epiphysis of the femoral head and the metaphysis (or neck) of the femur. The epiphysis becomes displaced and comes to lie behind and slightly below its normal attachment to the neck. The displacement can be gradual or sudden and its degree is variable. The condition may not be apparent in the early stages on an anteroposterior radiograph, but may be best shown on the lateral image. The main thrust of treatment is directed towards keeping the femoral head in the acetabulum until it reforms. Sometimes osteotomy is needed [**ref 2: 316**].

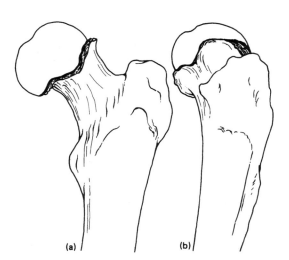

Figure 8.8 Slipped upper femoral epiphysis (a) anterior aspect (b) lateral aspect.

Coxa vara and valga

This is not a disease but a *deformity*. The angle between the neck of the femur and the shaft is normally about 135°; if it is *less than* 135° the condition of coxa vara is said to be present. This alignment abnormality can be related to certain congenital conditions or can be the result of diseases where bone is softened – for example – Paget's disease or osteomalacia. Mal-union of a fractured neck or trochanteric region of the femur is another cause. A femoral neck shaft angle of more than 135° is termed *coxa valga*.

Radiographic techniques – femur, lower third

An anteroposterior and lateral projection with or without a horizontal X-ray beam are taken. The patient and image receptor positions are the same as for the knee (*see* – projections (20 and 24) in Chapter 7) but using a larger X-ray field and image receptor.

Central ray direction – Perpendicular to the image receptor and long axis of the femur and centred over the condylar region of the femur.

Where the patient has an internally fixed supracondylar fracture include the whole of the 'implant' on the radiograph.

Radiographic techniques – femur, middle third

This area is examined almost exclusively for fractures and their treatment. The whole of the long bone with both knee and hip joints must be included on the radiographs.

(1) Anteroposterior femur

The patient lies supine with the hands resting upon the chest. The image receptor lies behind the femur. The affected leg is extended and the toes point upwards if possible.

Central ray direction – Perpendicular to the long axis of the femur and centred over the middle of the thigh.

Include soft tissues of the thigh to demonstrate subcutaneous haematoma or air. Include both knee and hip joints on the radiograph. Using two overlapping casettes if necessary, and use radiation protection on the gonads.

(2) Lateral femur

From the position for the anteroposterior projection the patient rotates to lie on the affected side. The image receptor lies behind the femur. Raise the foot of the affected side on a small pad and flex the knee and hip. The sound limb lies behind the affected limb. The pelvis is tilted backwards 45° so that the upper end of the femur is not obscured by soft tissues.

> *Central ray direction* – Perpendicular to the long axis of the femur and centred over the middle of the thigh.

Again include both joints on the image receptor using more than one cassette if necessary. Carefully use radiation protection for the gonads where appropriate.

Injuries

Preferably, the patient should be examined using an X-ray trolley. The anteroposterior radiograph is exposed in the cassette tray thus avoiding moving the patient. A lateral projection of the lower two-thirds of the bone and knee joint is taken with a horizontally directed central ray, the cassette being propped against the medial aspect of the leg. Even though a patient has a fractured femur the hip must *always* be included in the examination. It may not be possible to rotate the patient so a lateral projection of the upper third of the bone must be taken by other means (*see* projections (7i–iv)).

Radiographic techniques – upper third and hip joint

Radiation protection is of importance in radiography of the hip region. Use of gonad shields, however, may be inadvisable for an initial examination. A secondary radiation grid is usually required for radiography of this subject area.

(3) Anteroposterior single hip

The patient lies supine with the legs extended. The arms are folded across the chest. The pelvis must not be rotated therefore check that the anterior superior iliac spines are equidistant from the image receptor and place X-ray transparent pads under the subject to support him if necessary.

The legs must be equidistant about the median plane of the body. The toes point upwards if possible.

> *Central ray direction* – Perpendicular to the image receptor and centred to a point 2.5cm inferiorly along the bisector of an imaginary line drawn between the anterior superior iliac spine and upper border of the symphysis pubis of the side of interest.

Acetabulum
For techniques – *see* below.

Neck of femur and trochanters
The neck of femur is directed not only upwards and medially but also in a forward direction from the shaft of the bone. This means that in the position for the supine projection where the toes are pointing upwards (projections (3, 4)) the neck of the femur is not parallel to the image receptor. This produces a very slight degree of foreshortening of the neck of the femur. If the whole leg is medially rotated this has the effect of raising the *greater trochanter* away from the image receptor and reducing the foreshortening of the femoral neck. In injuries of the femoral neck or trochanteric region, the leg invariably falls outwards. This has the effect of increasing the degree of foreshortening but at the same time reveals the *lesser trochanter*. Where comparison of the two sides is made by referring to Shenton's line (*see* page 124); ideally both limbs and feet should be placed in the same degree of rotation although this is not always possible.

(4) Anteroposterior both hips

Same position as for projection (3). The arms are folded across the chest. In addition the median sagittal plane is placed to be coincident with the central longitudinal axis of the table. For comments on feet position – *see* [**ref 7:** 126].

Central ray direction – Vertical to a point 2.5 cm above the upper border of the symphysis pubis.

Congenital dislocation of the hip

See page 124.

(5) 'Turned lateral' single hip

From the supine position the patient is turned on to the affected side with the knee and hip flexed. The pelvis is tilted backwards through 45° and supported. The sound limb lies behind the affected limb.

Central ray direction – Perpendicular to the image receptor and centred over the upper third of the femur.

This position produces an oblique projection, for a 'true' lateral projection – *see* (7(i)).

(6) Lateral both hips ('frog's position')

The patient needs to have reasonably free movement at the hip and knee joints for this position. It is frequently used for children where comparisons of both sides are required. The patient lies supine with the hands placed on the chest. The hips and knees are flexed. From a position where the knees 'point' upwards the legs are externally rotated each through 60°. The soles of the feet are placed together. The knees should be supported on pads.

Central ray direction – Perpendicular to the image receptor and centred to a point 2.5 cm above the upper border of the symphysis pubis.

If the neck of femur is of special interest the outward degree of rotation should be reduced to 15° [**ref 7**: 130].

Injuries

The initial radiographic examination for fractures of the upper extremity of the femur should include an anteroposterior (3) and lateral projection (7(i)) of the hip. The lateral image is vital in the case of an *impacted fracture* of the neck of femur because it may not be apparent from the anteroposterior projection. It is also usual to take an anteroposterior view of the whole pelvis (*see* projection (8)) because the patient may have sustained other bony injuries

such as a fracture of the pubic rami. This is also necessary because of the occurrence of bilateral fractures [**ref 4**: 1617]. As so many of these patients are elderly and are most likely to have operative treatment, a chest radiograph taken at the same time avoids another visit to the radiology department for the patient.

(7) Lateral ('neck of femur')

The first projection (7(i)) is a 'true lateral' in the sense that it creates an image at 90° to the anteroposterior hip projection.

Projections (7(ii) – (iv)) are compromise solutions.

(i) *In cases of injury where the patient cannot be rotated, or when following up operative treatment.*

The patient remains supine. A cassette and grid is propped vertically against the affected side of the patient. The uppermost edge is pressed well into the patient's waist. The long axis of the cassette is parallel to the neck of the femur. Raise the sound limb from the table, flexing the knee and hip. The sound limb is rotated outwards at the hip joint and the foot should come to rest on a suitable support (*Figure 8.9*).

Central ray direction – Horizontal from the unaffected side of the patient to be perpendicular to and centred over the neck of the femur.

Collimate the X-ray beam as much as possible. Adequate flexion and external rotation of the sound hip is important in order to avoid superimposition of soft-tissue shadows of this leg over the head of femur on the side of interest.

For a discussion of patient dose reduction using an air gap technique rather than a secondary radiation grid – *see* [further reading **1**].

(ii) *Where the sound leg cannot be raised and the patient must not be rotated*

The cassette and grid is placed in the same position as for projection (7(i)) except that the cassette is tilted backwards by 25° and supported (*Figure 8.10*).

Central ray direction – Towards the neck of the femur as in projection (7(i)) except an additional tilt of 25° is made (from the horizontal and then towards the floor).

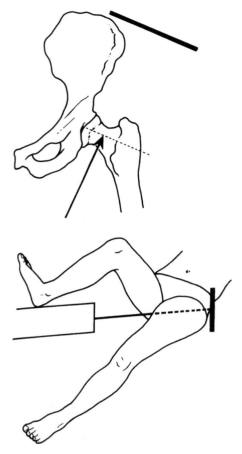

Figure 8.9 Position of the patient, cassette and direction of the x-ray beam in projection (7(i)) lateral 'neck of femur'.

The central ray should be perpendicular to the cassette.

(iii) If the sound leg cannot be raised but the trunk can be turned slightly.

From the anteroposterior position the pelvis is tilted so the hip under examination is raised above the level of the sound hip. Support the raised side on non-opaque pads. The cassette and grid are propped vertically against the outer aspect of the hip, its top edge pressed into the patient's waist. The long axis of the image receptor is parallel to the femoral neck.

Central ray direction – Horizontal and towards the upper end of the femur so the central ray is perpendicular to the cassette (Figure 8.11).

(iv) Where the patient cannot easily lie down or where there is limited movement at the hips.

The patient sits with his knees flexed over the end of the table. The cassette and grid is vertically supported at the side of the thigh and hip (*Figure 8.12*).

Central ray direction – Horizontal, from between the legs and towards the neck of femur.

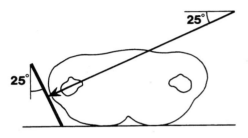

Figure 8.10 Position of cassette in projection (7(ii)).

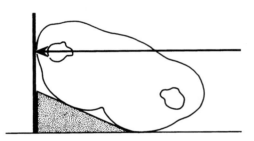

Figure 8.11 Position of cassette and direction of central ray in projection (7(iii)).

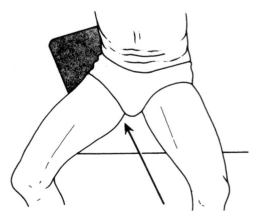

Figure 8.12 Position of cassette and direction of central ray in projection (7(iv)).

PELVIS: THE INNOMINATE BONES

Essential anatomical terminology *(Figure 8.13)*

The pelvic girdle is formed by the two *innominate bones* which are jointed anteriorly by the pubic *symphysis* (a cartilaginous joint). Posteriorly, the two *ilia* (wings) are separated by the wedge-shaped sacrum which forms the paired *sacroiliac joints*. The stable ring-like structure of the pelvis has two basic functions, to support the abdominal contents and to transmit the forces of weight bearing from the spine to the lower limbs. The term pelvis means basin. Anatomically it can be divided into two segments- the upper, wider *false pelvis* and the lower, narrow *true pelvis*. Intervening between the two segments is the *pelvic brim*. The characteristic differences between the male and the female pelvis have been the subject of much study for use in the fields of forensic science and anthropology. Anatomically the sacrum and coccyx form part of the vertebral column and are discussed in Chapter 9.

Indications for the X-ray examination

Injuries

Stable fractures of the pelvis

If the pelvic ring is broken either at its periphery or at one level (i.e. above or below hip level) then the fracture is stable (i.e. there will be no displacement). Sudden muscle contractions may lead to *avulsion fractures* of the anterior superior iliac spine (sartorius muscle), the anterior inferior iliac spine (rectus femoris) or the ischial tuberosity (hamstrings). Otherwise a single fracture may occur through the ilium or pubic ramus. This is usually caused by a direct blow and occurs rather more readily in the osteoporotic bones of the elderly. Double fractures of the pubic rami *(Figure 8.14)* may remain stable provided the sacroiliac ligaments are unaffected.

Complex fractures of the pelvis

Much more serious injuries exist where the continuity of the pelvic bony ring is broken. If

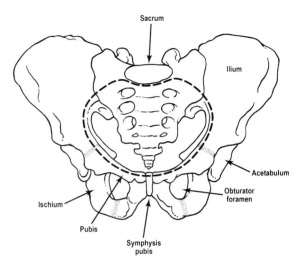

Figure 8.13 Bony pelvis. The pelvic brim is indicated by the dotted line.

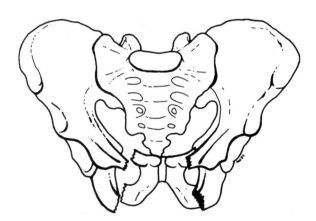

Figure 8.14 Fracture involving all four pubic rami.

there is disruption at two levels then there is potential for displacement. An example is given in *(Figure 8.15)*. Several combinations of injury are possible which may also include *diastasis* or widening of the symphysis or a sacroiliac joint. Pelvic ring fractures occur as the result of high-energy blunt trauma, such as encountered in road-traffic accidents and falls. The resultant pattern of injuries will reflect the direction of forces involved in its creation. *Anteroposterior compression* is often the result of a head-on motor vehicle collision where the patient is a passenger. *Lateral compression* injuries usually result from sideways impact motor vehicle collisions. *Vertical shear* injuries are

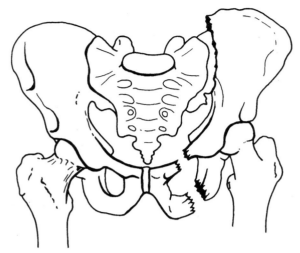

Figure 8.15 Disruption of the pelvic rim by a double fracture through the left ilium and both ischio-pubic rami.

typically the result of a fall from a height, but they can also occur in road-traffic accidents. Occasionally the direction of force is not solely aligned with one of the above three vectors and more than one pattern of injury may be evident [**ref 8**]. *CT* is indicated in all pelvic ring fractures or ligamentous disruptions in which stability is in question [**ref 3**: 3]. Complex injuries of the pelvis are often complicated by injury to pelvic blood vessels, nerves and viscera. Injury to the bladder and urethra are common because the lower ureters, bladder and urethra are closely related to the pelvis. The membranous part of the urethra is the most vulnerable part of the tract in the male. The rectum is usually only involved in more severe pelvic fractures in which case radiographically there may be fractures through the sacrum and coccyx and gas shadows outside the rectum may also be visible on the radiographs. The internal iliac artery is the main vessel involved in injuries of the pelvis; massive blood loss can occur and the patient may need large transfusions. Because of the serious nature of these complications, their treatment may take precedence over that of the bony injuries.

Fractures of the acetabulum

Fractures of the acetabulum disorder the hip joint and major disruption will usually lead to osteoarthritic degeneration in the long term.

[**ref 2**: 172]. The roof of the acetabulum may be fractured if the head of the femur is driven inwards and upwards towards the pelvic cavity. There are several degrees of injury, ranging from a small crack in the acetabulum to a complete medial displacement of both acetabulum and femoral head – *stove-in hip*. In about half the cases of *posterior dislocation* of the hip joint the head of the femur carries with it a fragment of bone from the posterior rim of the acetabulum. Otherwise the acetabulum may be involved in the more severe compression and vertically unstable fractures referred to above. Fractures of the acetabulum can be classified according to their location in the acetabulum. In the normal functioning pelvis, forces transmitted through the acetabulum are carried by two bony buttresses known as the *anterior (iliopubic) and posterior (ilioischial) column* (*Figure 8.16*). Either one or both of these columns may be fractured. Routine radiographs do not give sufficient detail of the acetabulum to allow

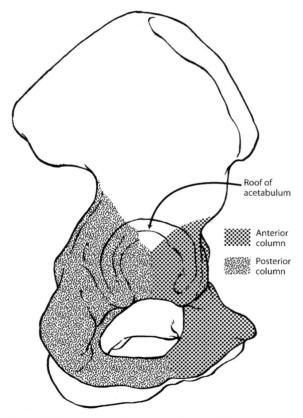

Roof of acetabulum

Anterior column

Posterior column

Figure 8.16 Anterior and posterior columns of the innominate bone.

classification of the type of fracture or the degree of displacement. Specialised projections and *CT* is usually required [**ref 2**: 172].

Other conditions of interest

Paget's disease

The pelvis is one of the bones commonly affected by Paget's disease. It may affect the pubis, ischium or ilium but sometimes only one side of the pelvis is involved. If the disease affects the acetabulum the hip joint may degenerate in a *secondary osteoarthritis* (*see* Chapter 3).

New growths

The pelvis may be affected by metastases from a primary tumour. A carcinoma of the prostate, for example, may spread via the bloodstream to the pubic bones.

Extrophy of the bladder

This is a rare congenital condition that involves the musculoskeletal structures of the lower abdomen and the genitourinary tract. There is a wide separation of the pubic bones, sometimes in association with rotational deformities of the pelvic bones around the sacroiliac joints.

Osteitis pubis

Osteitis pubis is a painful condition of uncertain aetiology that affects the pubic symphysis and surrounding tendinous attachments. One common cause stems from unusual biomechanical stress to the pelvis. The condition has been associated with parturition, trauma, non-urologic surgery, urinary tract infections, and arthritic disorders [**ref 10**]. The radiograph may show areas of sclerosis, bone destruction or both. Stress views (*see* below) may demonstrate instability of the symphysis.

Radiographic techniques – pelvis: innominate bones

Routinely only one projection is taken of the pelvis. In non-urgent cases bowel preparation may sometimes be necessary and protocols for radiography of women of childbearing age are adhered to; however, gonad protection in females may not be feasible and in males should be used with care.

(8) Anteroposterior pelvis

The patient is supine with the median sagittal plane coincident with the central longitudinal axis of the table. The arms folded across the chest. Both legs are extended and placed together and the positioning of the feet is symmetrical if possible. For a discussion on feet position – *see* [**ref 7**: 126]. A pillow can be placed under the patient's knees for comfort. The pelvis must be symmetrical – the anterior superior iliac spines must be positioned so that they are equidistant from the table top and image receptor. The position of the patient's legs may be used as a guide to any degree of rotation present. Correct the pelvis position using non-opaque pads.

> *Central ray direction* – Vertical and centred in the mid-line to a point between the level of the anterior superior iliac spines and the upper border of the symphysis pubis.

The whole pelvis must be included on the radiograph. If the patient is emaciated then the iliac bones may be over-exposed so a second radiograph may have to be taken. If the patient is of thin physique then the exposure may be made using only a cassette without a grid.

Injuries

Plain radiography is the initial imaging technique by which the pelvic ring is evaluated. Careful attempts should be made to place the patient in the standard position, but the degree of movement tolerated by the patient depends on the extent of injuries elsewhere. Serious fractures of the pelvic ring are nearly always caused by a crushing force therefore requests are also likely to be made for radiography of the abdomen and chest. Lateral projections of both abdomen and chest taken with a horizontally directed X-ray beam may show free gas in the peritoneal cavity from ruptured bowel and a lateral projection of the pelvis may also demonstrate a fracture of the sacrum or coccyx.

The anteroposterior projection (8) evaluates the anterior and posterior pelvic ring elements.

Supplementary techniques (12 and 13 and 14(ii)) should not be attempted with a badly injured patient. Projections (12) and (13) are sometimes referred to as *Judet's views* however that author did not specify either degree of patient rotation or direction of the central ray [**ref 7**].

(9) Pelvic inlet (caudad) projection

This shows the pelvic ring configuration better than projection (8). Any widening of narrowing of the ring diameter is immediately apparent. It is particularly useful for assessing medial displacement of fractures involving the acetabulum, iliopubic and ilioischical columns. It also demonstrates posterior displacement of the ilum at the sacroiliac joint. The patient position is the same for projection (8) however the central ray is directed 40° caudad to be approximately parallel to the long axis of the sacrum. The image receptor must be displaced downwards accordingly.

(10) Pelvic outlet or tangential (cephalad) projection

For evaluation of fractures of the ilium at the sacroiliac joint. This projection demonstrates the body of the sacrum and sacral foramina. The patient position is the same as for (8), however the central ray is directed 35° cephalad to be approximately perpendicular to the long axis of the sacrum.

(11) Lateral pelvis

With the patient remaining in the supine position, a cassette and grid are supported vertically at the side of the patient's pelvis.

Central ray direction – Horizontal and centred to a point 8 cm posterior to the anterior superior iliac spine of the side nearest the X-ray tube.

There is a tendency for the patient's sacrum and coccyx to sink into the mattress and thus be obscured by artefacts on the radiograph. Another problem is that this area may be projected off the bottom of the image receptor. To avoid this second situation, the cassette should be positioned so that its lower border is slightly below the level of the tabletop. A special cassette holder can be used for this purpose. To reduce magnification of the subject, position the patient as close to the cassette as possible.

(12) External (iliac) oblique projection

This demonstrates the posterior (ilioischial) column and anterior acetebular rim. From the supine position, the patient is rotated through 45 °, on to the affected side. The hips and knees are flexed and the raised side is supported. The image receptor lies behind the patient in the table bucky. (*See* also [**ref 7**: 138]).

Central ray direction – Perpendicular to the image receptor and centred over the hip joint of the affected side.

(13) Internal (obturator) oblique projection

This demonstrates the anterior (iliopubic) column and posterior acetabular rim. From the supine position the affected side is raised until the pelvis has been rotated through 45°. The posterior surface of the ilium of the raised side is now in profile. The hips and knees are flexed and the raised side is supported. The image receptor lies behind the patient in the table bucky. (*See* also [**ref 7**: 138]).

Central ray direction – Vertical and centred to a point 2.5 cm behind the anterior superior iliac spine of the raised side.

Increase the X-ray source to image receptor distance from the standard 100 cm to 120 cm to compensate for the larger subject to image receptor distance.

(14) Pubic bones and pubic symphysis

Localized projections:

(i) Position the patient as for projection (8): centre a vertical, collimated X-ray beam over the symphysis pubis.

(ii) *Profile projection* – From a sitting position, legs extended; the patient reclines backwards through 30° degrees and is supported. The patient's back makes an angle of 60° with the table. The pubic symphysis is now perpendicular to the image receptor placed beneath in the table bucky.

Central ray direction – Vertical and centred to a point over the symphysis pubis.

(iii) The pelvic inlet projection (9) will produce a similar appreearance.

Instability of the symphysis

These projections have been picturesquely named the 'flamingo views'. The patient stands with her back against the vertical bucky. Position otherwise as for projection (8). Two exposures are made, with the patient taking the full body weight on each leg in turn.

Central ray direction – Horizontal and centred to a point over the symphysis pubis.

This examination can be completed with the patient facing the image receptor.

References

1. Berquist TH (1991) *Imaging of Orthopaedic Trauma* New York: Raven Press

2. Dandy DJ and Edwards DJ (1998) *Essential Orthopaedics and Trauma (3rd Edition)* Edinburgh: Churchill Livingstone

3. Foster LM Barton ED (2001) Managing pelvic fractures, Part 2: physical and radiologic assessment *Journal of Critical Illness* May

4. Judet R Judet J Letournel E (1964) Fractures of the acetabulum: classification and surgical approaches for open reduction *Journal of Bone and Joint Surgery American* **46A**(8): 1615–1646

5. McRae R and Andrew W (1997) *Orthopaedics and trauma: an illustrated colour text* Edinburgh: Churchill Livingstone

6. Parker MJ (1992) Missed hip fractures *Archives of Emergency Medicine* **9**: 23–27

7. Swallow RA Naylor E Roebuck EJ Whitley AS (1986) *Clark's Positioning in Radiography (11th Edition)* London: Heinemann

8. Thornton DD (2002) *Pelvic Ring Fractures* http://www.emedicine.com/radio/topic546.htm accessed 08/10/2004

9. Trimble S (2000) Hip fractures: covering all angles *Synergy* November pages 8–11

10. Vitanzo PC McShane JM (2001) Osteitis pubis: solving a perplexing problem *The Physician and Sports Medicine* **29**(7)

Further reading

1. Barrall T (2004) Lateral hip air gap technique *Synergy* January pages 20–23

2. Pennal GF et al (1980) Pelvic disruption: assessment and classification *Clinical Orthopaedics* **151**: 12–21

The vertebral column

CHAPTER CONTENTS

Table of main and supplementary radiographic techniques

General anatomical area	Projection	Page	Common Indications
Cervical spine	1 AP C1-C3	144	Injury, pathology
	4 AP C3-C7 or	145	
	5 AP moving jaw	146	
	7 or 8 Lateral	147	
	9 Laterals flexion/extension	147	Instability
Neural arch, pillars, facet joints	10 Trauma obliques	148	Injury
	4 AP C3-C7 pillar view	146	
Intervertebral foraminae	6 AP obliques C1-C7	146	Foraminal encroachment Lateral root stenosis
Odontoid process	1 AP C1-C3 or	144	Injury
	5 AP moving jaw or	146	
	2iv AP axial or	144	
	2v PA axial	145	
	7 Lateral	147	
Atlanto-occipital joints	1 AP C1-C3	144	
	3ii Lateral	145	
Cervicothoracic junction	11 Lateral or	148	Injury
	12 'Swimmer's' lateral (*Twining*)	148	
Thoracic spine	13 AP	150	Injury, pathology
	14 Lateral	150–151	
	15 AP obliques	151	
Lumbar spine	16 AP L1-L5	155	Injury, pathology
	18 Lateral L1-S1	155–156	
	20 Laterals flexion/extension	156	Stability
	21 AP obliques	156	Spondylolisthesis
Lumbosacral junction	17 AP L5-S1	155	If not demonstrated
	19 Lateral L5-S1	156	on **16** and **18**
Sacrum, sacroiliac joints and coccyx	22 AP sacrum and coccyx	157–158	Injury, pathology
	23 Lateral sacrum and coccyx	158	
	24i Oblique sacroliliac joints	158	Ankylosing spondylitis
	24ii AP sacroiliac joints	158	

Typical effective radiation dose for a thoracic spine examination: **0.7 mSv**
Approximate equivalent period of natural background radiation: **4 months**
Typical effective radiation dose for a lumbar spine examination: **1 mSv**
Approximate equivalent period of natural background radiation: **5 months**

Essential anatomical terminology

The vertebral column is a complex anatomical structure. As part of the axial skeleton, it plays a role in transmission of body weight via the sacroiliac joints to the pelvis and lower limbs. The vertebral column is divided into five regions (*Figure 9.1*): the uppermost and more mobile *cervical spine*, the *thoracic (dorsal) spine* with which the ribs are articulated and the more massive *lumbar spine*. Below lie the fused, wedge-shaped *sacral* vertebrae articulating below with the rudimentary 'tail' (the *coccyx*) and on either side with the ilial section of the innominate bone forming the synovial *sacro-iliac joints*. When viewed from the side the normal vertebral column is seen to consist of a number of curves; a convex anterior-facing curve in the lumbar and cervical regions (*lordosis*) and a concave anterior-facing curve in the thoracic and sacral regions (*kyphosis*).

There are normally thirty-three vertebrae in all – seven cervical, twelve thoracic, five lumbar, five (fused) sacral and four coccygeal. Reference may be

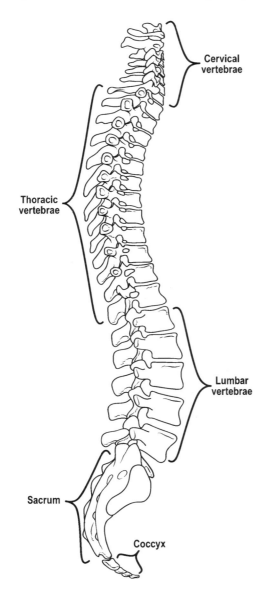

Cervical vertebrae

Thoracic vertebrae

Lumbar vertebrae

Sacrum

Coccyx

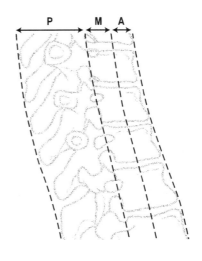

Figure 9.1 The regions of the vertebral column.
Inset shows the 'three column' spine:
A – anterior column
M – middle column
P – posterior column

made to individual vertebrae by naming each bone with a letter and number – for example – the second lumbar vertebra can be termed L2. Except for the uppermost two vertebral bones and the sacrum and coccyx; the cervical, dorsal and lumbar vertebrae are all roughly the same shape (*see – Figure* 9.2). There are two main component parts are the *body* and *neural arch*. The cylindrical *body* lies at the front forming symphyseal-type (anterior) cartilaginous joints with the bodies of the adjacent vertebrae via intervening *intervertebral discs*. These joints may be termed *discovertebral joints*. In the cervical region (C3–7) the body has a prominent lip on each side – the *uncinate processes*. These articulate with reciprocal grooves on the body of the vertebra above it. These are called *Luschka's joints* or *uncovertebral joints*. Their status as synovial or cartilaginous joints is uncertain (**ref 39:** 272). Posteriorly, the bony *neural arch* encloses the *spinal cord* or *spinal nerves* and *meningeal envelope*.

Each neural arch has a pair of superior and inferior articular processes carrying facets that form synovial plane (posterior) joints with the processes of the bones above and beneath it. These are also known as the *apophyseal* or *facet joints*. In the cervical region, the superior and inferior articular processes form an *articular pillar*, which bulges laterally at the junction of pedicle and lamina. The pillars may be termed the *lateral masses*. The first cervical vertebra (*atlas*) is ring-like in shape and articulates with the *occipital bone* of the skull forming the *atlanto-occipital joints*. The second cervical vertebra (*axis*) incorporates a peg-shaped process (*odontoid process*). This 'peg' articulates with the anterior arch of the atlas and is kept in place by a *transverse ligament*. Joints between axis and atlas may be termed *atlantoaxial*.

There are thirty-one pairs of spinal nerves, eight cervical, twelve thoracic, five lumbar, five sacral and one coccygeal. Individual spinal nerve pairs can be numbered using roman numerals to differentiate them from vertebral bones. Spinal nerves emerge from the *intervertebral foramina* (Figure 9.3). Cervical nerve roots exit above the level of the adjacent vertebral body (spinal nerve pair CVIII exits between vertebrae C7 and T1). In the rest of the spine the nerve roots exit below the adjacent bodies (spinal nerve pair TI at the intervertebral foramina between vertebrae T1 and T2).

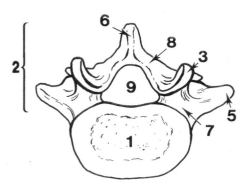

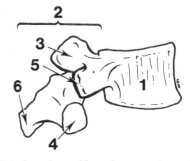

Figure 9.2 Superior and lateral aspects of a typical lumbar vertebra: **1,** *body;* **2,** *neural arch;* **3,** *superior articular process;* **4,** *inferior articular process;* **5,** *transverse process;* **6,** *spinous process;* **7,** *pedicle;* **8,** *lamina; and* **9,** *vertebral foramen.*

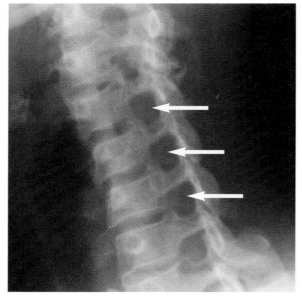

Figure 9.3 An anteroposteriorr oblique cervical spine radiograph. Intervertebral foramina are indicated with arrows.

Indications for the X-ray examination

Spinal injuries – general comments

An important element of vertebral column anatomy is the strong spinal ligaments that bind the vertebral bones. Trauma may result in damage to any of the bony or ligamentous structures of the spine either in isolation or in combination hence compromising the supportive role. Following trauma a critical element of assessment is determination of mechanical and neurological stability, i.e. to assess whether the spine is able to withstand stress without progressive deformity or further neurological damage [ref 24: 228].

Denis [ref 8] first described the concept of the 'three column spine' (*see* Figure 9.1) following a retrospective review of thoracolumbar spine injuries and observation of spinal instability. Allen [ref 1] extended this concept to the cervical spine. The three main elements or columns of the spine include both bony and ligamentous components. The columns may fail individually or in combination by four basic mechanisms of injury.

1. Compression
2. Distraction
3. Rotation
4. Shear

Major spinal injuries are classified into four different categories, all definable in terms of the degree of involvement of each of the three columns. The main concern is with the neurological elements and initially, radiography contributes to determining which structures are involved, the extent of the damage and assessment of risks of complication. *CT* provides essential additional information especially for occult fractures and for any spinal canal encroachment [ref 23: 64]. *MRI* provides visualisation of soft tissue and neural elements plus unsuspected traumatic disc herniations.

Categories of spinal injury are:

1. *Compression fracture* – failure of anterior column with intact middle column often caused by hyperflexion of the spine and results in *wedging* of vertebrae (*see – thoracic and lumbar spine injuries*, page 152).

2. *Burst fracture* – failure of both anterior and middle columns caused by axial loading of the spine. Bony fragments may be extruded into the spinal canal.

3. *Seat-belt fracture* – failure of posterior and middle columns caused by rapid deceleration exacerbated by use of lap-strap type seat belts. Failure entirely through the bone is termed a *Chance fracture* [ref 5].

4. *Fracture- dislocation* – all three columns fail from multi-directional forces (*see – thoracic and lumbar spine injuries*, page 152).

Further comments on spinal injuries in specific spinal regions are given below.

Other conditions of interest – general comments

There are many medical conditions that affect the vertebral column and are not features exclusive to a specific region. A few examples are degenerative changes such as *spondylosis, osteoarthritis* and *disc prolapse*. These may however be more common and have particular features in certain spinal regions, therefore additional related comments are made in each of the dedicated spinal sections below.

Spondylosis

Spondylosis is a term used particularly to describe degeneration of the intervertebral discs characterised by disc space narrowing and *osteophyte* formation (*Figure 9.4*). There is also likely to be chronic degeneration, i.e. *osteoarthritis* (*osteoarthrosis*) of the apophyseal and (in the cervical

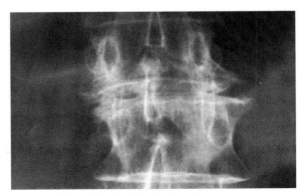

Figure 9.4 Spondylosis of the lumbar spine.

region) the uncovertebral joints. For practical purposes the two conditions may be considered together and treated as degenerative joint disease [**ref** 7: 421]. Degeneration of intervertebral discs is identifiable in some discs in nearly everyone over the age of sixty [**ref 34**: 2437]. Spondylosis may result in *spinal stenosis* (*see* – below) and foraminal encroachment by osteophytes (*lateral root stenosis*) leading to compression of spinal cord or spinal nerve roots respectively.

Osteoarthritis (osteoarthrosis)

For general comments and features – *see* Chapter 3.

Disc prolapse (slipped disc)

Each intervertebral disc consists of a dense fibrous collagenous tissue – the annulus fibrosus – which surrounds a softer gel-like centre – the nucleus pulposus. A major function of the discs is to act as 'shock absorbers' in the vertebral column. Problems are most likely to arise in the regions of the spine that are more mobile and also subject to the greatest strains and as part of a range of degenerative changes, lesions can occur in these discs. In *disc prolapse* the nucleus bulges through a rent in the annulus. This herniation can be in any direction and of varying degrees. If the disc prolapses backwards or posterolaterally, the nucleus may be extruded to impinge upon the contents of the spinal canal or on one of the issuing spinal nerves with resultant neuropathy. Plain radiographs will not demonstrate a disc prolapse (as will *MRI*) but they may exclude other pathology.

Spinal stenosis

The width of the spinal canal varies greatly in normal individuals [**ref 7**: 442] and stenosis is canal narrowing. Rarely it is congenital, more commonly it is acquired as a result of degenerative changes of *spondylosis* (*see* – above), trauma or *spondylolisthesis* (*see* page 153). Patients with stenosis are much more likely to develop *myelopathy* (dysfunction of the spinal cord). They are also more susceptible to cord or nerve root damage from minor trauma [**ref 36**: 147].

New growths

In the spine the majority of these are secondary metastatic deposits from a primary – usually a carcinoma of the breast or lung. The tumour may cause collapse of a vertebral body. Primary tumours arising from either the bone or the contents of the spinal canal are quite rare. Tumours of the nerve tissue only infrequently cause changes in the surrounding bony structures.

CERVICAL SPINE

Indications for the X-ray examination

Cervical spine injuries

For general comments on spinal injuries – *see* above.

For a discussion of patterns of cervical spine injury and percentage distribution of vertebral arch and body fractures – *see* [**ref 26**].

Injuries to the cervical spine are common and tend to occur in falls and in road traffic accidents. Neck injuries are often found in combination with head injuries and may be difficult to assess because the patient may be unconscious at the time of examination. These patients must be handled with care during the initial X-ray examination and until the extent of damage is known. In all injuries to the vertebral column there is always a danger of damage to the spinal cord. This damage may be in the form of interference with the blood supply, compression, contusion (bruising) or transection (tearing). In the cervical spine the canal is fairly wide so there is a greater chance of the cord escaping severe damage than if the injury were in a lower part of the spine. If cord injury does occur the outcome will either be fatal or the patient will have some degree of impairment. The most vulnerable part of the cord lies anteriorly, affecting firstly the motor supply of the upper limbs before the motor pathways to the lower limbs. Next to be involved are the spinothalamic tracts carrying pain and temperature, and lastly the posterior columns carrying proprioception and touch. The *phrenic nerve* provides the motor supply to the diaphragm and arises mainly from the fourth cervical segment (at about the level of the body of C4). Any injury to the spinal cord above this level may cause immediate cessation of respiration and death. The upper limbs are innervated by the fifth cervical to the first thoracic segments via the brachial plexus.

If the patient has injury at a lower cervical level (a common site) then the patient may have quadriplegia but it is still possible for a good deal of arm function to remain.

Injuries of the cervical spine are grouped according to the mechanism that caused them [**ref 24**: 234]. Traumatologists refer to *compression, flexion* and *extension* injuries – although rotational forces may also play a part. The *whiplash injury* is common in motorists whose cars are 'shunted' from behind and into another vehicle in front. The neck is hyperextended and then rapidly flexed; bony or soft tissue injuries result giving rise to clinical signs and symptoms. The term 'whiplash' has been devalued so that some now use it to refer to virtually any soft tissue injury to the neck [**ref 23**: 62].

Subluxation

Because the posterior intervertebral joints are more horizontally inclined and laterally placed in comparison with the same joints in the rest of the spine, subluxations and dislocations of these facet joints are far more common than elsewhere. Forceful flexion with rotation of the neck may cause subluxation of one or both of a pair of joints (*Figure 9.5*). A more serious injury involves true dislocation. It should be emphasized that the degree of anatomical abnormality demonstrated on the radiographs may not bear any relationship to the degree of cord damage present. Dislocation of the posterior vertebral joints may result in quadriplegia for the patient but the radiograph may be 'normal' because the dislocation has undergone a spontaneous reduction.

Extension injuries may cause tearing of the spinal longitudinal ligaments. Fracture of the lower spinous processes and neural arches may sometimes occur when the head is driven backwards. Extension injuries are particularly common in middle aged and elderly people where the spine is more rigid [**ref 24**:241].

Lateral mass (articular pillar) fractures

Fractures of this area of individual cervical vertebrae are relatively common in patients with *whiplash injury*. In one large study of 399 patients, 21% had a fracture at this site [**ref 26**].

Burst fractures (see – above)

Examples of causes include heavy objects falling on the head or where the vertex of the head strikes the ground as in falls or swimming-pool dives. Depending on the level of force a vertebral body may be simply split or – more seriously – comminuted such as in the *Jefferson fracture*.

Fracture of the atlas (Jefferson fracture) (Figure 9.6)

A quadripartite burst fracture of the atlas [**ref 20**]. Both lateral masses are displaced sideways. In some cases this injury will cause immediate death because of cord compression. 50% of patients survive this injury without significant neurological involvement [**ref 21**].

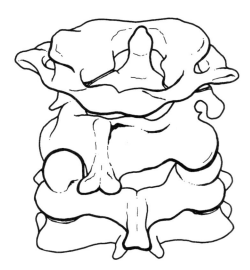

Figure 9.5 Posterior aspect of the upper cervical vertebrae, showing dislocation of an intervertebral joint on one side.

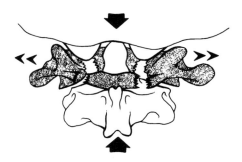

Figure 9.6 Jefferson fracture of the atlas. Forces directed along the axial skeleton results in the 'splitting' of the bone.

Posterior arch of the atlas (C1) fracture

Owing to hyperextension of the neck, the arch is compressed between the occiput and the posterior arch of the axis.

Fractures of the axis (C2) (Figure 9.7)

Fractures usually occur at the base of the odontoid peg [**ref 2**] as a result of severe flexion/extension injury of the neck. The fragment can be displaced together with the atlas in either a forward or backward direction. If there is a rupture of the transverse ligament of the atlas, which crosses immediately behind the peg, then the atlas can be dislocated and the outcome may be fatal cord compression.

Other conditions of interest

Cervical spondylosis

Cervical spondylosis is probably the commonest cause of the syndrome of neck and upper arm pain. Neck movements are likely to be restricted. Some patients may be symptom-free [**ref 23**: 56]. The vertebral joints between the fifth, sixth and seventh cervical vertebrae are most likely to be affected. (*See* also *lumbar spondylosis*, page 153).

Cervical disc prolapse

Wear and tear seems to have more effect on the lower region of the cervical vertebra, and the intervertebral discs that are involved in spondylosis are also the ones most likely to prolapse. This condition is not as common in the cervical spine as it is in the lumbar region but the disc lesion is the same in either case (*see* page 140). Irritation of a nerve root caused by the prolapsed disc may result in the patient experiencing pains radiating down the arm (*brachial neuralgia*) and motor nerve weakness.

Torticollis (wry neck)

The term means twisted neck. This is a condition in which the neck lies in abnormal lateral flexion with both the head and the neck also rotated to the same side. There is a host of underlying pathologies [**ref 32**] but torticollis may be caused by spasm in the sternomastoid and trapezius muscles following trauma to the neck. It is also often associated with cervical disc prolapse. *Congenital torticollis* is not a true developmental defect, but it is due to a birth injury that causes fibrosis in one sternomastoid muscle and as a result during growth a torticollis forms.

Thoracic outlet syndrome

Compression of the subclavian artery and the lower trunk of the brachial plexus may cause symptoms to arise in the limb of their supply. The area bounded by the first ribs is known as the thoracic outlet and symptoms arising from causes in this area are referred to as the thoracic outlet syndrome. The vessel and nerve trunk may be compressed by the tightness of the scalene muscles or by the presence of a supplementary rib arising from the seventh cervical vertebra. *Cervical ribs (Figure 9.8)* vary greatly in size and shape and clinical symptoms bear little relationship to the radiographic abnormality. A very small cervical rib may have a fibrous band attachment that causes much impairment for the patient, whereas a large rib may produce no problems at all. Cervical ribs occur in about 6% of the population [**ref 34**: 2412].

Rheumatoid arthritis

The transverse ligament restrains any backward travel of the odontoid peg but it may be torn in injury or become attenuated and ruptured in rheumatoid arthritis (**ref 24**: 221). Whilst rheumatoid arthritis in the cervical spine is common (**ref 23**: 56) many patients are relatively asymptomatic. The manipulation of the neck needed to intubate the patient for anaesthesia is

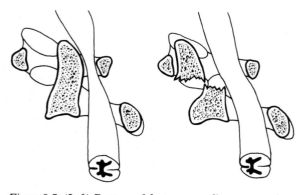

Figure 9.7 (Left) Rupture of the transverse ligament causing dislocation of the entire axis. (Right) Fracture at the base of the odontoid peg with posterior displacement of the rest of the bone.

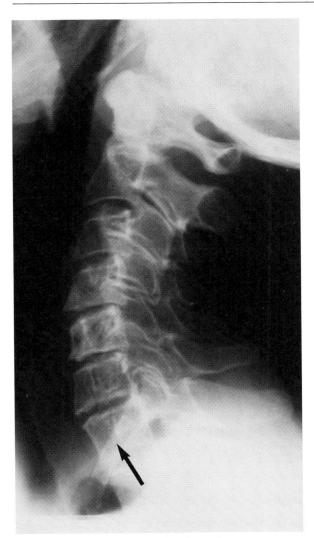

Figure 9.8 Cervical rib – lateral radiograph.

hazardous therefore a prior radiological assessment is required. Vertical subluxation of the odontoid process through the foramen magnum is one of most serious complications of rheumatoid disease [**ref 16**]. This condition may be termed *atlanto-axial impaction*. (*See* also *basilar invagination* page 169).

Developmental anomalies and anatomic variants

These can provide sources of diagnostic error, for example *os odontoideum* where the odontoid peg is completely detached from the body of the second cervical vertebrae. For a list of some of these anomalies of the upper cervical spine – *see* [**ref 36**: 46–7]

Klippel-Feil syndrome (Figure 9.9)

This is a developmental defect where two or more cervical vertebrae are fused, the neck is short and its movements are restricted. Other congenital anomalies such as *Sprengel's shoulder*, *spina bifida* and rib lesions usually coexist.

Radiographic techniques – general comments on projection radiography of the spine

Two projections of the specified area taken at right angles to each other were until relatively recently (in the UK) considered to be the minimal requirements for an examination of the spine.

Modern protocols may limit the number of projections to a single lateral (for example) in certain categories of patient complaining of back

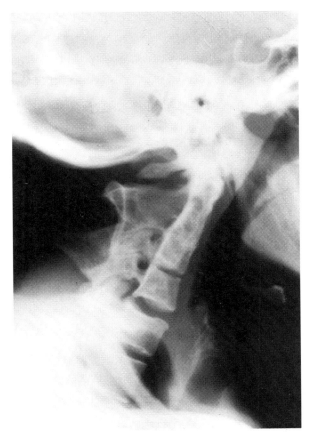

Figure 9.9 Lateral radiograph of the cervical spine in Klippel-Feil syndrome.

pain. Anteroposterior and lateral projections then, are otherwise the standard procedure. Where further information is needed concerning the neural arch, the *posterior, facet* or *apophyseal joints* between the superior and inferior articular processes and the *intervertebral foramina*, oblique projections are taken. For the thoracic and lumbar spines conventional radiographic technique requires images to be made with the subject recumbent. It is usual practice to use a secondary radiation grid when examining the spine with the lateral projection of the cervical spine as a possible exception. Effects of weight bearing on alignment are best visualised with the subject standing or sitting. (*See* also [further reading **12**]). Researchers have concluded that helical *CT* can depict significant fractures not shown by plain radiography and should be added routinely to the initial screening in polytrauma victims [**ref 29**].

Radiographic techniques – cervical spine

The positioning may be undertaken with the patient seated unless the patient's condition precludes this. This position is chosen first for reasons of convenience, and secondly because gravity tends to aid depression of the shoulders – important in the lateral projection (7). For planes and lines of reference for positioning of the head in cervical spine techniques refer to Chapter 10. For patients with suspected injury – *see* projection (7) and (8) first.

(1) Anteroposterior C1 – C3

To reveal the upper cervical vertebrae the patient must be radiographed with the mouth open. The head must be carefully positioned so that neither teeth, alveolar process of maxillae nor occiput obscure the vertebrae. The patient lies supine or stands erect facing the X-ray tube. The median sagittal plane remains perpendicular to the table and image receptor. The patient is asked to open the mouth wide and the head is adjusted until the maxillae are felt to be superimposed on the occiput (*Figure 9.10*). The head must be immobilized. The mouth can be held open with a non-opaque bite-block.

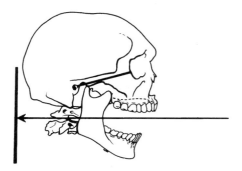

Figure 9.10 The principles of relative patient and X-ray beam positioning in projection (1). The dotted line represents the hard palate.

Central ray direction – Through the midline of the open mouth parallel to a line joining the upper incisors (or hard palate if edentulous) with the lower margin of the occipital bone.

Note – The central ray does not have to be perpendicular to the image receptor. Generally the X-ray tube makes an angle of 20° with the orbitomeatal base line. The important principle is that the beam is tangential to the obscuring bones of the base of skull and face.

The 'open-mouth' view is inadequate in intubated patients and will miss up to 17% of injuries to the upper cervical spine [**ref 15**]. It should be replaced by a *CT* scan from the occiput to C2.

(2) Odontoid process (dens)

This is demonstrated in the following projections:

(i)   *Anteroposterior CI–C3* – As for projection (1).

(ii) *Lateral CI–C7* – As for projection (7).

(iii) *Anteroposterior CI–C7* – As for projection (5) – moving jaw technique.

Where the patient cannot open the mouth or where visualization in the normal anteroposterior projection is impossible because of a condition such as *basilar invagination*, alternative projections (iv–vii) are available:

(iv) *Anteroposterior axial* – The patient lies supine or stands erect facing the X-ray tube. The median sagittal plane is placed perpendicular to the image receptor. The orbitomeatal base line is raised to be 45° to the image receptor.

Central ray direction – Central ray is angled 35 ° cephalad and centred to a point midway between the external auditory meatus (EAMs).

(*See* – also [**ref 3**: 299] *Fuch* method).

(v) *Posteroanterior axial* – The patient is prone or erect. The medial sagittal plane is placed perpendicular to the image receptor. The orbitomeatal base line is raised to be 45° to the image receptor.

Central ray direction – Central ray is angled 30° caudad and centred to a point midway between the EAMs.

(*See* – also [**ref 3**: 299] *Judd* method).

The odontoid process is also demonstrated in the following:

(vi) *Lateral* for atlanto-occipital joints [projection (3(ii))].

(vii) *Anteroposterior obliques* for atlanto-occipital joints – *see* [**ref 35**: 149].

(viii) *Submentovertical skull* (projection (7), page 175).

There may be doubt over the presence of a fracture of the process. This could be due to artefactual shadows. A common example is the cleft between the two upper incisor teeth which can be 'projected' on to the process in projection (1) and be mistaken for a vertical split. If doubt arises from the initial radiograph then a second anteroposterior projection (1) could be taken with the X-ray tube at a slightly different angle. (*See* also [further reading 5] for normal variants simulating disease and [further reading **6**] for pseudofractures (Mach bands) affecting the dens). Because of the problems associated with plain radiography of this area, use of *CT* is an important option.

(3) *Atlas and atlanto-occipital joints*

(i) *Anteroposterior C1-C3 (projection (1))* – The articulations can occasionally be demonstrated by the AP projection when the patient is edentulous [**ref 35**: 148]

(ii) *Lateral atlanto-occipital joints* – The median sagittal plane is placed parallel to the cassette and grid.

Central ray direction – Perpendicular to the image receptor and centred to a point 2.5 cm below the EAM.

The joints are overshadowed by the mastoid processes of the temporal bone in the lateral projection.

(4) *Anteroposterior C3 – C7*

The jaw or occiput will obscure the upper two vertebrae in this projection. The patient lies supine or stands erect facing the X-ray tube. The median sagittal plane is perpendicular to the image receptor. Raise the chin slightly with the overall aim to superimpose the lower border of the jaw on the occiput when the X-ray tube is angled appropriately. The lower border of the mandible is placed at 90° to the image receptor is a useful guide.

Central ray direction – Central ray is angled 5° – 15° cephalad and centred over the thyroid cartilage (C5) in the midline.

Another approach is to use a 'straight' X-ray beam directed towards the sternal notch with open collimators so that the beam will include C3 (*Figure 9.11*). Lead protection over the sternal area must be used in this case.

Neck held in flexion

Where the patient cannot raise the chin adequately an additional cephalad X-ray tube angulation can be made to project the jaw upwards away from the spine.

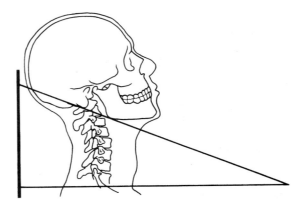

Figure 9.11 Patient positioning in projection (4). Centring over the sternal notch is an option provided that appropriate radiation protection is applied to the sternal area.

Torticollis

With the patient supine it may sometimes be possible to assist the patient *gently* to straighten the rotation of the head. Otherwise the anteroposterior projection will have to be taken in whatever position the patient can manage.

Cervical rib

A collimated view can also be taken of the area; position as for projection (4).

> *Central ray direction* – Central ray is angled 15° cephalad and centred over the sternal notch.

Pillar view (lateral mass, en-face view)

This is an anteroposterior projection with the patient's neck hyperextended and the X-ray beam angled 25 – 30° caudad and directed toward the thyroid cartilage [**ref 17**]. (*See* also [**further reading 13**]). Clark [**ref 35**: 157] recommends rotating the head to either side in turn so that the mandible will not be superimposed on the vertebral arches on that side. The beam is angled caudally 35° and centred to a point just posterior to the angle of the mandible remote from the image receptor. This projection helps to evaluate the articular pillars and laminae (but it is likely that *CT* would be used instead).

(5) Anteroposterior C1 – C7 (moving jaw, diffusion technique)

This can be used as an alternative to projections (1) and (4) although not following trauma. With the patient supine, position the head as for projection (1) and immobilize it adequately. Ask the patient to open and close the mouth gently and slowly in a continuous fashion. Rehearse this before making the exposure.

> *Central ray direction* – Perpendicular to the image receptor and centred over the lower tip of the symphysis menti.

Use a long exposure time – for example – 4 seconds. The mouth movement during the exposure causes the jaw image to be diffused over the cervical spine. An eponymous term for this projection is *Ottonello* [**ref 3**: 300]. It has also been picturesquely termed 'waggy jaw'.

(6) Anteroposterior obliques C1 – C7

These projections give more information about structures of the neural arch and allow assessment of the exit foramina. The patient sits on a rotating stool with his back to the vertical bucky and image receptor. Rotate the patient's whole body through 45° towards one side. Continue turning the head until the median sagittal plane of the head is parallel to the image receptor (*Figure 9.12*). Raise the chin slightly.

> *Central ray direction* – Perpendicular to the image receptor and centred over the sternomastoid muscle at mid-neck level of the side nearest the X-ray tube.

Angulation of the X-ray tube cephalad (e.g. by 15°) may improve visualization of the foramina especially where the cervical lordosis is exaggerated. Repeat for the other side. The foramina demonstrated are on the side of the neck nearest the X-ray tube. These 45° obliques may be carried out in a position for a posteroanterior oblique projection with appropriate reversed X-ray tube angulation, in which case the foramina demonstrated are on the side nearest the image receptor.

Figure 9.12 Patient positioning for a left anteroposterior oblique projection of the cervical spine.

(7) Lateral CI – C7

This is the most important radiographic view [**ref 4**: 42].

The patient sits in the general lateral position with the affected side (if relevant) nearest the image receptor. The shoulder touches the cassette. The median sagittal plane is placed parallel to the image receptor and the chin is raised slightly to move the jaw angle away from the vertebrae (*Figure 9.13*). The lower border of the cassette must be at shoulder level and the shoulders depressed as far as possible so that C7 is included on the radiograph. Where difficulty in demonstrating C7 is experienced refer to the techniques for the cervicothoracic junction (projections (11 and 12).

> *Central ray direction* – Perpendicular to the image receptor and centred 2.5 cm behind the angle of the jaw over C3.

The focus to image receptor distance is increased to 150cm from the standard 100cm because of the large subject to image receptor distance.

Alternative technique – projection (8).

Figure 9.13 Patient positioning for a left lateral projection of the cervical spine.

(8) Where the patient must be examined in a horizontal position

Patients with suspected bony injury to the neck will be brought to the department on a trolley.

The lateral projection (8) must be taken first with the orthopaedic collar or other support remaining in situ. The image is inspected before any further movement of the head and neck are permitted. The rule is always to seek medical advice or assistance – and take great care. For the lateral projection – the patient lies supine. The shoulders are equidistant from the tabletop. A cassette is propped vertically alongside the patient's neck, its lower border lying below the level of the shoulder. The head and neck are adjusted so that the median sagittal plane is parallel to the image receptor. If at the first attempt the cervicothoracic junction is not demonstrated then two assistants, i.e. usually medical and nursing professionals, co-ordinated by the radiographer (and given radiation protection) will pull downwards on the patient's arms so that the lower cervical vertebrae are shown on the radiograph. If possible the 'pull' takes place with the patient suspending expiration, the arm pressure is then increased and the exposure is made. A single person pulls asymmetrically, and poorly on one side, increasing the danger to both patient and puller.

> *Central ray direction* – As for projection (7).

Torticollis

The cassette for the initial radiograph should be positioned on the side away from the tilted neck and a horizontal beam centred just above the shoulder nearest the X-ray tube. Immobilization may be aided if the patient is supine. More than one lateral projection may be required in order to demonstrate all the cervical vertebrae.

(9) Laterals in flexion and extension

These will show changes in alignment of the cervical vertebrae in cases of instability caused by injury. They should not be undertaken at an initial examination unless under appropriate sanction and supervision. Flexion and extension views may be carried out later during treatment management to confirm that the spine is stable. Using fluoroscopy is an option [**ref 6**].

Rheumatoid arthritis – possible atlanto-axial subluxation

A single lateral cervical spine radiograph with the patient in supervised comfortable flexion is recommended [**ref 30**: 37].

(10) *Trauma oblique projections*

Projections similar to (6); these show the pedicles, articular processes and facet joints. The patient remains supine; the cassette is centered at the level of the thyroid prominence (C5) and displaced to one side to allow for the oblique direction of the X-ray beam.

> *Central ray direction* – Towards the middle of the neck on the side nearest the X-ray tube at the level of C5 with the central ray angled 45° transverse to the median sagittal plane and 15° cranially.

The procedure is repeated for the other side of the neck. A 30° transverse angulation has been recommended to improve delineation of posterior elements and facet joints compared with 45° [**ref 38**: 66].

Radiographic techniques – cervicothoracic junction

The shoulders largely obscure this region of the vertebral column in the lateral aspect. Failure to produce a lateral or alternative projection in cases of injury may result in an abnormality of C7 being missed unless *CT* can be accessed. Projection (11) may reveal C7 and T1 in the suitably ambulant subject. For a supine subject, if projection (8) has failed to show the junction then projection (12) is the popular alternative method for demonstrating the lower cervical and upper thoracic spine.

(11) *Lateral*

Position and direct the X-ray beam as for projection (7). Sandbags are held in each hand to aid depression of the shoulders. In most patients C7 will be shown. The exposure can be increased from projection (7).

(12) *'Swimmer's' lateral (Twining)*

The patient sits or lies with the median sagittal plane parallel to the image receptor. The arm nearest the image receptor is folded over the head. The posterior aspect of the raised arm and the axilla touch the support (Figure 9.14). The other arm lies in internal rotation along the side of the trunk, this shoulder being depressed as far as possible.

> *Central ray direction* – Perpendicular to the image receptor and centred to a point just above the shoulder nearest the X-ray tube so that the central ray passes through the axilla nearest the image receptor.

An eponymous term for this projection is *Twining* [**ref 3**: 279].

In a study [**ref 19**], it was concluded that 'swimmer's view' and trauma obliques show the alignment of the vertebral bodies with equal frequency. However it was found that supine oblique radiographs expose patients to less radiation and are more often successful in demonstrating the posterior elements.

Figure 9.14 Patient positioning for a right 'swimmer's projection of the cervical spine.

THORACIC SPINE

Indications for the X-ray examination

Injuries

For general comments on spinal injuries *see* – page 139 and for thoracic and lumbar spine injuries *see* – page 152.

Other conditions of interest

Kyphosis

The normal anteroposterior curve of the thoracic vertebrae is called the thoracic kyphosis and the range of convexity in normal subjects is discussed in [further reading **3**]. The term can also be used to denote an abnormally accentuated curve and there are several pathological causes. If a vertebral body collapses and becomes wedge shaped as a result of trauma or pathology such as tuberculosis then there tends to be an associated angular increase in the curve. This is known as a *kyphos* or *gibbus*. If pathological involvement includes several or all of the vertebral bodies then there will be a general rather than an angular increase in the curvature – for example – in *ankylosing spondylitis, Paget's disease* and *osteoporosis* (*see* Chapter 3).

Senile kyphosis

In old age some individuals tend to develop a kyphosis and consequently lose height. This can be because of a combination of vertebral flattening and wedging as the bones undergo changes of *senile osteoporosis* (*see* Chapter 3). Degenerating intervertebral discs also have a tendency to become reduced in thickness as age advances and this partially accounts for the loss in height.

Scheuermann's kyphosis *(Figure 9.15)*

In 1920 Scheuermann [**ref 33**] described a condition that causes an increase in the normal anteroposterior curve of the thoracic and thoracolumbar spine in adolescents. Until puberty the upper and lower surfaces of the vertebral bodies are cartilaginous. At this time two annular epiphyses for the circumferential parts of the upper and lower surfaces of the body appear. These secondary centres fuse with the rest of the bone at

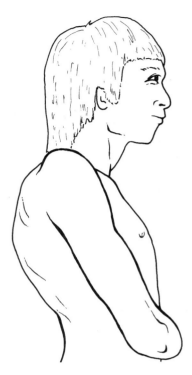

Figure 9.15 Adolescent kyphosis.

about the age of 25 years. In adolescent kyphosis these annular epiphyses seem to develop abnormally so the vertebral bodies fail to grow properly and become wedge shaped. This view is apparently controversial – many theories have been proposed for the etiology of this disease, but the true cause remains unclear [**ref 22**]. There is a multiplicity of synonyms for this condition.

Disc prolapse

This is rare, accounting for less than 0.5% of cases. It tends to occur at the level of T10 – T12, with chronic presentation [**ref 23**: 52].

Scoliosis

Scoliosis is a complex condition that is most simply defined as a lateral curve or tilt of a part of the spine. The Scoliosis Research Society has defined scoliosis as a lateral curvature of the spine greater than 10° as measured using the Cobb method [further reading **2**] on a standing radiograph [**ref 14**]. In addition to this lateral curvature there is often also a rotation of the vertebral column around its longitudinal axis. If the scoliosis is in the thoracic spine the ribs are distorted by the rotation, producing a hump on one side. This deformity of the chest cage may interfere with lung function. Patients with severely deformed chests are more prone to recurrent chest infections. These and other structural changes and defects are part of what is known as *structural scoliosis*. The most common type of structural scoliosis is *adolescent idiopathic scoliosis* (Figure 9.16). Its cause is thought to be multifactorial with genetic, metabolic and growth disorders all making a contribution [**ref 23**: 48]. Other structurally scoliotic spines can be attributed to some congenital vertebral defect or neuromuscular problem – for example – poliomyelitis. Treatment depends on severity and varies from observation for mild cases to bracing (external splinting) and surgery in more severe cases.

Tuberculosis of the spine (tuberculous spondylitis) (Pott's disease)

The thoracolumbar spine is the most common extrapulmonary site of tuberculsosis [**ref 18**]. The original focus of the disease is in a vertebral body

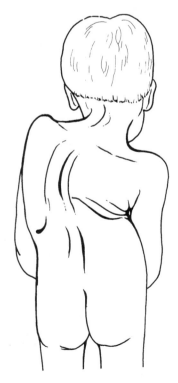

Figure 9.16 Untreated idiopathic scoliosis.

from where it spreads and destroys the neighbouring disc and adjacent vertebral body. As the bone collapses it may produce an angular deformity of the spine (kyphos). A paravertebral abscess is formed which surrounds the vertebral bodies. In the lower dorsal and lumbar regions, pus may spread into the neighbouring psoas muscle sheath to form a psoas abscess. If the disease in the thoracic region spreads posteriorly, the spinal canal may become narrowed and pressure on the spinal cord may result in *Pott's paraplegia*.

Developmental anomalies and anatomic variants

These can provide sources of diagnostic error. For a list of some of these anomalies of the thoracic spine (*see* [**ref 36**: 162]).

Radiographic techniques – thoracic spine

For general comments on projection radiography of the spine (*see* page 143).

(13)   *Anteroposterior thoracic spine*

The patient lies supine with the arms by the sides. The shoulders and anterior superior iliac spines of the pelvis are placed equidistant from the tabletop. The head should be supported on a pad or pillow. The image receptor is positioned to include cervico-thoracic and thoraco-lumbar spine junctions.

> *Central ray direction* – Perpendicular to the image receptor and centred to a point 2.5 cm below the sternal angle.

Expose on deep arrested inspiration. The steep variance in physical density of the overlying structures – trachea, heart and diaphragm – may make it necessary for separate radiographs to be exposed to demonstrate adequately all of the thoracic vertebrae. Specialised radiographic 'filters' placed between the X-ray source and patient have been produced to even out this subject density.

(14) *Lateral*

The patient lies on the affected side with his back to the radiographer. The patient's hips and knees are flexed for support. Raise both arms over the head, placing the lower arm under the pillow. The long axis of the vertebrae should be parallel to the image receptor and perpendicular to the central ray if the disc joint spaces are to be demonstrated. Adjust the position with non-opaque pads. The surface of the patient's back should be seen to be perpendicular to the tabletop, i.e. rotation must be avoided. Check that the ilia and shoulders are superimposed and that the patient is immobilized.

Central ray direction – Perpendicular to the long axis of the thoracic spine and centred over the mid-axillary line and the level of T6.

Expose on deep arrested inspiration; or if the patient's thorax is immobilized – for example – with a broad bucky band a long exposure time can be used with the patient breathing gently to produce diffusion of lung markings and ribs over the vertebrae. This latter technique has been discontinued due to concerns over high radiation dose (*see* [**ref 37**]). In the lower thoracic region there is an abrupt change in subject density due to the transition from over-shadowing by lung to diaphragm. More than one radiographic exposure may be necessary to demonstrate both lower thoracic and upper lumbar vertebrae.

(15) Anteroposterior obliques

These projections demonstrate the costo-vertebral joints on the side nearest the image receptor but do not demonstrate the apophyseal joints [**ref 35**: 164]. From the positioning for the anteroposterior projection the patient is rotated 45° to either side and supported appropriately.

Central ray direction – Perpendicular to the image receptor to a point 5 cm below the level of the sternal angle and in the mid-clavicular line of the raised side.

Kyphosis and kyphos

Where there is a generalized increase in spinal curvature supine positioning for the anteroposterior projection may be possible. To prevent discomfort non-opaque pads should be placed under the patient to give adequate support. Where a sharp angulation is present (possibly due to more acute pathology) or where the patient would suffer discomfort in lying on his back, erect positioning for the antero-posterior radiograph will be preferable.

Central ray direction – To the apex of the spinal curve (see Figure 9.17).

In extreme cases it may be difficult to produce an acceptable projection and more than one image may be required with appropriate tube angulation. Note that the lateral projection may require a lot less exposure than the anteroposterior because the vertebrae may be very prominent.

Adolescent idiopathic scoliosis

Once a diagnosis of scoliosis has been made, the primary concerns are whether there is an underlying cause and whether the curve will progress. Radiographic evaluation is undertaken with a posteroanterior projection to allow measurement of the spinal curvature. (Using a PA projection reduces the dose to breast tissue and bone marrow is six time less sensitive than breast tissue [**ref 34**: 2467]). Future growth potential is assessed by grading of the iliac apophysis. Posteroanterior projections with the patient side bending may be used pre-operatively for selecting fusion levels [**ref 34**: 2467]. For radiation dose reduction – *see* [**ref 10**] and for evaluation using digital radiography and fluoroscopy – *see* [**ref 11**].

Injuries – *see lumbar spine radiographic techniques*

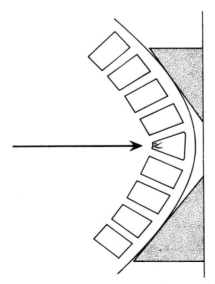

Figure 9.17 Centring the X-ray beam to the apex of the spinal curve.

LUMBAR SPINE

Indications for the X-ray examination

Lumbar (and thoracic) spine injuries

See page 139 for general comments on spinal injuries.

Wedge fractures of vertebral bodies

From the dorsal to the upper lumbar region the curve and movement of the spine are predominantly of flexion. If a force acts along the vertical axis of the spine in either direction then the vertebral column will probably *hyperflex*. The anterior portion of one or more vertebral bodies will be compressed. These crush or *wedge fractures* (*Figure 9.18*) are the commonest in the thoracic and thoracolumbar regions of the spine, especially in the osteoporotic bones of the elderly whose bones often need minimal trauma before they are damaged (*see* Chapter 3). Wedge compression fractures tend to heal fairly easily but there may be a residual wedge deformity in the affected bone (*see* also *kyphosis*, page 149).

Fracture–dislocations

In spinal injuries the danger of associated damage to nerve roots and cord is of prime importance and this danger is always greatly increased when fractures of the neural arch permits a fracture dislocation to develop. From the thoracic to lumbar regions, the joint facets of the superior and inferior articular processes become more vertically inclined. This makes pure dislocation of the joints almost impossible. A fracture through the articular processes would not necessarily make the spine unstable on movement simply because stability of the spine depends on the integrity of the discovertebral joints (anterior joints), the facet joints (posterior joints) and the spinal ligaments. The type of injury required to disrupt all of these components is a forceful flexion, distraction, rotation or shear of the spine – for example – caused by a fall from a height on to the shoulder or a rock fall over a flexed back. Effectively, all three columns fail (*see* – *spinal injuries* – general comments, page 139). Typically the injury occurs at a level somewhere between T10 and L2 and may produce a shearing fracture just below the disc (*Figure 9.19*). In this pattern, the upper vertebral body is displaced forwards on the lower and as the

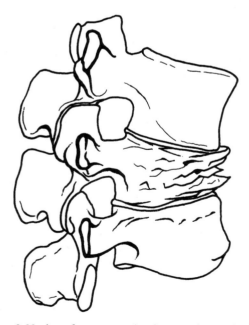

Figure 9.18 A crush or compression fracture of a vertebral body resulting in a wedge-like deformity, sometimes called a 'wedge-fracture'.

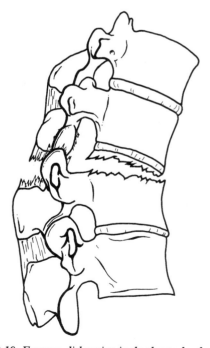

Figure 9.19 Fracture-dislocation in the thoracolumbar spine.

fracture is unstable the patient should be moved carefully, avoiding flexion and rotation of the back. Unfortunately, damage to the contents of the spinal canal is common, so there is a great risk of paraplegia.

Transverse process fractures in the lumbar spine

These commonly occur following either a direct injury (blunt abdominal trauma) or a sudden muscle pull – *avulsion fracture*. The fracture virtually always unites without requiring any special treatment. Lumbar transverse process fractures should be thought of as minor injuries but at the same time regarded as a significant marker for abdominal organ injuries [**ref 25**].

Nerve injuries at different levels of the thoracic and lumbar spines

Injury to the spinal cord and nerve roots is not a guaranteed outcome in fractures of the vertebral column, however the probability of nerve injury occurring varies according to the vertebral level involved:

(1) *Thoracic spine*: a fracture-dislocation usually causes complete transection of the cord. Complete paraplegia is common. *MRI* may shows that the cord is not transected but heavily compressed, still resulting in a complete lesion.

(2) *Thoracolumbar spine (Tl2/Ll)*: the lower segments of the spinal cord and the proximal roots of the cauda equina lie side by side in the spinal canal. A nerve lesion caused by a fracture may be a mixed one. Sometimes the cord may be damaged but not the nerve roots.

(3) *Lumbar spine*: below the level of Ll the vertebral canal contains the cauda equina (level of cord termination does vary) and this structure is more resistant to injury than the cord itself.

Other conditions of interest

Lumbago and sciatica

Lumbago means low back pain; this is often severe and usually benign. About 1% of patients have pain associated with serious spinal pathology, 4% with nerve root compression and 95% with mechanical (simple) low back pain [**ref 13**]. Renal pathology may cause back pain; however, this and other extra-spinal causes of back pain are usually excluded by clinical means as well as by radiology. An acute attack of lumbago pain and muscle spasm may be experienced in *lumbar disc prolapse (see – below)*. For patients with chronic back pain radiographic examinations have main value for patients under 20 or over 55 years of age. Acute back pain is usually due to conditions that cannot be diagnosed using radiography [**ref 30**: 38–39]. For a study of cost-effectiveness of lumbar spine radiography – *see* [**ref 27**]. *Sciatica or sciatic neuralgia* is characterized by pain radiating to the leg. The chief cause is compression of one of the lumbar nerve roots. This can occur in *lumbar disc prolapse (see – below)* or because of osteophytic encroachment of the intervertebral foramina in *spondylosis*.

Lumbar spondylosis

Lumbar spondylosis is present to some exent in everyone over the age of 40 [**ref 7**: 431]. In advanced spondylosis the disease is characterised by large osteophytes, narrowed disc spaces and sclerotic vertebral bodies [**ref 7**: 431] (*see* page 139).

Lumbar disc prolapse (slipped disc)

Prolapse of an intervertebral disc is most common in the lower lumbar spine between L4/5 or L5/SI in people between the ages of 25 and 45 [**ref 23**: 52] and can be an acute event during continuing disc degeneration (*see* page 140).

Spondylolisthesis and spondylolysis

Spondylolisthesis means a slipping vertebra – one slipping forwards on the vertebra below. There are several grades of slipping severity and classes of causes. The most common type is slipping at a *spondylolysis* (broken vertebra) – thought to be attributable to stress fractures of one or both sides of the neural arch through the relatively weak pars interarticularis. The pars may be incompletely fused with a fibrocartilaginous ring. Displacement occurs when the integrity of this ring is overwhelmed. Spondylolisthesis is most common in the fifth lumbar vertebra and the patient may be affected by lower back pain and symptoms of nerve root pressure. However spondylolysis is estimated to be present and asymptomatic in 5 – 6% of the population [**ref 23**: 54]. This area of a lumbar vertebra is best demonstrated in the oblique projection (*see* – projection (21)). In this view the outline of the lamina, superior (*Figure 9.20a*) and inferior (*Figure 9.20b*) articular processes and the transverse process (*Figure 9.20c*) resemble the silhouette of a Scots terrier, the pars interarticularis corresponding to the neck of the dog. A defect appears as a collar on the dog (*Figure 9.21*).

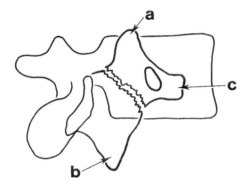

Figure 9.20 The left pars interarticularis defect as would be visible on the left anteroposterior oblique radiograph. For key – see text.

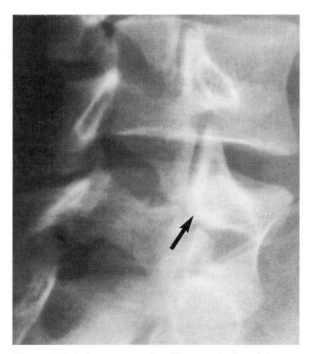

Figure 9.21 Left anteroposterior oblique projection of the lower lumbar spine. A defect is visible through the left pars interarticularis of the fifth lumbar vertebrae.

Ankylosing spondylitis

See page 157 and Chapter 3.

Lordosis

The normal anteroposterior curve in the lumbar spine is convex in the forward direction. This is known as the lumbar lordosis. An abnormal increase in this curve can be produced where there is incorrect distribution of the weight of the trunk through the lumbar vertebrae. This has the effect of tiring the muscles of the back and an unsupported spine sags in its most mobile region – the lumbar region. The condition is sometimes called *swayback*. An increased lordosis may also be the result of compensation for an exaggerated kyphosis in the thoracic spine.

Developmental anomalies and anatomic variants

Some developmental anomalies are very common but most do not have clinical significance [**ref 34**: 2412]. They may however provide sources of diagnostic error plus a *transitional vertebra* (*see* – below) may have significance if it causes a vertebral level to be wrongly identified pre-operatively. *Sacralization and lumbarization* are anomalies that may be associated with low back pain. Sacralization is the complete or partial fusion of L5 with S1. This is seen in over 6% of the normal population [**ref 34**: 2412]. In some individuals the transverse process of the fifth lumbar vertebra on one or both sides may be enlarged and sometimes fused with the sacrum and ilium. Lumbarization is where the first sacral segment is not part of the sacrum but anatomically is similar to a lumbar vertebra and is separated from the second sacral segment by a rudimentary intervertebral disc. Another anomaly is that L1 may have rudimentary ribs. For a list of some other of these anomalies of the lumbar spine – *see* [**ref 36**: 224–225].

Spina bifida

Incomplete development of the neural arches of the vertebrae such that they are not completely fused posteriorly – leaving the vertebral canal open dorsally. This can simply be a small gap in the spinous processes bridged by unossified cartilage – *spina bifida occulta*. As many as 20% of the population have radiological spina bifida occulta without serious symptoms [**ref 7**: 446]. When the defect is more extensive, the contents of the spinal canal may be exposed on the surface – *myelomeningocele* – usually in the lumbar region. In severe forms of spina bifida there may be other abnormalities of the vertebrae and ribs. The patient may also have *hydrocephalus* due to obstruction to the outflow of cerebrospinal fluid from the fourth ventricle by a protrusion of the cerebellum into the foramen magnum – *Arnold-Chiari* malformation (*see* Chapter 10). If nerve tissue is involved in spina bifida the patient will have functional impairment of the lower limbs and some degree of loss of bowel and bladder control. As a result of muscle imbalance, various lower limb deformities may develop.

Radiographic techniques – lumbar spine

For general comments on projection radiography of the spine – *see* page 141.

(16) Anteroposterior L1–L5

The patient lies supine with the arms by the sides. The shoulders and anterior superior iliac spines are placed equidistant from the tabletop. Flexing the hips and knees to rest the soles of the feet on the tabletop will flatten the lumbar lordosis bringing the spine in a more parallel direction to the image receptor.

> *Cental ray direction* – Perpendicular to the image receptor and centred in the mid-line at the level of the lower costal margin (over L3).

Expose on arrested expiration. The image should show soft-tissue outlines of the psoas muscle and kidney on either side of the spine.

Weight bearing

Changes in vertebral alignment can be seen if the anteroposterior projection is taken in the erect position – *see* (further reading **12**].

(17) Anteroposterior L5 – S1 joint space

Using the same position as in projection (16). The X-ray tube is angled cephalad between 5° and 25° so that the central ray passes through the joint space (*Figure 9.22*). The degree of angulation depends on the lumbosacral angle.

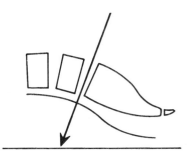

Figure 9.22 The central ray, angulated upwards to pass through the joint space between the body of L5 and the sacrum in projection (17).

> *Central ray direction* – Central ray is angled 5° to 25° cephalad and centred over the mid-line at the level of the anterior superior iliac spines.

The image receptor must be sufficiently displaced in alignment with the beam.

(18) Lateral L1 – S1

The patient lies on the affected side or with his back to the radiographer. The knees and hips are flexed for support. The position is adjusted so the ilia and shoulders are superimposed. The long axis of the spine should be parallel to the image receptor and perpendicular to the central ray (*Figures 9.23 and 9.24*). This can be achieved by placing non-opaque pads under the chest, waist and between the legs. Compensatory X-ray tube angulation may also be needed.

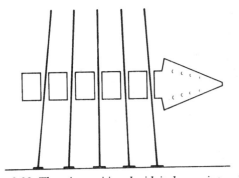

Figure 9.23 The spine positioned with its long axis parallel to the image receptor in projection (18). The X-ray beam passes through the vertebral body joint spaces and these are clearly demonstrated on the resultant image.

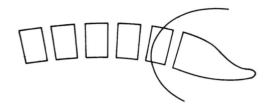

Figure 9.24 Outline appearance of the lumbar vertebral bodies and their joint spaces as seen on the lateral lumbar spine radiograph in projection (18).

Central ray direction – Perpendicular to the image receptor (or with compensatory angulation) and centred over the body of L3 at the level of the lower costal margin.

Exposed on arrested expiration. Place a piece of lead rubber on the table top just behind the patient's back. This will prevent scattered radiation produced in the subject from reaching the image receptor and affecting the image. (For a detailed discussion of this assertion – *see* [further reading **8** and **9**]). If the patient has a lumbar scoliosis (*Figure 9.25*), position him so that the convexity of the curve is directed towards the image receptor.

(19) Lateral L5 – S1

The patient remains in the same position as in (18). The direction of the L5–S1 body joint space is assessed by palpating the dimples next to the posterior superior iliac spines. The central ray should pass directly through the space therefore X-ray tube angulation may be needed.

Figure 9.25 Placing a lumbar scoliosis curve with the convexity towards the image receptor.

Central ray direction – Perpendicular to the image receptor (or with compensatory angulation) and centred to a point 7.5 cm in front of the spinous process of L5.

A much higher kilovoltage may be needed to penetrate the mass of bone in the lateral position. Often the state or angle of the joint can be determined by looking at the anteroposterior LI – L5 radiograph. Where repeated attempts at producing a joint space fail, the radiographer should repeat the radiograph but with the patient lying on the other side. If the fifth lumbar vertebra is sacralized a joint space cannot be shown.

(20) Laterals in flexion and extension

These demonstrate any instability of the spine by showing changes in alignment of the bodies. The patient is erect standing in the general lateral position with one side touching the vertical bucky. Instruct the patient to bend forwards and then backwards and take a radiograph in each position. Adequate safe support must be provided. The image receptor should be large enough to include the lumbosacral region or the entire lumbar spine as necessary.

(21) Anteroposterior obliques lumbar spine

From the supine position the patient is rotated to one side through 45°. The hips and knees are flexed and supported.

Central ray direction – Perpendicular to the image receptor and centred at the level of the lower costal margin on the mid-clavicular line of the raised side.

Repeat raising the opposite side. The pars interarticularis and facet joints on the side nearest the image receptor are shown (*see Figures 9.20 and 9.21*). If L5 – S1 is the area of interest in *spondylolisthesis* then the centring point may be lowered. For a discussion on centring techniques for this projection – *see* [further reading **4**].

Injuries

In more serious spinal trauma two projections must be taken without moving the patient. Use of a casualty table system is preferable. The anteroposterior projection must be adequately exposed if a fracture is suspected in the thoracolumbar region. If the patient must remain prone then a posteroanterior projection is a sufficient temporary alternative. For a second projection, the patient's arms are raised (if allowable), and a lateral radiograph is taken using a horizontal X-ray beam. The cassette and grid are propped alongside the patient's chest. The spine may be partially obscured by the mattress shadow if the patient is supine. There is little that can be done about this but major bony displacements should be visible. The cassette positioning level and exposure should be adjusted if both thoracic and lumbar spines are to be shown. *CT* scanning is carried for any abnormal, suspicious or inadequately visualised areas.

SACRUM, SACROILIAC JOINTS AND THE COCCYX

Indications for the X-ray examination

Injuries

Physical injury may involve the sacrum, coccyx or sacroiliac joints alone or in combination with each other, or with other spinal, pelvic and abdominal visceral injuries [ref 36: 331].

Fractures of the sacrum

This injury is caused by a fall or direct blow on the sacral region. The fracture may be no more than a crack but there can be complications if the sacral foramina are involved where nerves may be damaged.

Traumatic dislocation of a sacroiliac joint

In serious pelvic injuries the continuity of the pelvic ring is disrupted in two places. This can be brought about by a fracture of the pelvis (both above the level of the hip – usually through the ilium – and below through the pubic bones). The fracture of the ilium may extend into the sacroiliac joint but sometimes widening (*diastasis*) of a sacroiliac joint may occur although this is rare [ref 36: 338].

Other conditions of interest

Ankylosing spondylitis

The sacroiliac joints are usually the first to be affected in this disease, the bony surfaces undergo degeneration and the joint space may be widened. Later on the joints may become completely fused – ankylosis. The sacroiliac joints may be affected by other inflammatory diseases (*see* Chapter 3).

Congenital abnormalities

There are two congenital defects of the sacrum which although very rare result in a deformity of the pelvic inlet and thus have obstetric importance:

(1) *Naegele's pelvis*: one wing of the sacrum is absent with ankylosis of the sacroiliac joint on the affected side. This produces an obliquely contracted pelvis [ref 28].

(2) *Robert's pelvis*: a faulty development of the sacral alae producing a transversely contracted pelvis [ref 12].

Coccydynia

This is pain in the region of the coccyx on sitting, especially on a hard surface; it tends to occur in women, usually after a fall but sometimes after childbirth. Radiographs may show an abnormally long coccyx or acute anterior angulation of it however guidelines [ref 30: 104–5] state that normal appearance is misleading and findings do not alter management. Radiography is indicated only in specific circumstances.

Radiographic techniques – sacrum, sacroiliac joints, coccyx

(22) Anteroposterior sacrum and coccyx

The patient lies supine with the legs extended and both knees rest on a pillow. The anterior superior iliac spines are positioned equidistant from the tabletop. Use gonad protection where appropriate for males.

For the sacrum

Central ray direction – Central ray is angled between 5° and 15° degrees cephalad from the vertical and centred in the mid-line above the symphysis pubis.

Because of the lumbosacral lordosis the anterior surface of the sacrum faces both forwards and downwards when the patient is supine. To produce an undistorted image the X-ray beam must be perpendicular to the sacral long axis. The cephalad beam angle is increased for females.

For the coccyx

Central ray direction – Central ray is angled 15° caudally from the vertical and centred in the midline 5 cm above the symphysis pubis.

(23) Lateral sacrum and coccyx

Position as for projection (18); the median sagittal plane of the pelvis should be parallel to the image receptor.

For the sacrum

Central ray direction – Perpendicular to the image receptor and centred 7.5 cm anterior to the skin surface, over the posterior superior iliac spines. This distance will vary according to the thickness of soft tissues.

A relatively large kilovoltage is required to penetrate the density of bone. The beam should be collimated and lead rubber placed on the tabletop surface as in projection (18). (In most patients the coccyx is superficial and will be over-exposed in this projection).

For the coccyx

Central ray direction – Perpendicular to the image receptor and centred to the coccyx which lies between the buttocks.

Accurate centring is needed otherwise the subject will be projected off the radiograph because of the large subject to image receptor distance. The exposure can be substantially reduced from that used for the lateral sacrum.

(24) Sacroiliac joints

(i) Oblique projection

The joint surfaces are orientated both in an anteroposterior and lateromedial direction as they pass from the front to the back of the posterior pelvic wall. For a relatively clear visualization of the joint space the side of interest must be raised (from the supine position) until the joint is perpendicular to the image receptor (*Figure 9.26*).

Central ray direction – Perpendicular to the image receptor and 2.5 cm medial to the anterior superior iliac spine of the raised side.

The X-ray tube may be angled cephalad 5°–15° from the vertical according to the angle of the sacrum (*see* projection (22)). Repeat for the other side for comparison.

(ii) Anteroposterior

Position and centre the patient as for projection (22, sacrum). The tube angulation is 10°–25° cephalad. Both sacroiliac joints are demonstrated. Note that rotation of the pelvis may result in a simulation of joint space narrowing [ref 36: 335].

(iii) Posteroanterior

This is an alternative projection to (24(ii)) and may be preferred because the diverging rays pass through the joint spaces. The patient lies prone with a pillow placed under the ankles. Check that there is no rotation of the pelvis.

Central ray direction – Central ray is angled 5°–15° caudally from the vertical and centred in the midline at the level of the dimples over the posterior superior iliac spines.

Subluxation

Two erect anteroposterior views are taken with the patient weight bearing on alternate feet (*see – instability of the symphysis*, page 133).

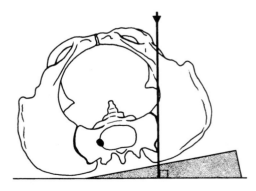

Figure 9.26 Principle of the patient positioning and direction of the central ray in projection (24(i)).

References

1. Allen BL (1989) Recognition of injuries to the lower cervical spine *in Cervical Spine Research Committee: the Cervical Spine* Philadelphia: Lippincott

2. Anderson LD D'Alonzo RT (1974) Fractures of the odontoid process of the axis *Journal of Bone and Joint Surgery American* **56**:1663–1674

3. Bontrager KL (2001) *Textbook of Radiographic Positioning and Related Anatomy (5th Edition)* St Louis: Mosby

4. Berquist TH (1992) *Imaging of Sports Injuries* Aspen: Gaithersburg

5. Chance CQ (1948) Note on the types of flexion fractures of the spine *British Journal Radiology* **21**: 452

6. Cox MW McCarthy M Lemmon G Wenker J (2001) Cervical spine instability: clearance using dynamic fluoroscopy *Current Surgery* **58** (1): 96–100

7. Dandy DJ and Edwards DJ (2003) *Essential Orthopaedics and Trauma (4th Edition)* Edinburgh: Churchill Livingstone

8. Denis F (1984) Spinal instability as defined by the 3-column concept in acute spinal trauma *Clinical orthopaedics* **189**: 65–96

9. Fon GT Pitt MJ Cole Thies A (1980) Thoracic Kyphosis: range in normal subjects *American Journal of Roentgenology* **134**: 979–983

10. Gray JE Hoffman AD Peterson HA (1983) Reduction of radiation exposure during radiography for scoliosis *Journal of Bone and Joint Surgery* **65** (1): 5–12

11. Håkan G Beckman K Jonsson B Andersson T Persliden J (2001) Digital radiography of scoliosis with a scanning method: initial evaluation *Radiology* **218**: 402–410

12. http://ww.hpv.informatics.bangor.ac.uk/Sim/Pelvis/ *The Virtual Pelvis Museum* (accessed 28/01/05)

13. http://www.nice.org.uk *Acute low back pain – Referral advice – version under pilot* (accessed 14/01/05)

14. http://www.srs.org/patients/glossary.asp *The Scoliosis Society* (accessed 16/02/05)

15. http://www.trauma.org/spine/spine-unconscious.html *Clearance of Cervical Spine Injury – Unconscious, Intubated Patients* Karim Brohi April 2002 (accessed 03/02/05)

16. http://www.wheelessonline.com/o11/165.htm *Atlanto-axial Impaction (Basilar Invagination)* (accessed 15/12/04)

17. http://www.wheelessonline.com/o11/154.htm *Pillar View* (accessed 03/02/05)

18. http://www.wheelessonline.com/oa3/83.htm *Tuberculous Spondylitis* (accessed 07/01/05)

19. Ireland AJ Britton I Forrester AW (1998) Do supine oblique views provide better imaging of the cervicothoracic junction than swimmer's views? *Journal of Accident and Emergency Medicine* **15** (3): 151–154

20. Jefferson G (1920) Fracture of the atlas vertebra: report of four cases, and a review of those previously recorded *British Journal of Surgery* **7**: 407–22

21. Levine AM Edwards CC (1991) Fractures of the atlas *Journal of Bone and Joint Surgery American* **73**: 680–691

22. Lowe TG (1990) Current Concepts Review: Scheuermann Disease *Journal of Bone and Joint Surgery American* **72**: 940–945

23. McRae R and Andrew W (1997) *Orthopaedics and trauma: an illustrated colour text* Edinburgh: Churchill Livingstone

24. McRae R Esser M (2002) *Practical Fracture Treatment (Fourth Edition)* Edinburgh: Churchill Livingstone

25. Miller CD Blyth P Civil ID (2000) Lumbar transverse process fractures – a sentinel of abdominal organ injuries *Injury* **31**(10): 773–6

26. Miller MD Gehweiler JA Martinez S Charlton OP Daffner RH (1978) Significant new observations on cervical spine trauma *American Journal of Roentgenology* **130**: 659–663

27. Miller P Kendrick D Bentley E and Fielding K (2002) Cost-effectiveness of lumbar spine radiography in primary care patients with low back pain *Spine* **27**(20): 2291–2297

28. Naegele FC (1839) *The Obliquely Contracted Pelvis* Mainz: Victor bon Zabern

29. Nunez DB Zuluaga A Fuentes-Bernardo Rivas LA Becerra JL (1996) Cervical spine trauma: how much more do we learn by routinely using helical CT? *Radiographics* **16** (6): 1307–1318

30. RCR Working Party (2003) *Making the Best Use of a Department of Clinical Radiology: Guidelines for Doctors (5th Edition)* London: The Royal College of Radiologists

31. Reamy BV Slakey JB (2001) Adolescent Idiopathic Scoliosis: Review and Current Concepts *American Family Physician* **64**(1)

32. Ross M Dufel S *Torticollis* http://emedicine.com/emerg/topic597.htm (accessed 20/12/04)

33. Scheuermann HW (1920) Kyphosis dorsalis juvenilis *Ugeskrift for Lægar, Copenhagen* pages 385–393

34. Stevens JM Rich PM in Grainger R Allison D Adam A Dixon A (eds) (2001) *Grainger and Allison's Diagnostic Radiology (Volume 3) (4th Edition)* London: Churchill Livingstone

35. Swallow RA Naylor E Roebuck EJ Whitley AS (1986) *Clark's Positioning in Radiography (11th Edition)* London: Heinemann

36. Taylor JAM Resnick DMD (2000) *Skeletal Imaging. Atlas of the Spine and Extremities* Philadelphia: Saunders

37. Trimble S (2000) Do lateral thoracic spine radiographs need an antiscatter grid? *Synergy* February page 22

38. Turetsky DB Vines FS Clayman DA Northup HM (1993) Technique and use of supine oblique views in acute cervical spine trauma *Annals of Emergency Medicine* **22** (4): 65–69

39. Williams P Warwick R (Eds) (1980) *Gray's Anatomy (36th Edition)* Edinburgh: Churchill Livingstone

Further Reading

1. Burrows H Younger K (1991) Adolescent idiopathic scoliosis *Radiography today* **57**(646): 12–17

2. Cobb RJ (1948) Outline for the study of scoliosis *American Academy of Orthopaedic Surgery* **5**: 261–275

3. Fon GT Pitt MJ Thies AC (1980) Thoracic kyphosis: range in normal subjects *American Journal Roentgenology* **134**: 979

4. Francis C (1993) Centring technique for posterior obliques of lumbar vertebrae *Radiography today* **59**(669): 20

5. Keats TE Anderson MW (2001) *Atlas of Normal Roentgen Variants that may Simulate Disease (7th Edition)* St Louis: Mosby

6. Daffner RH (1977) Pseudofracture of the dens: Mach bands *American Journal of Roentgenology* **128**: 607–612

7. MacNab I (1975) Cervical spondylosis *Clinical Orthopaedics* **109**: 69

8. Mitchell FE (1991) Scattered radiation and the lateral lumbar spine – part 1: initial research *Radiography today* **57**(644): 18

9. Mitchell FE Leung C Lo YF Ahuja A Metreweli C (1991) Scattered radiation and the lateral lumbar spine – part 2: clinical research *Radiography today* **57**(645): 12

10. Ridley N et al (1998) Radiology of skeletal tuberculosis *Orthopedics* **21**(11): 1213

11. Thomas A (2003) Imaging the lateral thoracic spine *Synergy* August page 10 – 13

12. Wood A (2000) Imaging the spine: Why take it lying down? *Synergy* December page16

13. Woodford MJ (1985) Radiography of the acute cervical spine *Radiography* **53**: 3–8

CHAPTER CONTENTS

Table of main and supplementary radiographic techniques

General anatomical area	Projection	Page	Common Indications
Survey projections			
Frontal bone, skull vault	**1i** Occipitofrontal or	171–172	Bone injury, pathology affecting bone itself, foreign bodies
	2i Fronto-occipital	172	
Frontal bone, frontal and ethmoid sinuses, orbits, superior orbital fissure, skull vault	**1ii** Occipitofrontal 15–20° *or*	172	
	2ii Fronto-occipital	172	
Vault and base – sides superimposed	**3** or **4** Lateral	172–173	
Occipital bone, posterior parietal bones, parts of temporal bones	**5** Fronto-occipital 30° half axial (*Towne*) *or*	173–174	
	6 Reverse half axial (*Haas*)	175	
Base of skull	**7** Submentovertical (*Hirtz*)	175	
Localised projections			
Pituitary fossa	**8i** Lateral	175	Enlarged fossa
	8ii Occipitofrontal 10°	175	
	8iii Fronto-occipital 30°	175	
Foramen magnum	**9i** Submentovertical	175	
	9ii Fronto-occipital 30°	175	
	9iii Lateral	175	
Cribriform plate ethmoid	**10i** Submentovertical	175	
	10ii Occipitomental	175	
	10iii Posteroanterior oblique (*Johnson and Dutt*)	176	
Optic foramen (canal), obits ethmoid, sphenoid sinuses	**11** Posteroanterior oblique (*Rhese*)	176	Enlargement of optic canal
Superior orbital fissure	**12** Occipitofrontal 20°	176	
Jugular foramina	**13** Modified SMV	176	Enlargement
Foramina rotundum	**14** Occipitomental	176	
Foramina ovale, lacerum, spinosum	**15** Submentovertical	176	
Petrous temporal bone	**16i** Fronto-occipital 30°	176	
	16ii Submentovertical	177	
	16iii Posteroanterior oblique (*Stenver*)	177	
	16iv Transorbital	177	
Mastoid complex	**17i** Fronto-occipital	177	
	17ii Submentovertical	177	
	17iii Lateral oblique (*Schüller*)	177	
	17iv Lateral oblique (*Law*)	177	
	17v Profile mastoid tip (*Hickey*)	177	

Effective radiation dose for a skull examination: **0.06mSv**
Equivalent period of natural background radiation: **3 days**

CRANIUM

Introduction

Some anatomists equate the cranium with the whole skull including the mandible, and divide it into *cranium cerebrale* and *cranium viscerale* (facial bones) [**ref 3**]. This chapter deals with a range of indications and techniques for radiography of the head excluding the facial bones and mandible which are to be found in Chapter 11. In the modern imaging department, most radiographers encounter limited numbers of requests for head radiography. Usually this is carried out in the context of head and neck (and facial) injury. Other conditions essentially involving neurological and associated tissues are investigated using the gold standard modalities of *CT* and *MRI*. Most likely the latter is undertaken within sub-specialising imaging departments. Specificity and sensitivity of these modalities far exceed anything possible using plain projection radiography. However, in the interests of attempting to complete the picture of head radiography, the supplementary techniques for localized areas of the cranium such as the temporal bone are included. They may be of historical interest only to some people, although it is always possible that a request for this specialist radiography may be encountered. Accordingly some of the better-known indications for medical imaging of lesions associated with these areas are included below, even though it is recognised that use of the modalities mentioned above will either be a priority or they will be used exclusively. Finally it should be noted that radiography is still essential in lesions affecting the bony skull including bony tumours and inflammatory lesions [**ref 30: 1617**]; to assess conditions that cause remodelling of the skull secondary to either local destruction or increased raised intracranial pressure and to assess cases of gross facial and skull fractures [**ref 7: 392**]. With the advent of MRI, radiographs are often needed to exclude radio-opaque foreign bodies prior to the examination.

Essential anatomical terminology

The cranium is the box-like structure that encloses the brain and its membranes, the cerebral circulation and sense organs. It can be arbitrarily divided into the *vault* (lid) and the *base* and is made up of several bones immovably fixed by *sutures* (fibrous joints). The bones forming the vault are thin, plate-like structures each having a compact bony inner and outer table separated by marrow-filled *diploë*. These bones include mainly the *frontal*, *parietal* and part of the *occipital* bones. The vault is sometimes referred to as the *calvaria* or skullcap (*Figure 10.1*). The base of the cranium (*Figure 10.2*), especially in its mid-section, is

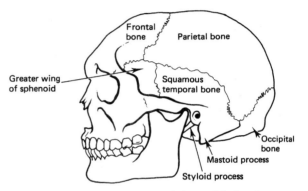

Figure 10.1 Lateral aspect of the skeleton of the head showing the bones of the cranium.

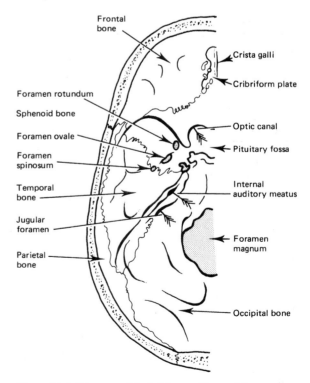

Figure 10.2 Diagram of the left internal base of the cranium.

perforated by the *foramina* that transmit cranial nerves and blood vessels. The base of the cranial box is formed anteriorly by the frontal bone forming the roof of the orbits. Behind this the 'bird-shaped' *sphenoid* bone with its outstretched 'wings'. Lying between the sphenoid and the occipital bone are the bilateral wedges of the *temporal* bones. For a diagram of the frontal aspect of the skull – *see Figure 11.1.* Two imortant features of each temporal bone are as follows:

(1) The *petrous* part of the temporal is wedged between the sphenoid and occipital bones of the skull base. The *internal auditory canal* transmits the vestibulocochlear and facial nerves across the petrous bone in a mediolateral direction and terminates posteriorly just above the jugular foramen. Normally each canal is approximately 10mm in length.

(2) Extending throughout the posterior part of the temporal bone and into the *mastoid process* is a system of *air cells* which interconnect with each other and the *mastoid antrum*. The antrum is an air sinus that communicates with the middle ear.

Indications for the X-ray examination

Head injuries – whether to use CT or radiography

Historically, skull radiography was used to evaluate trauma patients because of an erroneous assumption that significant injury would be reflected by the existence or otherwise of injury to the cranial vault [ref 6: 272]. Between 20–35% of severely head injured patients have no identifiable fracture [ref 21]. Detecting the presence or absence of an intracranial injury is much more important than detecting a skull fracture [ref 6: 273] and the received approach would be that if there has been sufficient injury to necessitate an examination then *CT* should be performed [ref 36: 271]. In the United Kingdom patients may be selected for *CT* imaging of the head by application of the National Institute for Clincal Excellence (NICE) criteria [ref 22]. These are an adaptation of the Canadian CT Head Rule [ref 29] that was developed by researchers wishing to reach a consensus of the

definition of 'clinically important brain injury'. These criteria enable adults with minor head injury requiring *CT* to be identified. If *CT* is done then skull radiography is deemed unnecessary and can be safely omitted or at least delayed [ref 6: 273]. However where *CT* is unavailable then plain skull radiographs still have a role in the management of less serious head injuries [ref 15: 23].

Head injuries – pathology

When considering injuries the head can be divided into three main regions – the cranium, the facial bones and the mandible. NICE [ref 22: 5] defines head injury as any trauma to the head other than superficial injuries to face. The term head injury, however, tends to be used in the situation where there has been trauma to the bones of the cranium and more importantly to its contents – the brain.

There is no strong correlation between a fracture of the skull and the symptoms (or complications) experienced by the patient. Thus a patient may suffer a severe head injury but no bony injury. On the other hand, extensive fractures of the skull may be present with relatively little brain damage.

The principal causes of head injury in the UK are road traffic accidents (accounting for 40–50%) [ref 11]. Falls and assaults with blunt instruments are amongst other causes. About 10% of the patients treated in accident and emergency units will have suffered a head injury [ref 4: 34]. Head injuries may be classified according to severity and causal mechanism. *Blunt trauma* – for example – the moving head striking an 'immovable' object such as in a fall, accounts for the majority of *closed head injuries*. Penetrating or *open head injuries* are caused by sharp objects at low impact or high-impact [ref 15: 19]. This type of injury may result in containment of foreign bodies such as gunshot, knife blades or nails. The severity of brain injury may be established by evaluation against the *Glasgow Coma Scale*. This is a scale that is used to evaluate the patient's level of awareness, indirectly indicating the extent of neurologic injury [ref 12].

Mechanism of brain injury

The brain floats in a fluid-filled cavity with little freedom of movement. A blow to the head produces a sudden acceleration (or deceleration) of the skull which the brain does not initially share and so the brain strikes the internal surfaces of the skull contusing (bruising) or lacerating itself on internal projections. In man, the brain stem joins the cerebrum at right angles so acceleration or deceleration tends to rotate the cerebrum, around its junction with the midbrain thus stretching the structures running through this junction. Of these structures the most susceptible is a group of synapses that maintain consciousness – the reticular formation. Traction on these synapses may interrupt conduction; hence the patient may suffer loss of consciousness for a period that varies from seconds to months.

Haemorrhage inside the cranium

This occurs to some degree in all but very minor head injuries but it is significant only if severe enough to produce a space-occupying clot – *a haematoma*. Haematomas can occur anywhere inside the cranium and are usually classified according to their anatomical site. They may be *intracerebral*, located for example in a ventricle, or they may lie outside the brain between the surrounding layers of meninges. The *extradural haematoma* lies in the potential space between the dura mater and skull whereas a *subdural* haematoma lies in the potential space between the dura and arachnoid membranes. (Various combinations are possible.) The source of these collections of blood can be a torn meningeal or cerebral artery. Alternatively the haemorrhage could originate from a vein or venous sinus. Whatever the case, this expanding mass presses on the brain (*Figure 10.3*). The cerebral hemisphere of the affected side is pushed away from the haematoma. This can cause a shift in the mid-line structures of the brain that may possibly be detected on the plain fronto-occipital radiographs (if taken) as a shift in the calcified pineal gland. This gland is calcified and visualised on about 50% of Caucasian adult skull radiographs after the age of 40 years [ref 35]. High intracranial pressure alone is unlikely to directly damage nervous tissue, but brain damage occurs as a result of *tonsillar* or *tentorial herniation* [ref 19: 217]. As the volume above the tentorium increases, the medial temporal lobes are pushed further down through the tentorial opening, finally becoming impacted there and compressing the midbrain. An alternative term for this condition is *pressure cone*.

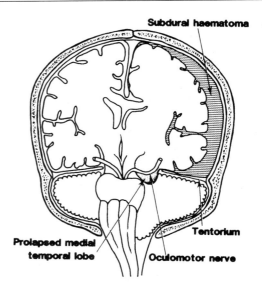

Figure 10.3 Subdural haematoma and its effects.

The patient can be observed for certain signs. The first of these is a deterioration of the conscious state as the midbrain reticular formation is compressed. Interference with the oculomotor nerve (3rd cranial nerve) may cause changes in the pupil's size and its ability to react to light. The pressure of the herniation is now transmitted into the posterior fossa of the skull where the cerebellum and structures of the brain stem are forced downwards into the spinal canal. Compression of vital brain centres during 'coning' is often fatal. Haematomas may be treated with drugs to reduce intracranial pressure and by opening the cranium – *craniotomy* – or in the operative procedure of *burr holes*.

Fractures of the skull

Fractures of the skull have a tendency to occur through the 'weakest' areas of bone. The squamous part of the temporal bone – for instance – is particularly vulnerable because even in adults it may have little more than egg shell thickness.

Fractures may be classified as

(1) linear
(2) diastatic
(3) depressed

(1) Linear fractures – 80% of fractures of the calvaria are of this kind [ref 6: 287] and in most cases are easy to identify especially when the X-

ray beam passes vertically through the fracture (*Figure 10.4*). They appear as sharp, straight radiolucent hair-like lines but they must not be confused with normal vascular markings or suture lines. The majority occur in the parietal region of the vault and may extend down through the squamous portion of the temporal bone to involve the base of the skull. Linear fractures are slow in healing and may be visible for periods up to 4 years or longer.

(2) *Diastatic fractures* – Represent about 5% of fractures [**ref 6**: 287]. This is traumatic splitting of the sutures.

(3) *Depressed fractures* – These are fairly uncommon (about 15% [**ref 6**: 287]). A fragment of bone is detached from its surround and depressed or pushed into the brain (*Figure 10.5*). This 'fragment' may be comminuted but there can also be a pathway between the fracture and the outside air in which case it is said to be *compound* or *open*. These fractures are often best seen when the fragment is in profile and its degree of depression and position must be assessed. Tangential projections of the skull may therefore be required if *CT* is unavailable.

Fractures of the skull base (*basal fractures*) are the result of a blow to the front of the skull and are accompanied by signs of soft tissue injury to the forehead [**ref 6**: 297]. Basal skull fractures are

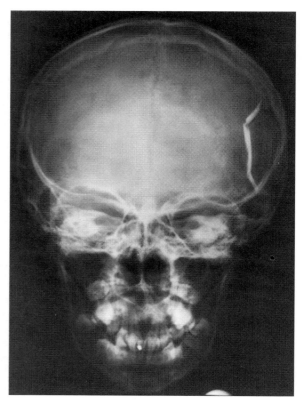

Figure 10.5 A depressed skull fracture in the region of the left parietal bone.

diagnosed clinically with signs including *periorbital heamatoma* ('panda eyes'), *mastoid haematoma* (Battle's sign), *cerebrospinal rhinorrhoea* or *cerebrospinal otorrhoea*. *Haemotympanum* is another sign that may be indicative of basal fracture [**ref 15**: 24].

Temporal bone injuries are usually due to severe blunt trauma. *Temporal bone fractures* are classified as longitudinal or transverse. Fracture of the labyrinth may cause sensorineural hearing loss, vertigo or facial nerve palsy. Related complications may include cerebrospinal fluid leak (*see* – below) or meningitis. High resolution *CT* is likely to be the modality of choice to demonstrate a temporal bone fracture.

Complications of skull fractures

These include the following:

(1) *Haemorrhage* – i.e. bleeding into the scalp, extra or epidural, subdural, or bleeding into brain or ventricular system (*see* – above). Intracranial bleeding can occur without any bony injury.

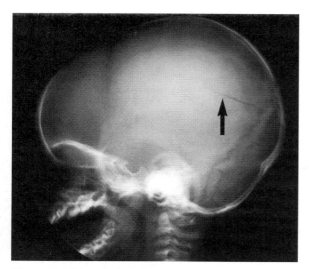

Figure 10.4 Lateral skull showing a linear fracture across the parietal bone.

(2) Entry of air and infection – *pneumocephalus* or *aerocele* results from the disruption of a bony wall of a paranasal sinus or mastoid air cell contiguous with the cranial cavity. Lateral skull radiographs should always be taken with a horizontal X-ray beam and the patient in the 'brow-up' position so air and air/fluid levels can be best visualized behind the frontal bone. The danger of air entry in any compound fracture of the skull lies in the possibility that it may carry with it bacteria and hence infection. Foreign bodies and fragments of scalp and hair can also admit microrganisms, with meningitis or cerebral abscess possible outcomes.

(3) Escape of cerebrospinal fluid into nasal cavity or ear – cerebrospinal fluid rhinorrhoea or otorrhoea.

(4) Cranial nerve damage. Cranial nerves may be ruptured by the trauma of a head injury and quite often fractures of the skull base may pass through foramina. Symptoms and effects will depend on which nerve has been damaged. The *abducent nerve* is occasionally involved in fractures of the skull base; paralysis of this nerve results in a medial squint as the lateral rectus muscle of the eye is affected. If the internal auditory meatus is involved then tearing of the *vestibulocochlear nerve* will cause impairment.

(5) *Growing skull fractures* – these usually occur after severe head injury in early life [ref 28: 2395]. There is progressive widening of the fracture line over a period of time due to exposure of the remodelling bone to pulsation of cerebrospinal fluid.

Tumours and other space-occupying lesions

Use of radiography

Plain skull radiography is unlikely to give additional information in the evaluation of central nervous system disease and has lost its central role as the initial examination of the brain and skull [ref 7: 392]. When introduced in 1972 (in the UK), CT had an accuracy approaching 100% in confirming and localising a lesion. Also the tumour was characterised in a high proportion of cases. Radiographs identified fewer than 50% of patients with intracranial tumours and had an even poorer record in localisation and characterisation [ref 30: 1461].

Pathology and radiographic appearances

Until its nature is more accurately determined an *intracranial tumour* may be called a *space-occupying lesion*. This is a blanket term that can also be used to describe an abscess or cyst. Intracranial haematomas can be classified as space-occupying lesions and are dealt with above.

Intracranial tumours may insinuate or infiltrate adjacent structures or they may engulf cranial nerves or vessels thus potentially producing a range of associated symptoms. Where by definition the lesion 'takes up' space within the closed box of the skull, the increase in volume of contents causes the intracranial pressure to rise. The changes may be insidious in onset and after a period of time, plain radiographs may produce very definite signs, the nature of which usually depends on whether the patient is a child or an adult. In a child widening of the sutures – *suture diastasis* – will occur where the joints have not yet fused. Young infants and neonates with raised intracranial pressure will also have large heads with markedly thin skull vaults. *Hydrocephalus* is the usual cause of raised intracranial pressure in the new born (*see* – below). In adults, *erosion* of the lamina dura of the dorsum sellae [ref 13: 2325] represents an 'early change' due to raised intracranial pressure. Eventually enlargement of the whole sella [ref 7: 395] may be visualised (*Figure 10.6(b)*).

Other signs of an intracranial space-occupying lesion in an adult include the following:

(1) *Mid-line displacement of normally calcified structures* i.e. the pineal gland (*see* – above), choroids plexus, falx cerebri or habenula.

(2) *Abnormal calcification* – such as in *meningioma*.

(3) *Abnormal vascular markings* on the bony walls of the skull. An example of this is in a *meningioma* where the tumour derives part of its blood supply from the middle meningeal artery. The artery (which grooves the lateral wall of the skull) becomes enlarged on the affected side.

(a)

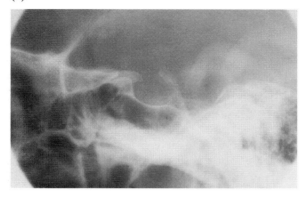

(b)

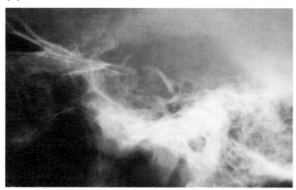

Figure 10.6 Radiographs of normal (a) and enlarged (b) pituitary fossa.

Its vascular channels consequently become more deepened and thus more obvious on the lateral skull radiograph. The middle meningeal artery passes through the foramen spinosum – so enlargement of this orifice when seen on a submentovertical projection would be another clue to the abnormality.

(4) *Remodelling of skull due to local erosion*

Examples are:

(i) *Pituitary adenoma* causing enlargement of the pituitary fossa. In adults it will result in *acromegaly*. Radiographs of the skull show thickening and enlargement of the bones of the vault, the sinuses and protrusion of the jaw (*see* Chapter 3).

(ii) *Acoustic neuroma (acoustic schwannoma)*. This is a benign tumour that arises from the schwann cells that wrap the vestibulocochlear nerve. It is a common intracranial tumour which acts as a space-occupying lesion causing erosion and expansion of the internal auditory meatus and sometimes erosion of the petrous apex. This condition is investigated by *MRI*.

(iii) *Optic glioma (astrocytoma)* is a rare tumour usually affecting children. It causes enlargement of the optic canal and optic foramen. Changes in the optic foramina and the sphenoid fissure may also indicate the presence of an intraorbital lesion.

(iv) *Glomus jugulare tumours* arise from paraganglion cells, the precursors of chemo and baroreceptors of great blood vessels. A common site is the jugular bulb resulting in enlargement and destruction of the jugular foramen [**ref 13**: 2431].

Tumours of the bone

These may be primary or secondary. *Primary tumours* of the skull causing bone erosion are exceedingly rare [**ref 28**: 2402]. *Secondary or metastatic tumours* of the skull where bone erosion is produced are more common. Examples are: *secondary carcinoma* from a primary in the lung and *myelomatosis* with its widespread deposits usually involving the vault of the skull.

Hyperostosis

This is thickening of the skull vault and may be generalized or local. *Hyperostosis frontalis interna* is a common normal variant seen most frequently in middle-aged women [**ref 7**: 394]. There is sclerosis and thickening of the inner table of diploë of the frontal bone. Generalized hyperostosis also occurs in *Paget's disease* where there is an increase in the thickness of the skull. The bones also become softer and the texture changes so the radiographs show a 'woolly' mottled appearance (*see Figure 10.7*).

Platybasia

This is flattening of the skull base. The term may be used to include basilar impression and invagination. *Basilar impression* is elevation of the floor of the posterior fossa and is a congenital anomaly. *Basilar invagination* is acquired resulting from diseases that cause bone softening [**ref 30**: 1469] such as *Paget's disease (Figure 10.7)*, *rickets* and *osteomalacia (see* Chapter 3 and *rheumatoid arthritis* Chapter 9, page 142). The degree of platybasia and basilar impression can be assessed from plain radiographs of the skull and a number of lines and measurements have been used for this purpose. These conditions are commonly symptomless but they can cause problems resulting from pressure and distortion of the brainstem and from obstruction of cerebrospinal fluid flow [**ref 30**: 1469].

Developmental abnormalities

There are several variations in the size and shape of the skull that do not necessarily have any clinical significance. Many descriptive terms are used, for example *dolichocephaly* means that the skull is long in relation to its transverse diameter whereas *brachycephaly* means that it is wide in relation to its length. Note that a skull may be normally asymmetrical – one side is slightly smaller or larger than the other. This can pose problems for an unwary operator when the aim is to produce 'non-rotated' frontal or occipital projections of the head!

Craniosynostosis

This condition produces an abnormal skull shape due to premature fusion of the sutures. This can be clearly demonstrated with CT using three-dimensional reconstruction [**ref 30**: 1467].

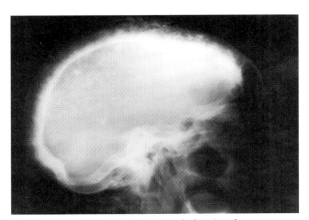

Figure 10.7 Lateral skull radiograph showing the characteristic appearance of Paget's disease. The patient has basilar invagination.

Craniocleidodysostosis

This is a rare condition where normal ossification of membranous bone is affected. The skull is rather flat and broad and shows prominent suture lines that are sometimes widely separated owing to the lack of bone development. There is also either complete or partial absence of the clavicles (*see* Chapter 6).

Hydrocephalus

Cerebrospinal fluid secreted by the choroid plexuses circulates through the ventricles and cisterns of the brain and around the subarachnoid space of the spinal cord and cerebral hemispheres. It eventually returns to the blood via the arachnoid villi which are situated mainly in the walls of the cerebral venous sinuses. If this flow is obstructed then fluid will accumulate under pressure in the ventricles – in *non-communicating or obstructive hydrocephalus*. The obstruction may be caused by a tumour, subarachnoid haemorrhage or a consequence of congenital abnormality. The commonest congenital causes of hydrocephalus are *aqueduct stenosis* and *Arnold-Chiari malformation*. In the Arnold-Chiari malformation part of the medulla oblongata and part of the cerebellum lie below the level of the foramen magnum in the spinal canal (*cerebellar tonsillar herniation*). The foramen magnum becomes plugged by these structures so that the cerebrospinal fluid is unable to escape through the foramina of Luschka and Magendie and is dammed back. The ventricles and the aqueduct dilate with fluid that continues to be secreted by the choroid plexuses and as intracranial pressure rises the unfused bones of the skull separate. The Arnold-Chiari malformation accompanies *spina bifida* (*see* Chapter 9). Ventriculo-peritoneal or programmable valve shunt systems may be used to control hydrocephalus. Radiographs of head, chest and abdomen may be required to show the extent and position of shunts.

Other conditions of interest

Acute mastoiditis – The middle ear communicates with the nasopharynx via the Eustachian tube. Physiologically the tube serves to equalize pressure between the middle ear and the atmosphere but it can also act as a potential route for the spread of infection between the two points. Infection in the middle ear is called *otitis media*. Usually, antibiotics treat this condition and it spreads no further. If the infection is allowed to develop then the mastoid air cells are also affected.

Chronic mastoiditis – This can occur as a sequel to acute mastoiditis when the infection has failed to resolve. Obliteration of the mastoid air cells now occurs as new bone is formed following the breakdown of the air-cell walls.

Cholesteatoma is a mass of stratified squamous epithelial cells abnormally sited and proliferating in the middle ear and mastoid. The mass may erode the bony walls of the attic, antrum or middle ear and can destroy the ossicular chain. *CT* and *MRI* are imaging modalities of choice.

Congenital abnormalities temporal bone

Deformities or even absence of part or parts of the hearing/equilibrium apparatus in the petrous part of the bone occur. Examples are *external auditory canal atresia* and *cochlear dysplasia*.

Bell's Palsy (BsP)

This is a disorder of the facial nerve with resultant paralysis involving both upper and lower facial muscles and an inability to shut the eye or even to blink on the affected side. BsP is now called *herpetic facial paralysis* because of evidence linking herpes simplex virus. In the early stages no imaging may be needed and 90% of patients recover facial nerve function spontaneously within two months [ref 8: 89].

Radiographic techniques – general comments

Because of the anatomically complex, spherical structure of the skull a single radiograph produces a composite picture. Strictly speaking several views are needed in order to fulfil projection radiographic requirements. Quite early in the history of radiography a great many projections and their variations were described. These were usually named after the person who had suggested them [ref 16: 1]. This caused confusion (eponymous terminology still does so). Lysholm suggested that skull radiographic projections and nomenclature should be standardised [ref 20]. In 1961 a commission [ref 23] accepted four projections described by Lysholm as the fundamental views for radiography of the skull [ref 16: 3] however as with other radiographic subjects, the selection and exact execution of projections is subject to local protocol and operator variation. Before the advent of CT when skull surveys were more widely practised it was considered an acceptable compromise to take four standard views of the skull [ref 30: 1461] thus displaying information about the front, back and sides of the cranium. Nowadays it may be standard practice to take only a lateral projection unless there is clinical evidence to suggest more is needed. The experience of this author however is that where head injury patients are referred for radiography, three basic projections (*projections* 1, 4 and 5) continue to be commonly requested.

Anatomical points, lines and planes
(Figure 10.8)

Reference must be made to certain anatomical points, lines and planes on the head. Using these helps the operator to standardise projections.

Median sagittal plane – This divides the skull in the mid-line from front to back.

Interorbital/interpupillary line – This joins the centre of the two orbits. It is at right angles (perpendicular) to the median sagittal plane.

Orbitomeatal base line – This is often referred to as the *base line* or *radiographic base line*. This joins the outer canthus of the eye to the central point of the extrernal auditory meatus (EAM). **This is the one used throughout the text.**

External occipital protruberance (EOP) and *glabella* are both relevant bony landmarks.

General patient position

During radiography, general patient position can be either erect or horizontal depending on preference and patient condition. Positioning the patient with the aspect of the head required for investigation closest to the image receptor is best practice, as this reduces geometric magnification and blurring. Positioning the head with the face turned away from the X-ray source (i.e. positioned

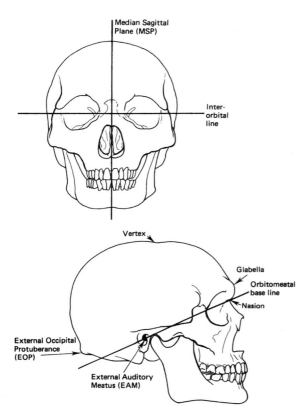

Figure 10.8 Anatomical lines, planes and land-marks that are important in radiography of the head.

for posteroanterior or occipitofrontal projection) helps to keep eye lens radiation dose to a mimimum [**ref 33**].

Radiographic equipment

With very few exceptions a secondary radiation grid is always used in radiography of the skull. The following techniques assume that a conventional horizontal or vertical bucky table is in use. Distinctive techniques have been devised for use with specialized, i.e. Lysholm skull table or *isocentric* equipment – for example – 'Orbix'. Generally speaking, use of this equipment incorporates *positioning* methods that will produce similar (but not the same) results to conventional techniques but with improved patient comfort, convenience and immobilisation. Specialist immobilizing devices can be used for the head, however in practice few operators tend to do this placing more reliance on short exposure times.

Radiographic techniques – cranium – general survey

Techniques (1–7) include the general survey projections for the cranium, the first six being the ones most commonly encountered or performed. Projections (8–17) include those for localized parts of the cranium.

(1) Occipitofrontal (posteroanterior) skull *(Figure 10.9)*

The patient is seated erect or lies prone facing the support. The forehead rests on the table. The orbitomeatal base line is positioned to lie at 90° to the image receptor. The median sagittal plane is placed perpendicular to the image receptor. This is achieved by placing the midpoint between the orbits (i.e. the nasion) and the lambda in the same vertical plane [**ref 5**: 358]. A useful suggestion is to locate the posterior end of the sagittal plane by feeling for the nuchal ligament lying in the furrow below the external occipital protruberance. For comments on skull asymmetry – *see* above (developmental abnormalities).

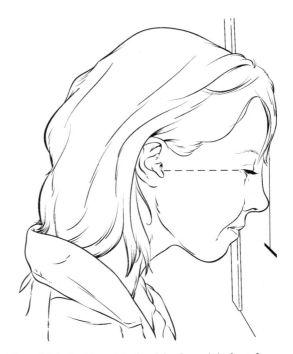

Figure 10.9 Position of the head for the occipitofrontal projection (1).

Central ray direction – Either (i) with the X-ray beam perpendicular to the image receptor and centred in the mid-line so that the central ray emerges through the glabella.

This radiograph shows the petrous bones lying within the orbits.

Or (ii) With the X-ray beam angled 20° caudad and centred in the mid-line so that the central ray emerges through the nasion.

The upper border of the petrous bones are seen at the level of the lower border of the orbits. The Commission [**ref 23**] recommended 15° caudal X-ray tube angle. Du Boulay [**ref 5**: 365] thought that there seemed no point in recommending the exact degree of inclination that should be used.

This projection (ii) is sometimes attributed to *Caldwell* [**ref 2**] whose original intent was to demonstrate the frontal and ethmoid sinuses and orbits.

Alternative technique – projection (2).

(2) Fronto-occipital (anteroposterior) skull

This projection is used where the patient must remain supine and only conventional X-ray equipment (as opposed to isocentric units) is available *or* in cases where the back of the skull is of interest. Rest the back of the head on a narrow wedge foam pad. The median sagittal plane is placed perpendicular to the image receptor. Either of the following projections may be performed, starting with the base line at 90° to the image receptor:

(i) Raise the chin slightly so the base line is 20° above a position where it is perpendicular to the image receptor. On the radiograph – the orbits will be visible *above* the petrous bones.

(ii) Keep the chin depressed so that the base line remains perpendicular to the image receptor (difficult for many patients). On the radiograph – the petrous bones are seen lying within the orbits.

Central ray direction – Perpendicular to the image receptor and centred through the nasion.

In projection (2(ii)), if the patient cannot produce or maintain the position, additional caudal angulation of the tube may be necessary to compensate for the raised base line.

(3) Lateral skull (head and neck turned) *(Figure 10.10)*

The patient faces the X-ray table. The head is turned on to the affected side, and the opposite shoulder is raised slightly. The side of the face and head rests against the support. The median sagittal plane is placed parallel to the image receptor. The interpupillary line is placed 90° to the image receptor. Pads may be needed to support the head and chin in this position.

Central ray direction – Perpendicular to the median sagittal plane and image receptor and centred midway between glabella and external occipital protruberance (EOP).

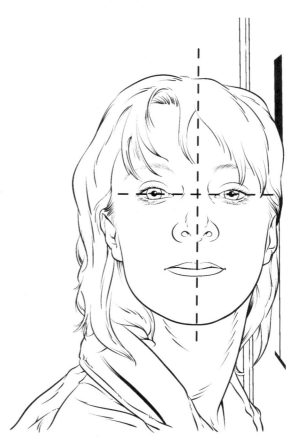

Figure 10.10 Position of the head for the lateral projection (3).

Some patients, especially elderly with more limited movement of the neck, find maintaining this position difficult. If the interpupillary line is not at 90° to the image receptor then a compensatory tube angulation may have to be made to produce a 'true' lateral projection. The direction of the central ray should be parallel to the interpupillary line. If this position proves unsuitable projection (4) should be attempted.

(4) Lateral skull (head and neck remaining straight)

The patient can be supine or erect. If erect, place a 30 x 24 cm cassette and grid in the vertically placed cassette holder. The patient is seated in the general lateral position and the median sagittal plane of the head is placed parallel to the image receptor. The affected side touches the cassette and grid. If the patient is supine, a foam pad is placed under the head to accommodate it within the field of a cassette and grid propped vertically alongside the head.

> *Central ray direction* – As for projection (3), whether the patient is erect or supine.

Projection (4) produces a lateral projection of the upper cervical spine provided the image receptor and field are extended to include it.

(5) Fronto-occipital (half axial) skull (Towne) *(Figure 10.11)*

The patient sits or lies with the back of the head touching the table or cassette with grid. A small foam pad is placed behind the head and the chin is depressed until the base line is perpendicular to the image receptor. The median sagittal plane is also positioned perpendicular to the image receptor.

> *Central ray direction* – Central ray is angled 30° caudad (see – below) and centred in the mid-line through the frontal bone so the central ray emerges through the foramen magnum.

The cassette should be displaced downwards to be centralized with the X-ray beam.

This is the best-known eponymous projection but note that *Towne* [ref 32] did not specify the degree of caudal X-ray tube angulation. Opinions differ as to what X-ray beam tilt is desirable [ref 14: 2304].

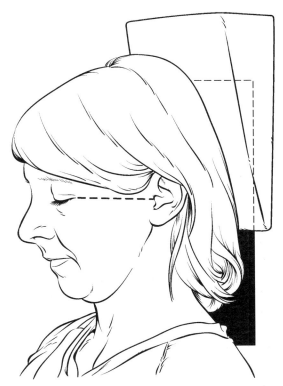

Figure 10.11 *Patient position for a fronto-occipital (half-axial) skull projection (5).*

The Commission suggested that (if the base line is perpendicular to the image receptor) then the central ray makes an angle of 25–30° craniocaudally to the base line [ref 23]. A *true* half axial projection will by definition be obtained by using an angle of 45° [ref 5: 365]. Clark's single description [ref 31: 205] (and that of other authors) of this projection as using a 30° caudal tilt has contributed to the received wisdom that 'Towne's' means use of this precise degree of tilt. Positioning the base line at 90° to the image receptor may be difficult for the patient; additional caudal tube angulation can be used to compensate for a slightly raised base line. On the radiograph the front of the skull is projected downwards leaving the structures that form the back of the skull – the foramen magnum, occipital and posterior parietal bones – relatively undistorted. The dorsum sellae is seen within the foramen magnum and the temporal bones lie on either side. If calcified, the pineal gland should lie in the mid-line (provided that there is nothing causing a mid-line shift).

Kyphosis

Difficulty is experienced in producing an acceptable image in patients with a pronounced spinal curvature and/or limited neck movement where the patient cannot depress the chin adequately (*Figure 10.12*). To overcome this, the patient lies on the couch. A 24 x 30 cm cassette and grid are placed under the head. Support the head and cassette on a pad. The base line is unlikely to be at 90° to the image receptor. Unfortunately, compensatory additional tube angulation projects the occipital bone downwards even further. Since it is usually impossible – owing to the curve of the dorsal spine – to position the cassette low enough, the foramen magnum will not be seen on the radiograph. Positioning a 35° foam pad underneath the knees and a pillow underneath the hips may help the patient flex the neck and depress the chin. Projection (6) may be used as an alternative.

Unconscious or seriously head-injured patients

Clinically significant head injuries will require *CT*. Where radiography is requested the technique of examination must be modified according to the patient's condition. Several rules are followed:

(1) The patient should be under supervision to detect changes in condition.

(2) The examination should be executed in the shortest possible time.

(3) The patient is examined in the supine position.

(4) There may be significant patient movement due to cerebral irritation, confusion or isorientation underscoring need for attempts at patient immobilisation and short exposure times.

(5) The patient's head may need to be held by an assistant.

(6) Take into consideration *other* injuries the patient may have. Head and neck injuries occur together. A lateral cervical spine radiograph is often routinely requested. Caution should be exercised if the head has to be lifted.

(7) The lateral projection will be taken with a horizontal X-ray beam – projection (4). Air/fluid levels may be present inside the cranium. A fluid level in the sphenoid sinuses may be caused by blood indicating a basal fracture.

Tangential projections

Should *CT* be unavailable these are used in the assessment of depressed fractures and also to gain further information about the inner and outer tables of the vault bones. The head is rotated to position the depressed fragment in *profile*. The central ray must be *tangential* to the fragment (*Figure 10.13*).

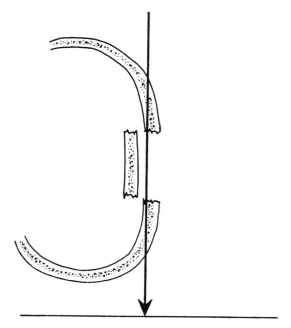

Figure 10.13 The principle of the tangential projection.

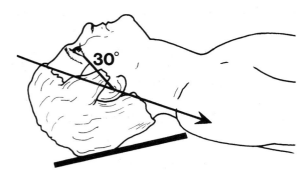

Figure 10.12 The problem of obtaining a fronto-occipital skull radiograph on a patient who is unable to flex the neck.

(6) 'Reverse' fronto-occipital (half axial) skull (Haas)

The patient sits facing the vertical bucky with the forehead touching the support. The base line is placed at 90° to the image receptor and the median sagittal plane is positioned perpendicular to the image receptor.

> *Central ray direction* – Central ray is angled 30° cephalad and centred in the midline below the external occipital protruberance so that the X-ray beam emerges through the glabella.

The disadvantage of the reverse projection is that the back of the skull is no longer close to the image receptor and the image will be magnified to some extent. The eponymous term for this projection is *Haas* [**ref 1**: 375]. (*See* also [**ref 9**]).

(7) Submentovertical (SMV/axial) skull (Hirtz)

Performance of this is easiest for the patient if undertaken using a Lysholm skull table that can be positioned and tilted thus:

The patient lies supine on a couch or trolley and is positioned so the shoulders are just beyond the end of the couch. The neck is extended backwards until the vertex of the skull touches the support (*Figure 10.14*) The median sagittal plane is positioned perpendicular to the image receptor. The skull table and head are mutually arranged so that the base line is parallel to the image receptor.

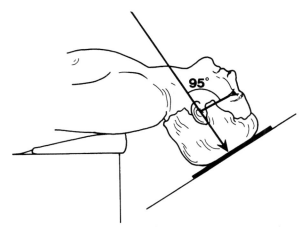

Figure 10.14 Positioning of the patient and angulation of the X-ray beam for the SMV projection (7).

> *Central ray direction* – Central ray is angled 5° cephalad and centred between the angles of the jaw in the mid-line. The central ray makes an angle of 95° with the base line.

Use of a *vertical bucky* is possible but the position is more difficult to achieve and maintain.

The eponymous term for this projection is *Hirtz* [**ref 16**].

Radiographic techniques – cranium – localized areas

Most of the following projections are adaptations of projections (1–7).

(8) Pituitary fossa

Additional projections are as follows:

(i) *Lateral* – As for projection (3) or (4). *Centre*: 2.5 cm above and in front of the uppermost EAM using a collimated X-ray beam.

(ii) *Occipitofrontal* – As for projection (1). *Centre*: 5 cm below the external occipital protuberance with the X-ray tube angled 10° cephalad using a collimated X-ray beam.

(iii) *Fronto-occipital 30° half axial* – As for projection (5), using a collimated X-ray beam.

(9) Foramen magnum

Additional localized projections are as follows:

(i) *SMV* – As for projection (7). *Centre*: Midway between the EAMs using a collimated X-ray beam.

(ii) *Fronto-occipital 30°*. *Centre*: As for projection (5), using a collimated X-ray beam.

(iii) *Lateral* – As for projection (3) or (4). *Centre*: 2.5cm below the EAM uppermost using a collimated X-ray beam.

(10) Cribriform plate of the ethmoid

Additional projections are as follows:

(i) *SMV* – As for projection (7).

(ii) *Occipitomental* – Position patient as for projection (1) Chapter 11, page 186.

Central ray direction – Central ray is angled 40° caudad and centred in the mid-line through the vertex just anterior to the EAMs

(iii) *Posteroanterior oblique* – From the position for an occipitofrontal projection (projection (1)), rotate the head to one side through 45°. Raise the base line through 35°.

Central ray direction – With the X-ray beam angled 10° caudad through the orbit in contact with the table.

> Repeat, moving the head in the opposite direction. The eponymous term for this projection is *Johnson and Dutt*.

In cases of cribriform plate fractures refer to projection (4), Chapter 11, page 188.

Crista galli

This is usually shown on the occipitofrontal 20°, projection (1 (ii)).

(11) Optic foramen (optic canal)

This is the passageway for the optic nerve and ophthalmic artery lying in the lesser wing of the sphenoid bone. A posteroanterior oblique projection is used and the central ray must coincide with the central axis of the canal [ref 5: 367]. The patient is seated and the head is placed in the position for the occipitofrontal position (projection (1)). The base line is then raised through 35° and the head is rotated through 45° bringing the orbit of the side under examination closest to the image receptor.

Central ray direction – Perpendicular to the image receptor and centred directly through the orbit nearest the image receptor.

Repeat the procedure for the other side. The two foramina will be compared; therefore the positioning must be comparable. There are several variants of this projection using differing head and X-ray tube angulations. Readers will note the similarity with projection (10(iii)) above and projection (26) Chapter 11. The eponymous term for posteroanterior oblique projections demonstrating ethmoid and sphenoid sinuses, orbits and optic foramina is *Rhese* [ref 24].

(12) Superior orbital fissure

This transmits the oculomotor, trochlear, ophthalmic and abducent nerves. The fissure is demonstrated on the occipitofrontal 20° projection of the skull (l(ii)).

(13) Jugular foramina

These lie at the posterior ends of the petro-occipital suture. Each transmits the internal jugular vein, and the glossopharyngeal, vagus and accessory nerves. Note that there is great anatomical variation and asymmetry of the region [ref 5: 369]. This is the best-known projection:

Modified SMV – This shows both foramina; the patient head position is the same as in projection (7).

Central ray direction – Central ray is angled 20° caudad and centred midway between the EAMs. Use a narrow rectangular field.

For an easier alternative *see* [ref 31: 211].

(14) Foramen rotundum

This transmits the maxillary nerve (a branch of the trigeminal). The foramen can be seen inside the maxillary antrum, below the orbit on the occipitomental projection projection (1), Chapter 11, page 186).

(15) Foramina ovale, lacerum, spinosum

The foramen ovale transmits the mandibular branch of the trigeminal nerve, the foramen lacerum the internal carotid artery and the foramen spinosum the middle meningeal artery. These foramina can be visualized on the SMV projection (7).

(16) Petrous part of the temporal bones

The list below is by no means comprehensive. Many projections have been proposed – both for the petrous and mastoid – several by Schüller [ref 25].

(i) *Fronto-occipital 35°* – As for projection (5) but with an additional 5° caudal angulation. *Centre:* Using a rectangular diaphragm in the mid-line so the X-ray beam passes between the EAMs.

(ii) *SMV* – As for projection (7). *Centre:* Midway between the EAMs with a rectangular diaphragm.

(iii) *Posteroanterior oblique* – This is a version of Stenver's projection [**ref 27**]. In this projection the long axis of the petrous bone is parallel to the plane of the image receptor and perpendicular to the central ray. Positioning starts with the patient in the position for the occipitofrontal projection (1). The head is 'off-centred' 2.5 cm so the orbit of the side of interest is over the cross-lines of the table. The head and neck are tilted axially 15° away from the side of interest. The head is now rotated through 45°, the side of interest remaining closest to the image receptor.

Central ray direction – With the X-ray beam angled 12° cephalad, midway between the external occipital protruberance and the EAM of the side nearest the X-ray tube.

Repeat for the other side. For a 'reverse Stenver's projection – *see* [**ref 5**: 369].

(iv) *Trans-orbital (per-orbital projection)* – This allows comparison of the internal auditory meatuses on the two sides. Previous recommendations were for positioning as for projection (2), i.e. patient facing the X-ray tube, but radiation dose to the eyes is of concern therefore posteroanterior positioning, i.e. as for projection (1) is preferable.

Central ray direction – Perpendicular to the image receptor and centred in the mid-line to emerge between the orbits.

(17) Mastoid complex

This is the air cells and the mastoid process.

(i) *Fronto-occipital 35 °* – The same comments apply as for projection (16(i)).

(ii) *SMV* – The same comments apply as for projection (16(ii)).

(iii) *Lateral oblique* – The head is positioned for the true lateral projection (3). The pinna of the ear next to table top may be folded forwards to avoid superimposition of the soft-tissue shadows on the mastoid area.

Central ray direction – Central ray is angled 25° caudad and centred 5 cm above and behind the EAM remote from the image receptor. This tube angulation can be varied i.e. to 15° or 30°.

Repeat for the opposite side. The eponymous term for the lateral oblique projection with 25° caudal angle is *Schüller* [**ref 26**]. This projection was used mainly for assessment of trauma and pneumatisation of the temporal bone [**ref 34**]

(iv) *Law's projection* – This is a lateral oblique projection. The head is positioned for the true lateral projection (3). with the X-ray beam angled

Central ray direction – Central ray is angled 15° caudad and 15° towards the face [ref 17] and centred 5cm above and 5cm behind the EAM away from the image receptor.

(v) *Profile mastoid process* – The tip is superficial and does not require a large exposure. The patient is supine in the position for the fronto-occipital projection (2). The base line is perpendicular to the image receptor. The face is rotated through 35° away from the side of interest. The aim is to project the mastoid process below the occipital bone and clear of the cervical vertebrae.

Central ray direction – With a 15° caudad angle centre directly over the mastoid process. Repeat for the opposite side.

The eponymous term for this projection is *Hickey.*

References

1. Bontrager KL (2001) *Textbook of Radiographic Positioning and Related Anatomy (5th Edition)* St Louis: Mosby

2. Caldwell EW (1907) Skiagraphy of the accessory nasal sinuses *American Journal of Roentgenology* 1: 27–30

3. *Churchill's Medical Dictionary* (1989) New York: Churchill Livingstone

4. Driscoll P Skinner D Earlam R (eds) (2000) *ABC of Major Trauma* London: BMJ Publishing

5. Du Boulay E (1980) *Principles of X-ray Diagnosis of the Skull* London: Butterworths

6. Given CA Williams DW in Rogers LF (ed) (2002) *Radiology of Skeletal Trauma (Volume 1) (3ʳᵈ Edition)* Edinburgh: Churchill Livingstone

7. Hadley DM in Armstrong P Wastie ML (eds) (2001) *A Concise Textbook of Radiology* London: Arnold

8. Harnsberger HR Hudgins PA Wiggins RH Davidson HC (2002) *Pocket Radiologist Head and Neck 100 Top Diagnoses* Salt Lake City: Amirsys Inc

9. Haas L (1927) Verfahren zur sagittalen Aufnahme der Sellage gend *Fortscr Roentgenstr* **36**: 1198–1203

10. Hoban W (1998) Supine skull radiography in A&E using ORBIX skull unit *Synergy* February pages 16–17

11. http://www.bbc.co.uk/health/awareness campaigns/mar_braininjury.shtml *BBC Health Awareness campaigns – Brain Injury Awareness Week* accessed 24/02/05

12. http://www.finr.com/glossary.html *Glasgow Coma Scale* accessed 03/03/05

13. Jäger R Rich P in Grainger R Allison D Adam A Dixon A (eds) (2001) *Grainger and Allison's Diagnostic Radiology (Volume 3) (4ᵗʰ Edition)* London: Churchill Livingstone

14. Jäger R Saunders D Murray A Stevens JM in Grainger R Allison D Adam A Dixon A (eds) (2001) *Grainger and Allison's Diagnostic Radiology (Volume 3) (4ᵗʰ Edition)* London: Churchill Livingstone

15. Jones N (ed) (1997) *Craniofacial Trauma: An Interdisciplinary Approach* Oxford: OUP

16. Kimber PM (1983) *Radiography of the Head* Edinburgh: Churchill Livingstone

17. Law F (1913) Radiography as an aid in the diagnosis of mastoid disease *Ann Otol Rhino Laryngol* **22**: 635–637

18. Lewis S (1995) Head imaging and craniometry: a historical note on a base line error *Radiography today* **61**(698): 410

19. Lindsay KW Bone I (1997) *Neurology and Neurology Illustrated (2ⁿᵈ Edition)* Edinburgh: Churchill Livingstone

20. Lysholm E (1931) Apparatus and technique for roentgen examination of the skull *Acta Radiologica Supplementum* **12**: 1–120

21. MacPherson BCM MacPherson P Jennett B (1990) CT incidence of intracranial contusion and haematoma in relation to the presence, site and type of skull fracture *Clinical Radiology* **42**: 321–6

22. National Institute for Clinical Excellence (2003) *Head Injury Clinical Guideline 4*

23. *Problem Commission Of Neuroradiology – study meeting on projections and nomenclature* Milan June 16th –18ᵗʰ 1961 *British Journal Radiology* **35**: 501–503

24. Rhese E (1910) Die diagnostik der erkrankungen des siebbeinlabyrinthes und der keilbeinhohlen durch das roengenverfahren *Dt Med Wschr* **36**:1756–1761

25. Schindler E (1997) Arthur Schüller: pioneer of neuroradiology *American Journal Neuroradiology* **18**: 1297–1302

26. Schüller A (1905) *Die schadelbasis im roentgenbilde* Hamburg: Grafe & Sillern

27. Stenver HW (1928) *Roentgenologie des felsenbeines und des bitemporalen schadelbieldes* Berlin: Springer

28. Stevens JM Murray AD Saunders D Lane B in Grainger R Allison D Adam A Dixon A (eds) (2001) *Grainger and Allison's Diagnostic Radiology (Volume 3) (4ᵗʰ Edition)* Edinburgh: Churchill Livingstone

29. Stiell IG Wells GA Vandemheen K Clement C Lesiuk H Laupacis A et al (2001) The Canadian CT head rule for patients with minor head injury *Lancet* **357**: 1391–1396

30. Sutton D in Sutton D (ed) (2003) *Textbook of Radiology and Imaging (Volume 2) (7ᵗʰ Edition)* Edinburgh: Churchill Livingstone

31. Swallow RA Naylor E Roebuck EJ Whitley AS (1986) *Clark's Positioning in Radiography (11ᵗʰ Edition)* London: Heinemann

32. Towne EB (1926) Erosion Of The Petrous Bone By Acoustic Nerve Tumor: Demonstration By Roentgen Ray *Archives Otolaryngology* **4**: 515–519

33. Waring L (1992) Changing to isocentric skull radiography *Radiography today* **58**(659): 16

34. Weber AL (2001) History of head and neck radiology: past, present, and future *Radiology* **218**: 15–24

35. Wurtman RJ Axelrod J Barchas JD (1964) Age and enzyme activity in human pineal. Letter to the Editor *J Clin Endocrinol Metabol* **24**: 299–301

36. Young JW in Sutton D (ed) (1998) *Textbook of Radiology and Imaging (6th Edition)* Edinburgh: Churchill Livingstone

CHAPTER CONTENTS

Table of main and supplementary radiographic techniques

General anatomical area	Projection	Page	Common Indications
Facial bones, upper – mid third	1 Occipitomental (*Water's*) or 2 Alternatives 3 Occipitomental 30° (*Titterington*) 4 Lateral	186–187 187 187–188 188	Injury
Zygomatic arches	5i Fronto-occipital 30° 5ii Reverse FO 30° 5iii Submentovertical	188 188 188	Injury
Nasal bones	6i Occipitomental 6ii Lateral	188 188	
Orbits	7i Occipitomental 7ii Modified OM 7iii Occipitomental 30° 7iv Lateral 7v Occipitofrontal 20°	188 189 189 189 189	Injury, blow-out fractures Foreign bodies
Maxillae	8i Obliques 8ii Occlusal and periapical	189 189	Minor injuries
Mandible	9 PA or 11 AP 12 Lateral 13–15 Lateral oblique and alternatives 17 Dental panoral tomography (DPT)	189 190 190 190 191	Injury
Symphysis menti/ central mandible	16 Occlusal 10 PA oblique	191 189–190	Injury
Temporomandibular joints	18 Lateral oblique 19 Transpharyngeal 20 Fronto-occipital *and* alternative 21 Dental panoral tomography (DPT)	191 191 192 192	Internal derangement Secondary osteoarthritis Fracture-dislocation
Paranasal sinuses			Persistent sinusitis New growth
Maxillary sinuses (antra)	22 Occipitomental 23ii Occipitofrontal 24 Lateral	193 193 194	
Frontal and anterior ethmoidal sinuses	23i Occipitofrontal (*Caldwell*) 24 Lateral	193 194	
Sphenoid sinuses	23iii Occipitofrontal 25 Submentovertical	193 194	
Posterior ethmoids	25 Submentovertical 26 Posterior obliques	194 194	

Effective radiation dose for a skull examination: **0.06mSv**
Equivalent period of natural background radiation: **3 days**

FACIAL BONES

Essential anatomical terminology

The skeleton of the face can be divided into three parts. The *upper third* above the superior orbital ridges belongs to the cranium. The *middle third* lies between the superior orbital ridges and the occlusal line of the upper teeth – or if the patient is edentulous, the upper alveolus. Bones of the middle third of the face (*Figure 11.1*) include:

(1) The maxillae and palatine bones above the upper teeth.

(2) The nasal, ethmoid and lacrymal bones between the orbits.

(3) The zygomatic or cheekbones.

(4) The sphenoid and frontal bones of the posterior and upper walls of the orbit.

(5) The paired pterygoid processes of the sphenoid bone lying directly behind the maxillae.

The mandible forms the *lower third* of the facial skeleton. It consists of a horseshoe-shaped bone – the *body* with its upper border – the *alveolar part* – containing sockets for the teeth. The mandibular *rami* have two prominent processes – the *coronoid* and *condylar processes*. The *temporomandibular joints* are the articulations between the condyles of the

mandible and squamous portion of the temporal bone on each side (*Figure 11.2*). These synovial joints each contain a meniscus – a fibrous structure that separates the condyle from the temporal bone. In normal functioning – when the mouth opens; the condyle translates forwards beneath the articular eminence and the intervening meniscus. A discussion of dental pathology and radiography is outside the scope of this book.

Indications for the X-ray examination

Facial injuries

Contemporary causes of facial bone fractures include road traffic accidents, interpersonal violence, sports

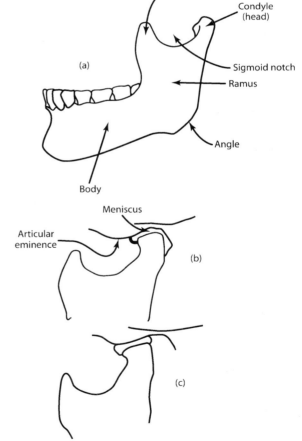

Figure 11.2 (a) Features of the mandible – lateral aspect.
(b) Closed temporomandibular joint.
(c) Open temporomandibular joint.

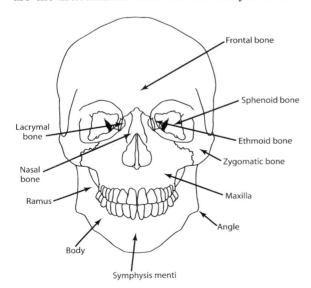

Figure 11.1 Bones of the face and features of the mandible.

injuries, falls, and industrial trauma [**ref 1**: 2]. Significant injuries to the face may be subsidiary to more serous injuries and therefore they may go unnoticed particularly if the patient develops gross facial oedema, making fractures difficult to diagnose either clinically or radiologically.

The maxillae consist of thin plates or sheets of bone connected together with some parts reinforced to form strong vertical buttresses designed to withstand the stress of mastication. These thin plates do not offer much resistance to horizontal forces, and as they enclose air-filled cavities, injury tends to shatter them. Overall, the facial bones have a very low tolerance to impact forces and the nasal bones have the least resistance of all. Bones of the mid-face articulate and interdigitate in a complex fashion and it is difficult for one bone to fracture without disruption to others. In a severe fracture there may be as many as 60–70 fragments [**ref 1**: 1].

The facial bones can fracture in several patterns and in any combination depending on the direction and severity of the blow. Different methods of classification can be used but it is usual to group the fractures according to the region of the face affected. Examples include fractures of the zygomatic region (zygomatic complex), fractures of the nasal region, bilateral fractures of the mid-face (Le Fort fractures), and orbital 'blow-out' fractures.

Generally, plain radiography provides a guide and indications for the use of other modalities such as *CT*, reformatted *3D CT* and *MRI*. Use of these is particularly important in cases of extensive fractures of the mid face and orbital trauma.

Le Fort fractures

These complex and bilateral mid-face fractures involving several bones produce detached segments of bone that are often freely movable. There are three types based upon studies conducted by René Le Fort in 1901 [**ref 6**]:

(1) *Le Fort 1 – Low-level fracture.* A horizontal fracture that separates the hard palate and the alveolar process from the middle face (*Figure 11.3*).

(2) *Le Fort II – Pyramidal or subzygomatic fracture.* The fracture line involves the nasal bones and the orbital floor, passing through walls of the maxillary sinus to the pterygoid plates of the sphenoid (*Figure 11.4*). This separates the mid-portion of the face from the cranium and lateral aspects of the face. If this detached segment is displaced backwards, then in the lateral radiograph the face will have a 'dish-face' appearance.

(3) *Le Fort III – High transverse or suprazygomatic fracture.* There is a detachment of the whole of the mid-facial skeleton from the cranial base (*Figure 11.5*). The fracture lines involve the

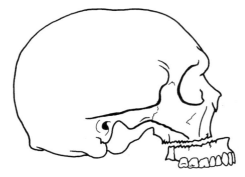

Figure 11.3 Le Fort type I fracture, lateral aspect.

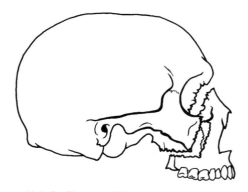

Figure 11.4 Le Fort type II fracture, lateral aspect.

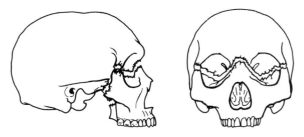

Figure 11.5 Le Forte type III fracture, lateral and frontal aspects.

nasal bones at a high level. They cross the medial wall of the orbit, extending into the inferior orbital fissure and continue along the lateral orbital wall to the zygomaticofrontal suture. The zygomatic arch and pterygoid plates are also fractured.

Le Fort fractures can occur in various combinations and sometimes two or all three types can occur simultaneously. (*See* also [**ref 2**: 591]). Considerable force is required to produce fractures of this magnitude. The patient will have associated and varying degrees of involvement of soft-tissues, eyes, nasal airways, sinuses and tongue. Air from the sinuses may leak into the facial soft tissues causing *surgical emphysema*. Displacement of the bony segments resulting in haemorrhage or airway obstruction is likely to require urgent surgery.

Orbital 'blow-out' fractures

A direct blow to the eye may cause a fracture of the thin orbital floor without there being any damage to the orbital margins (*Figure 11.6*). The blow distorts the globe of the eye and the force is transmitted to the bony walls. As the orbital floor is the weakest area it fractures. Periorbital tissue – muscle and fat – is displaced downwards into the maxillary antrum. Interference with the actions of ocular muscles causes *diplopia* or double vision. *Enopthalmos* – a sinking of the eye – is another sign and difficult outcome of this type of injury. Plain radiographs may incidentally show evidence of orbital floor or wall fractures but are notoriously

unreliable in excluding such an injury or determining its extent [**ref 1**: 70]. *CT* provides appropriate information.

Nasal injuries

According to the Royal College of Radiologists [**ref 9**: 101] 'X-rays' are unreliable in diagnosing nasal fractures and even when positive, they do not usually influence patient management. They may be requested at ENT (ear nose throat) or maxillofacial department follow-up depending on local policy.

Fractures of the mandible

A fracture can occur at any place in the mandible but there are certain sites that are more vulnerable because of their relative inherent weakness. These are:

(1) The condylar neck which is slender.

(2) The mandibular angle which is weakened by the change in direction of structural bone grain and sometimes by the presence of an unerupted eighth molar.

(3) The body where tooth sockets weaken the bone for example at the canine tooth socket. Alveolar resorption which follows a tooth loss also weakens the mandible and pathological fractures may occur. Resorption may cause the mandibular body to become no thicker than a pencil and fractures in this situation are difficult to treat [**ref 1**: 11].

Mandible fractures are often compound because they 'open' into the mouth. A *flail mandible* (*Figure 11.7*) is a serious injury where the bone is broken at the symphysis and also on both sides through the ramus or condyles. These multiple fractures may result in loss of bony support for the tongue and the

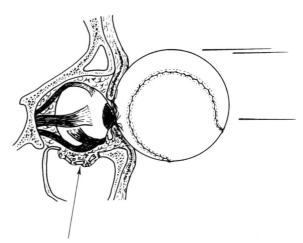

Figure 11.6 The mechanism of the orbital 'blow-out' fracture.

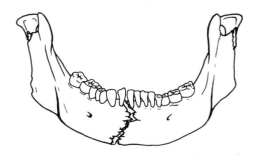

Figure 11.7 Flail mandible

floor of the mouth and thus permit posterior displacement of these structures causing airway obstruction. The most common multiple fracture is caused by a fall on the mid-point of the chin resulting in fractures of symphysis and both condyles. This may occur in epilepsy, the elderly who lose consciousness and soldiers fainting whilst standing on parade – hence the term *guardsman's fracture*. Blows to the mandible are transmitted to the skull base (*see* Chapter 10) and relatively minor mandible injury may be associated with a more serious degree of head injury [**ref 1**: 10].

Dislocation of the mandibular condyles

When dislocated, the condyle lies in front of the articular eminence of the temporal bone. It can be dislocated, on one or both sides. Fracture-dislocation also occurs. The articular disc or meniscus may be damaged following trauma and the joint may subsequently degenerate in a *secondary osteoarthrits* (*see* Chapter 3).

Temporomandibular joint (TMJ) problems

This joint is a common site for complaint of abnormality. Clicking sounds and pain are indicative of *internal derangement* – a structural abnormality within the joint, which most often affects females [**ref 12**]. In this condition there is an abnormal positional and functional relationship between the disk and articulating surfaces. The Royal College of Radiologists [**ref 9**: 34] comments that (conventional) X-rays do not often add information as the majority of TMJ problems are due to soft tissue dysfunction rather than bony changes. Both *CT* and *MRI* may be used to diagnose derangement and other disorders and are preferable to *arthrography* which is invasive.

Radiographic techniques – upper and middle thirds of face

General comments

The reference lines and planes used in positioning of the head are defined and illustrated in Chapter 10. The comments concerning the use of a grid and immobilizing devices for the skull are equally applicable to techniques for the facial bones.

Techniques described refer to standard radiographic equipment (i.e. isocentric techniques are not included). Techniques (1–4) give a general picture of the facial bones. Using the standard occipitomental projection (1), images may be examined systematically along lines where bone dysjunction can be clearly seen [**ref 7** and **14**] – *see Figure 11.8*. Techniques (5–8) include supplementary projections for localized areas.

(1) Occipitomental facial bones (Water's) (Figure 11.9)

The occipitomental projection with various modifications is the most useful view of the facial bones [**ref 11**]. Two British radiologists introduced the principles of this projection in 1915 [**ref 15**]. The projection is famously named after one of the pair, i.e. *Water's*.

The patient is seated erect facing the bucky table. The median sagittal plane is 90° to the image receptor and aligned with the midline of the table. The chin is raised and rests on the table surface so that the orbitomeatal base line makes an angle of 45° with the image receptor.

Central ray direction – Perpendicular to the image receptor and centred in the midline so the central ray emerges at the level of the lower orbital margins.

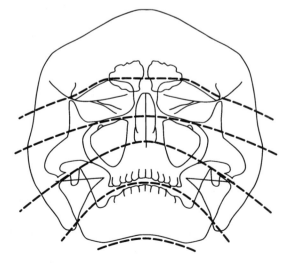

Figure 11.8 McGrigor's lines (or Campbell's lines) used for systematic evaluation of possible bone dysjunction on the occipitomental radiograph. The lower two lines are attributed to Trapnell [ref 14].

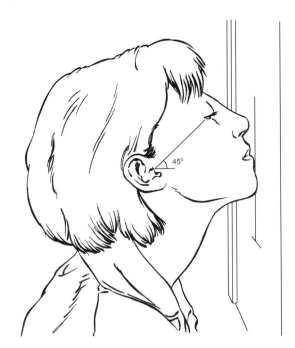

Figure 11.9 Patient position for projection (1) occipitomental facial bones and (3) occipitomental 30° facial bones.

On the radiograph the petrous bones appear as projected below the maxillary sinuses (antra). In using erect positioning with a horizontal X-ray beam, the presence of any fluid levels in the maxillary antra (e.g. presence of blood) may be disclosed. Air may be seen collecting above the orbit in *orbital emphysema* denoting a possible fracture extending into the ethmoid sinuses.

Some authorities prefer use of a 10° caudad X-ray beam direction for the OM projection – *see* [**ref 1: 69**]. Alternative techniques – projections (2).

(2) *Where the patient must remain horizontal*

(i) A *'reverse' occipitomental* can be taken.
     Some authorities rightly claim that reverse projections are of little use [**ref 1: 65**] but it is possible to take this projection using a *substantially increased* X-ray source to image distance (but without a grid) thereby reducing magnification and geometric unsharpness. However the standard occipitomental projection is always superior to the reverse view.

The patient is supine. The median sagittal plane is placed perpendicular to the image receptor. The chin is raised (if possible).

Central ray direction – Central ray should make an angle of 45° with the orbitomeatal base line and be centred over the upper lip in the mid-line. A cephalad tube angle may be required. (Backward tilting of the head may not be permissible.)

The aim is to project the maxillae above the petrous bone. Alternative methods of obtaining these occipitomental projections on an injured patient in the supine position are as follows:

(ii) *Occipitomental head turned*
      If permissible, rotate the head and neck over to one side, raising the shoulder so that an occipitomental projection with a horizontal beam can be taken (*Figure 11.10*). The cassette and grid are supported in front of the patient's face with the base line at 45° to the image receptor.

(iii) *Use of special equipment* – Isocentric units permit standard occipitomental projections on recumbent, supine subjects – or where the patient cannot extend the neck.

(iv) For an adapted protocol for a recumbent patient – *see* [**ref 5**].

(3) *Occipitomental 30° facial bones (Titterington)* (Figure 11.9)

The occipitomental 30° projection gives further information about the lower orbital margins and zygoma. The same patient position is used as in projection (1).

Central ray direction – Central ray is angled 30° caudally and centred through the vertex of the head so the central ray emerges in the mid-line at the level of the lower orbital margins.

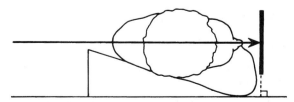

Figure 11.10 Position of the head and the cassette and the direction of the central ray in projection 2(ii).

The cassette must be displaced well down. The exposure should be increased from projection (1). With the base line at 45° this projection may be considered to be 'over-tilted'. It may be preferable to rest both chin and tip of nose on the table thus reducing the base line angle. Note that various degrees of tube tilt can be used with a conventional occipitomental position (*see* projection (1)).

The eponymous term for this projection is *Titterington*. A 'reverse' occipitomental 30° projection is *not* recommended as the degree of image distortion may be unacceptable; however (*see* [**ref 5**] and [**ref 8**] for an adapted protocol for a recumbent patient).

(4) Lateral facial bones

The patient is erect, facing the vertical bucky table. The head and body are rotated until the affected side of the face is nearest the image receptor and rests on the table. The median sagittal plane is parallel to the image receptor. The interpupillary line is perpendicular to the image receptor (*see Figure 10.10*, Chapter 10).

> *Central ray direction* – Horizontal and to a point 2.5cm below the outer canthus of the eye.

A horizontal beam should always be used for the lateral projection. This may show fluid levels in a sinus or possibly air/fluid levels inside the cranium (indicating a cribriform plate fracture). If the patient must remain recumbent (supine) then the cassette and grid are propped by the side of the face with the horizontal X-ray beam directed 'across table'.

Injured patients

Where serious injuries of the face have been sustained, speed and accuracy of technique are vital. The patient may have to be intubated by an anaesthetist as normal breathing may become impossible. Radiographs should be obtained before intubation takes place wherever possible.

If there are teeth, crowns or dentures missing or unaccounted for then it may be advisable to undertake additional chest and lateral soft tissue neck radiographs.

(5) Zygomatic arches

Any of the following may be used:

(i) *Fronto-occipital 30° 'jug-handle view'* – Position as for projection (5) Chapter 10, page 173. Collimate the beam to a rectangle.

> *Central ray direction* – Central ray is angled caudally from above the nasion so that the X-ray beam makes an angle of 30° to the orbitomeatal baseline and passes through the zygomatic arches on both sides. Centre in the midline.

Some reduction in exposure is appropriate depending on whether grid or non-grid technique is used.

(ii) For a reverse occipitofrontal 30° (*see* projection (6) Chapter 10, page 175). This technique may be preferred to reduce radiation exposure to the eyes.

(iii) *Submentovertical* – Position as for projection (7) Chapter 10, page 175.

> *Central ray direction* – From below the chin and centred in the mid-line between the mandibular bodies; angled cephalad so that the X-ray beam makes and angle of 5° with the orbitomeatal baseline.

Collimate the beam to include the zygomatic arches. Similar comments on exposure apply as for (5(i)).

(6) Nasal bones

(i) *Occipitomental* – As for projection (1). Collimate the beam to the nasal area.

(ii) *Lateral* – Position of patient and cassette as for projection (4).

> *Central ray direction* – Perpendicular to the image receptor and centred over the root of the nose.

The X-ray source to image receptor distance can be increased to compensate for the larger subject to image receptor distance.

(7) Orbits

The orbits are shown on the following projections:

(i) *Occipitomental* – As for projection (1).

(ii) *Modified occipitomental* – Position of patient and direction of central ray is the same as for projection (1), except the orbitomeatal base line is adjusted to be 35° to the central ray which is perpendicular to the image receptor [**ref 13**: 239]. The central X-ray beam passes along the line of the orbital floors.

(iii) *Occipitomental 30°* – As for projection (3).

(iv) *Lateral* – As for projection (4).

(v) *Occipitofrontal 20°* – As for projection (1 (ii)), Chapter 10, page 172. The X-ray beam can be collimated to include just the orbits.

Foreign Bodies

One method to determine the presence and location of a foreign body in the eye is to perform two separate localised occipitomental projections using one or two cassettes with the patient looking up and down . Two laterals may also be taken with a similar routine. A common request is for radiography to exclude foreign body prior to MRI scanning. This is usually limited to one occipitomental projection (eyes straight) and radiological opinion is then sought.

(8) Maxillae

These projections give information concerning minor injuries.

(i) Obliques

The patient faces the vertical bucky. The orbitomeatal base line is raised 10 ° from the horizontal. The head is rotated through 40° to either side in turn. The nose, forehead and chin are in contact with the table.

> *Central ray direction* – Central ray is angled 10° cephalad and centred below the mastoid process remote from the image receptor – see [ref 13: 240].

(ii) Occlusal projections and dental periapical imaging

These demonstrate the hard palate, the alveolar parts of the maxillae and the teeth within; for examples of techniques (*see* [**ref 16**]).

Radiographic techniques – mandible

General comments

Fractures can occur on the side of the mandible opposite to that which received the blow – *contre coup* injury. The mandible can also often fracture in more than one place; therefore it is important that both sides should be adequately demonstrated. Dental panoral tomograms (DPT) provide the best overall view of the mandible and is especially valuable for demonstrating fractures in the condylar region. DPT can only be attempted in co-operative patients plus the technology has some shortcomings. As the image is formed by *tomography*, there is some lack of definition produced by anatomical structures outside the focal trough and notably the front of the mouth is the least clearly depicted due to the superimposition of the cervical spine [**ref 10**: 12]. Plain radiographs are therefore a viable alternative and adjunct to DPT in which case lateral and lateral oblique projections of both sides should be taken for comparison, (*see* projections (12) and (13)). If the patient has no teeth, i.e. is edentulous, then the exposure may need to be reduced from the normal situation. Lateral and lateral oblique projections of the mandible can be taken without a secondary radiation grid.

(9) Posteroanterior mandible.

This is usually done with the patient erect facing the image receptor. The projection shows the body and angles of mandible and demonstrates any displacement of fractures. The condylar head is obscured by superimposition of the mastoid process. Position as for an occipitofrontal skull projection (*see* – projection (1), Chapter 10 and *Figure 10.9*, page 171).

> *Central ray direction* – Perpendicular to the image receptor and centred in the mid-line 7.5 cm below the external occipital protruberance.

Alternative technique – projection (11).

(10) Symphysis menti

From the patient position for the occipitofrontal projection (projection (1), Chapter 10) rotate the head through 20° to either side in turn.

Central ray direction – Perpendicular to the image receptor and centred 5 cm lateral to the cervical spinous processes. The central ray passes directly through the symphysis menti for the right and left sides (in turn).

Reduce the exposure from the posteroanterior mandible projection (9). (*See* also occlusal projections (16)).

(11) *Anteroposterior mandible*

An alternative to projection (9). The patient faces the X-ray tube. Place the head on a small pad to bring the orbitomeatal base line 90° to the image receptor. It may not be possible for the patient to depress the chin so if the base line remains slightly elevated then this is acceptable.

Central ray direction – Perpendicular to the image receptor and centred in the mid-line over the lower lip.

(12) *Lateral mandible*

With the patient seated in a chair, ask him to support a cassette by the side of the face. The cassette should be placed parallel to the median sagittal plane and 90° to the interorbital line. Raise the chin slightly to bring the mandibular rami away from the cervical spine.

Central ray direction – Perpendicular to the image receptor and 4 cm behind the symphysis menti.

Both sides of the mandibular arch are superimposed, but any displaced fracture fragments may be demonstrated. Further projections are needed to separate the two sides of the bone.

(13) *Lateral oblique mandible*

Arrange the patient and cassette as for projection (12). Now turn the face towards the cassette to bring the body of the mandible parallel to the image receptor, keeping the chin raised (*Figure 11.11*), the central ray is perpendicular to the image receptor. Then – to separate the two sides of the jaw – *either* (i) tilt both head and cassette over to one side by 25°, the X-ray tube position is not altered (*Figure 11.12*) (*Centre*: 5 cm below the angle of the jaw on the side nearest the X-ray tube); *or* (ii)

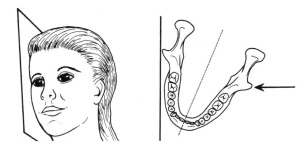

Figure 11.11 The first stage of the positioning in projection (13) – turning the face towards the cassette so that the body of the mandible is parallel to the image receptor.

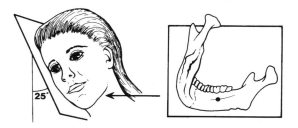

Figure 11.12 Positioning of patient and cassette and direction of the central ray in projection (13(i)).

keeping the head and cassette in the same position (*Figure 11.13*) (*Centre*: 5cm below the angle of the jaw but angle the central ray 25° cephalad).

Alternative techniques – projections (14 and 15).

(14) *Where the patient remains supine and cannot turn the head*

Prop the cassette vertically alongside the face. The head should rest on a foam pad to raise it from the table. Raise the chin if possible. Keep the median sagittal plane parallel to the image receptor and the interorbital line 90° to the image receptor.

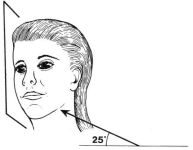

Figure 11.13 Position of patient and cassette in projection (13(ii)).

Central ray direction – Central ray is angled cephalad 25–30° and centred 5 cm anatomically inferior to the angle of the jaw remote from the image receptor.

Take care that the shoulder nearest the X-ray tube does not obstruct the X-ray beam – *see* [**ref 13**: 243].

(15) If the patient can turn the head and neck

From the supine position the head and neck are rotated towards the side of interest. Raise the opposite shoulder on a pillow. A cassette is supported beneath the face, the median sagittal plane being parallel to the image receptor.

Central ray direction – Central ray is angled 30° degrees cephalad from the vertical and should make an angle of 60° with the cassette – see [ref 13: 243]. Centre 5 cm anatomically inferior to the angle of the jaw remote from the image receptor.

(16) Occlusal projections

These are undertaken for a more localized picture of the central mandible and may show small fractures and any involvement with the teeth. The occlusal image receptor is placed and held between the teeth, long axis cross-wise; the X-ray tube side faces downwards.

Central ray direction – Perpendicular to the image receptor and centred to the submental aspect of the jaw.

An intra-oral dental X-ray set is more convenient but conventional equipment can be used. (It may not always be possible to introduce an image receptor into the mouth if there are injuries to the soft tissues).

(17) Dental panoral tomography (DPT)

For comments on use of DPT – *see* above. For a detailed discussion and examples of techniques – *see* [**ref 16**].

Radiographic techniques – temporomandibular joints (TMJs)

When the mouth is opened the condyle of the mandible glides forwards on to the condylar eminence of the temporal bone. By asking the patient to open and close the mouth, the radiographer can locate the joint whilst touching the patient's face.

(18) Lateral oblique TMJ

In a true lateral projection both joints would be superimposed and obscured by the temporal bones. This projection separates the two sides while the subject remains close to the image receptor. Position as for the lateral skull (projection (3), Chapter 10, page 172). Immobilize the head. Three separate exposures for each side are made with the mouth:

(i)   Open

(ii)   Closed

(iii)   Teeth clenched together

Explain the procedure carefully to the patient. Use a non-opaque bite block for (i).

Central ray direction – Central ray is angled 25° degrees caudad (in some patients 30° is required.) and centred to a point 5 cm above the joint remote from the image receptor.

Collimate the beam. Repeat the procedure for the other side. These projections may be taken without using a secondary radiation grid. The image receptors should be carefully marked.

(19) Transpharyngeal projection

This shows the condylar head free from overlying bone structures. The projection is taken through the sigmoid notch (between coronoid process and condyle) of the opposite side of the mandible, across the nasopharyngeal air space. The head is in a position for a true lateral projection. A cassette is held by the patient against the side of the face.

Central ray direction – The central ray is perpendicular to the median sagittal plane. The beam is then angled 5° cephalad and 5° in a posterior direction and centred to the sigmoid notch of the uppermost side 2.5 cm below the zygomatic arch; and 5 cm anterior to the tragus. The patient's mouth is open.

Repeat for the other side. (*See* [**ref 16**]).

(20) Fronto-occipital both joints

The patient's head is in the position for the fronto-occipital projection (projection (2), Chapter 10 and *Figure 10.11*). A non-opaque bite block should be used to keep the mouth open.

> *Central ray direction* – Central ray is angled 30–35° caudad from above the glabella and centred in the mid-line.

This projection can be taken with the mouth closed. The X-ray beam must be suitably collimated.

An alternative projection is the 'reverse' fronto-occipital projection (projection (6) Chapter 10, page 175).

(21) Dental panoral tomography (DPT)

For comments on use of DPT – *see* above. For a detailed discussion and examples of techniques – *see* [**ref 16**].

PARANASAL SINUSES

Essential anatomical terminology

The paired paranasal sinuses together with the nasal cavities are air-filled bony boxes lying within the facial and basal head skeleton. Changes in their radiopacity, the thickness or shape of their mucous membrane lining and the state of their bony walls tell the person assessing the image about their normality. *CT* is useful to demonstrate the complex sinonasal anatomy and if available would be the modality of choice.

Indications for the X-ray examination

Infections (sinusitis)

Infection of the sinuses produces swelling of the lining mucous membrane and filling of the cavity with fluid exudates – a product of the inflamed tissues. The thickness of the mucosa can be seen on the radiographs but if the sinus is filled with fluid then it will appear uniformly opaque when compared with an unaffected side. Where there is sufficient air and fluid present in the sinus then a *fluid level* will form (*Figure 11.14*). Fluid levels are most easily demonstrated in the maxillary sinuses. If infection persists in a sinus when its outlet is blocked then it may become filled with pus – *empyema*. Other conditions can produce changes in the lining mucosa without the formation of fluid levels. Royal College of Radiologists guidelines [**ref 9**: 29] state that acute sinusitis can be diagnosed and treated clinically. Radiological 'signs' on sinus radiographs are often non-specific and encountered in asymptomatic individuals; however radiography may be required if the sinusitis is persistent.

Polypus

This is an outgrowth of mucosa attached to the wall of the nasal cavity or sinus by a stalk. Nasal polyps can occur as a sequel to infective or allergic changes in the mucous membranes.

Barotrauma

This is a form of trauma that may affect the paranasal sinuses (and the mastoid air cells) as a result of alterations in atmospheric pressure. If

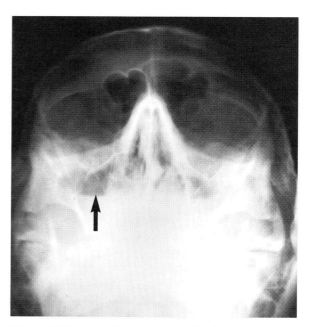

Figure 11.14 An occipitomental projection showing fluid levels in the maxillary sinuses.

there is a failure of equalization of pressure in a sinus because of some obstruction of its opening then thickening of its mucosal lining may result.

These changes can affect divers or sub-aqua swimmers for example.

New growths

A tumour of the sinuses is most likely to be a carcinoma – a malignant tumour of the epithelial lining and not of the bone. These most frequently arise in the maxillary or ethmoid sinuses. Radiographically the sinus will become opaque and the bony walls will gradually be eroded as the tumour infiltrates and destroys it. *CT* is indicated if malignancy is suspected.

Radiographic techniques – sinuses

General comments

Projections of the paranasal sinuses should be standardized as far as possible so that they are reproducible and thus easily compared. A sinus protractor or similar angle-measuring device can be used when the head is positioned. Collimation of the beam is of special importance and a beam-limiting device – usually a cone – may be used. Patient positioning is usually erect.

(22) Occipitomental sinuses

The same position in projection (1) is used, with the patient erect (*see – Figure 11.9*).

> *Central ray direction* – Horizontal and centred in the midline so the central ray emerges at the level of the lower orbital margins.

The petrous bones must be projected below the lower border of the maxillary antra (sinuses). If they are not then the head is described as 'undertilted'. If movement of the neck is restricted a compensatory caudal X-ray tube angulation will be needed. If the chin is raised too far then the teeth may obscure the lower antra and this tends to occur more readily in children. The occipitomental projection shows the *maxillary sinuses (antra)*.

If the mouth is kept open the *sphenoid sinuses* and *nasopharynx* are seen (especially in an edentulous patient). The *frontal sinuses* are shown but are foreshortened.

Fluid levels

With a horizontal beam, fluid levels in the antra may be shown. For further proof that an opacity is fluid and not mucosal thickening, repeat the occipitomental projection but tilt the head and neck to one side through 30°. The fluid will 'settle' because of gravity in a direction parallel to the floor.

(23) Occipitofrontal sinuses (Caldwell)

(i) Position as for the occipitofrontal skull (projection (1), Chapter 10 and *Figure 10.9*).

> *Central ray direction* – Central ray angled is caudad between 10° and 15° and centred above the external occipital protruberance to emerge through the nasion.

This demonstrates the *frontal sinuses* and the *anterior ethmoids* which are projected above the sphenoid sinuses. Development of this projection is attributed to *Caldwell* [ref 3].

Alternative

(ii) Central ray is perpendicular to the image receptor, directed towards the maxillary sinuses and centred 4 cm below the external occipital protruberance.

This demonstrates the *maxillary sinuses* below the level of the petrous temporal bones. The sphenoid sinuses are superimposed on the anterior ethmoids.

Alternative

(iii) Central ray is angled 10° cephalad, directed towards the nasion and centred in the midline.

This projects the *sphenoid* sinuses above the ethmoids to be superimposed on the frontal bone.

Fluid levels frontal sinuses

These can be confirmed by the following projection. With the patient supine, the head is turned through 90° (one shoulder is raised). A cassette is propped vertically in front of the face. The median sagittal plane is positioned 90° to the image receptor and parallel to the tabletop. Direct the central X-ray as for the occipitofrontal 15° projection (23(i)) except using a horizontal beam.

(24) Lateral sinuses

Position as for the lateral skull (projection (3), Chapter 10 and *Figure 10.10*).

> *Central ray direction* – Perpendicular to the image receptor and centred to a point 2.5 cm posterior the outer canthus of the eye along the orbitomeatal base line.

All groups of sinuses are shown but the pairs are superimposed.

(25) Submentovertical sinuses

Position as for the submentovertical skull (projection (7), Chapter 10, page 175).

> *Central ray direction* – As for projection (7), Chapter 10.

This demonstrates the *sphenoid* sinuses, the *posterior ethmoids* and also the maxillary antra and orbital walls.

Plan projection, frontal sinuses

The patient position remains the same as in projection (25).

> *Central ray direction* – Centre the X-ray beam inside the arch of the mandible so the central ray passes tangentially through the frontal sinuses.

(26) Posteroanterior oblique sinuses

The patient sits facing the bucky table. The chin is raised so that the base line is 30° from the horizontal. The head is rotated to right and left sides in turn so that the median sagittal plane makes an angle of 40° with the image receptor. The patient's nose, chin and cheek bone touch the table surface.

> *Central ray direction* – Perpendicular to the image receptor and centred through the orbit nearest the image receptor.

The *posterior ethmoids* are projected through the orbit. The *optic foramen* may also be shown. (*See also* projection (10(iii)) Chapter 10.)

References

1. Banks P Brown A (2001) *Fractures of the Facial Skeleton* Oxford: Wright

2. Bowerman JE *Fractures of the middle third of the facial skeleton* in JL Williams (ed) (1994) *Rowe & Williams Maxillofacial Injuries* Edinburgh: Churchill Livingstone

3. Caldwell EW (1907) Skiagraphy of the accessory nasal sinuses *American Journal Roentgenology* **1**: 27–30

4. Driscoll P Skinner D Earlam R (eds) (2000) *ABC of Major Trauma* London: BMJ Publishing

5. Leach M (2001) Horizontal beam facial bone views on the supine patient *Synergy* May p 4–8

6. Le Fort R (1901) Étude experimentale sure les fractures de la machoire supérieure *Revue Chir* **23**: 208

7. McGrigor DB Campbell W (1950) The radiology of war injuries Part VI: wounds of the face and jaw *British Journal Radiology* **23**: 685–96

8. Ponsford A Clements R (1991) A modified view of the facial bones in the seriously injured *Radiography today* **57**(646): 10–12

9. RCR Working Party (2003) *Making the Best Use of a Department of Clincal Radiology: Guidelines for Doctors (Fifth Edition)* London: the Royal College of Radiologists

10. Semple J Gibb D (Undated) *The Place of Panoramic Tomography in Dental Radiography* London: College of Radiographers

11. Sidebottom AJ Cornelius P Allen PE Cobby M and Rogers SN (1996) Routine post-traumatic screening of mid-facial injuries: is one view sufficient? *Injury* **27**: 311–13

12. Sommer OJ Aigner F Rudisch A Gruber H Fritsch H Millesi W Stiskal M (2003) Cross-sectional and functional imaging of the temporomandibular joint: radiology, pathology and basic biomechanics of the jaw *Radiographics* **23**: 14

13. Swallow RA Naylor E Roebuck EJ Whitley AS (1986) *Clark's Positioning in Radiography (11th Edition)* London: Heinemann

14. Trapnell DH in NL Rowe JL Williams (eds) (1985) *Diagnostic Radiography in Maxillofacial Injuries* Edinburgh: Churchill Livingstone

15. Waters CA Waldron CW (1915) Roentgenology of accessory nasal sinuses describing modification of occipito-frontal projection *American Journal Roentgenology* 2: 633–639

16. Whaites E (2002) *Essentials of Dental Radiography (3rd Edition)* Edinburgh: Churchill Livingstone

Further Reading

1. Cruz AA Eichenberger GC (2004) Epidemiology and management of orbital fractures *Current Opinions in Ophthalmology* **15**(5): 416–21

2. McGhee A Guse J (2000) Radiography for midfacial trauma: is a single OM 15 degrees radiograph as sensitive as OM 15 degrees and OM 30 degrees combined? *British Journal Radiology* **73** (872): 883–885

Index